A SHORT HISTORY OF
CAMBODIA

Short History of Asia Series

Other books in the series
Short History of Bali, Robert Pringle
Short History of China and Southeast Asia, Martin Stuart-Fox
Short History of Indonesia, Colin Brown
Short History of Japan, Curtis Andressen
Short History of Laos, Grant Evans
Short History of Malaysia, Virginia Matheson Hooker

Series Editor
Milton Osborne has had an association with the Asian region for over 40 years as an academic, public servant and independent writer. He is the author of many books on Asian topics, including *Southeast Asia: An introductory history*, first published in 1979 and now in its ninth edition, and *The Mekong: Turbulent past, uncertain future*, published in 2000.

A SHORT HISTORY OF

CAMBODIA

FROM EMPIRE TO SURVIVAL

By John Tully

SILKWORM BOOKS

First published in Australia in 2006 by Allen & Unwin
First published in Thailand, Cambodia, Laos, Vietnam and Burma
by Silkworm Books in 2006.

Silkworm Books
6 Sukkasem Road, T. Suthep
Chiang Mai 50200 Thailand
Email: info@silkwormbooks.com

National Library of Australia
Cataloguing-in-Publication entry:

Tully, John.
    A short history of Cambodia : from empire to survival

    Bibliography.
    Includes index.
    ISBN–10: 974 93619 1 1
    ISBN–13: 978 974 93619 1 7

    1. Cambodia — History. 2. Cambodia — Politics and
    government. 3. Cambodia — Economic conditions. I. Title.
    (Series : Short history of Asia).

959.6

Set in 11/14 pt Goudy by Midland Typesetters, Australia
Printed by O. S. Printing House, Thailand

10 9 8 7 6 5 4 3 2

Contents

For my parents, Matthew and Ethel

Preface

This book traces the history of Cambodia from the Indian-influenced state of Funan, which predated Angkor (founded in 802), to the present: a grand sweep of over 2000 years. Also included is a brief discussion of the pre-history of what is today Cambodia in Chapter 2. The Cambodian monarchy is over 1200 years old; King Sihamoni, who sits on the throne today, is the latest incumbent in a line dating from the reign of King Jayavarman II, the shadowy founder of Angkor, the first unified polity of Cambodia. It is not an unbroken bloodline of kings, but was disrupted by usurpers on many occasions. The institution, however, has remained constant for almost all of this time. If we count Jayavarman II's predecessors, the monarchy is even older, and epigraphic evidence indicates that Khmer culture predates him by around 200 years. Whether those that lived here before were Khmers, we cannot say, although it is probable that they were.

If the monarchy has been remarkably resilient, so too have been the Khmer people and their culture, which sustained the kingdom. Although there have been some sharp discontinuities in Cambodian history, the Khmers today, particularly the rural dwellers who still make up the majority of the population, live much as their ancestors did. In their heyday, the martial Khmers carved out an immensely powerful empire with Angkor, the largest city of antiquity, at its centre. Today we see only the stone heart of a city that has long since rotted away, and can trace the pattern of the city's veins, the network of canals that carried life-giving water from the distant heights of Kulen. Then, as now, the largest class was the peasantry, although they doubled as soldiers and builders. When the first European visitors arrived in the 16th century, the empire was in decline and the centre of gravity of the Cambodian state had shifted downstream to the Quatre Bras region at the head of the Mekong delta, where it remains today. The possible reasons for this shift are discussed in Chapter 3.

Later years saw Cambodia gradually squeezed on two sides by powerful enemies, the Siamese (today's Thais) to the west in the Menam Valley, and the Vietnamese to the east. The Vietnamese, who had migrated much earlier from what is today the Canton region of China to the Hanoi region, steadily pushed southwards and by 1780 they had completed their occupation of *Kampuchea Krom*, the formerly Khmer lands around what is today Saigon in the lower Mekong delta. In the same period, the Siamese kings carved off chunks of Cambodian territory, and both neighbours demanded tribute. Cambodia had gone from empire to vassal state and by the late 18th century its sovereignty was in peril. The country had entered into a Dark Age. Rival armies of foreigners fought on Cambodia's soil and sacked its towns. The Vietnamese directly administered the country for 30 years during the first half of the 19th century, placing puppets on the throne and striving to assimilate the Khmers, whom they regarded as 'barbarians', into Vietnamese culture. Cambodia almost became a Vietnamese province: the earlier fate of the Khmer lower Mekong delta lands. King Ang Duang restored order and a measure of sovereignty, but after his death in 1860 the country was once again plunged into chaos. This period is discussed in Chapter 4.

Most historians conclude that Cambodia would have disappeared if Duang's successor and eldest son, King Norodom, had not negotiated a treaty with France to keep his neighbours at bay. Under the terms of the treaty, as discussed in Chapter 5, his kingdom became a protectorate in 1863. The Siamese seethed, but could do little against superior force. The French gradually tightened control over the Kingdom to create a de facto colony, administered by a powerful official known as the *Résident Supérieur*. In 1887, Cambodia became part of the newly created Indochinese Federation under a governor-general with his capital at Hanoi. Along the way, French heavy-handedness provoked a huge revolt and Norodom died some years later a broken old man. Despite this, the French did preserve the country's territorial integrity and much of its traditional way of life. The downside of the colonial period was that the French left a model of authoritarian rule and failed to develop the country socially and economically, thus contributing to later tragedies that befell Cambodia.

The colonial period lasted until 1953, when King Norodom Sihanouk led his 'royal crusade for independence', which saw the restoration of Cambodian sovereignty even before the 1954 Geneva peace conference agreed to independence for the rest of French Indochina. Sihanouk was a complex man and although an unpredictable autocrat, he managed to sustain his country's neutrality throughout the 1950s and 1960s. In this he resembled an acrobat on a high wire; when he slipped—or was, rather, pushed in a right-wing pro-American coup in March 1970—his pride was badly damaged, but the consequences for his subjects were much direr. The 'Sihanoukist' period is the subject of Chapter 6.

Between 1970 and 1979, Cambodia blundered into a modern Dark Age. Civil war, cataclysmic aerial bombardment and Pol Pot's bloody revolution almost destroyed the country. These disasters are examined in Chapters 7 and 8. Since the overthrow of the Pol Pot regime by Vietnamese forces in 1979, the country has struggled against the odds to rebuild itself, and this is the subject of Chapters 9 and 10. The rebuilding was not straightforward, but was a confused and contradictory process. As the American writer Evan Gottesman has noted in his insightful book on post-DK Cambodia, 'Cambodia did not *arise* from the ashes of the Khmer Rouge with anything approaching ideological clarity. Rather, it *emerged*—after twelve years of conflict and confusion . . . [emphasis added]'. Cambodia today is beset with myriad problems, most notably underdevelopment, corruption and authoritarian rule, and one can only hope that the tenacity of the Khmers, which has sustained them through the long centuries since the decline of their empire, will prevail.

Footnotes have been kept to a minimum, as these tend to impede the flow of the work, but a full bibliographic essay and glossary of terms are to be found in this book. Also included is a list of abbreviations on page 234. The book is intended for tourists, students and general readers with an interest in Southeast Asia and world affairs. Many will be drawn to a discussion of Cambodia's more recent past, but I hope they will also take the time to read about the more distant history of what is a fascinating country. Others might begin by only considering Angkor, and might wish to explore other periods of the country's history. Perhaps even young Khmers might wish to look at this book as the first step in the study of their history. Finally, I should add that this book is not a guide to the Angkor ruins. A number of excellent guides, some lavishly illustrated, do exist and I have listed some of these in the bibliographic essay. My chapter on Angkor is more concerned with social history than with the monuments as works of art, although this is not to belittle them.

Acknowledgments

Firstly, I would like to thank Dr Milton Osborne, the series editor, for inviting me to write the Cambodia volume of the Allen & Unwin Short Histories of Asia series. Milton has been an attentive editor, making many thoughtful suggestions and intervening (as a Cambodia specialist himself) to remove some of my more egregious errors. I would also like to thank my wife Professor Dorothy Bruck for her painstaking reading of the manuscript. She brought her acute intelligence to bear on the manuscript, making many helpful suggestions for changes in style and asking, as an intelligent non-specialist, for elaboration of points that I had taken for granted. I should not forget, either, to thank my friend Tony Dewberry for reading the chapter on the Pol Pot regime and discussing its implications. I should also thank my friend and old teacher Professor David Chandler for his encouragement and advice on several occasions, and Catherine Earl for her index. More generally, I must thank the School of Social Sciences at Victoria University for making the time available for me to work on the book. Finally, I would like to thank Rebecca Kaiser, Allen & Unwin's editorial manager, for her patience in waiting for this work to be completed. Naturally, any errors are my own responsibility.

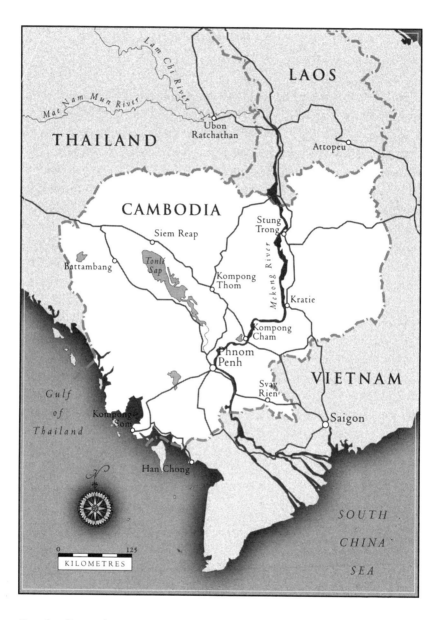

Cambodia today

1
THE PEOPLE
AND THEIR
ENVIRONMENT

The modern Khmers are the inheritors of an ancient tradition, the most noteworthy signs of which are the ruins of Angkor. Although other archaeological sites are widely spread across the country, from the Mekong delta to the vicinity of Battambang, the Dangrek Mountains and even into countries which are today separate states, most tourists come to visit Angkor. Some, indeed, fly in and out of nearby Siem Reap airport from Thailand or Vietnam and remain ignorant of the rest of this fascinating country. Its fascination is not lessened by the fact that Cambodia is among the poorest countries in Asia. While it has made much progress since the end of the destructive Pol Pot regime in 1979, there are disturbing recent signs of retrogression within under-development, with rising infant mortality rates and declining economic growth. On the other hand, the literacy rate of rural women, who are the poorest and most downtrodden of the poor, increased from 52.7 per cent in 1998 to 65.3 per cent in 2004, according to the United Nations-assisted National Institute of Statistics at Phnom Penh. (Some of the problems of underdevelopment are discussed in Chapter 9.)

The land of Cambodia

During the Angkorean period Cambodia stretched between the South China and Andaman Seas, but today it comprises a little over 181 000 square kilometres: not a large country, but not a tiny one either. It is roughly half the size of Germany and three times as large as Belgium. It has a tropical climate: warm the whole year round, with a six-month dry season with frequent drought, and a monsoon of astonishingly intense rains.

Physically, Cambodia is a vast, shallow bowl with the edges rising steeply to the north, the east and the south into wild, jungle-cloaked mountains and plateaux. These jungles are home to a variety of birds and animals, including tigers, wild cats, wild buffaloes, monkeys, elephants and rhinoceros, various kinds of snakes including the cobra, and the Siamese crocodile. Their numbers, however, are falling steadily due to logging, hunting and the encroachment of human settlement. The Siamese crocodile was thought to be extinct, but zoologists recently found small numbers of them living in the remote Cardamom Mountains, protected by the people of a nearby village. That tigers still exist is attested to by my friend Mathieu Guérin, who was stalked by one in the isolated mountains of Mondulkiri province while doing fieldwork in the late 1990s.

On the west and the south-east of the great central basin of Cambodia, the flatlands stretch across into Thailand and Vietnam, forming 'gates' as it were into the kingdom, through which throughout the centuries invading armies have often poured. The central basin is dominated by an intriguing natural hydraulic system, on which the prosperity of the kingdom has long depended. At the centre of it is a vast cocoa-coloured sheet of water, Lake Tonlé Sap (the Great Lake), the largest freshwater lake in Southeast Asia. In the north of the country, the Mekong, one of the largest rivers of the world, rushes from Laos over a series of spectacular rapids and falls. Then, at a more sedate pace, it courses into the Cambodian basin, past the towns of Stung Treng, Kratie and Kompong Cham, to the capital city of Phnom Penh, where the waters form a giant St Andrews shaped cross known to the French as the *Quatre Bras*, or 'Four Arms'. Here, the main river splits into two channels, the Mekong proper and the Bassac, the first of the many distributaries of the Mekong delta, through which the waters pour through Vietnamese territory into the South China Sea. Another river, known as the Tonlé Sap, which most of the time is a tributary of the Mekong, forms the fourth arm of the cross, winding upstream from Phnom Penh.

A remarkable ecosystem

The Mekong, the world's 12th longest river, rises thousands of kilometres away on the Tibetan plateau and every year, after the spring thaw in the mountains, the snow-fed waters surge downstream in a mighty flood. In fact, so great is the volume of water that it is unable to drain through the delta and backs up into the Tonlé Sap past the capital, reversing the flow so that the water flows upstream, past the old capital at Udong and into the lake of the same name as the river. When this happens, the surface area of the lake expands enormously, forming an immense inland sea of over 13 000 square kilometres and attaining a depth of up to 10 metres. In October or November, the direction of flow changes and the waters are carried away to the sea. The enormous volumes of water, silt and nutrients give rise to a teeming population of over 200 varieties of fish, and these form the major source of protein for the people of Cambodia. Over one million people earn their living directly from fishing and some three million live around the lake, some by flood retreat farming.

Contrary to popular perception, not all of Cambodia's soils are fertile, but the most fertile tend to be in the vicinity of Lake Tonlé Sap and the Mekong, and it is here that the densest concentrations of people are found. This invaluable ecosystem, sadly, is under threat from both logging and pollution from chemicals and sewage. Already, many species of fish, birds, turtles, snakes and crocodiles have disappeared. During Sihanouk's time, signs warned people (roughly translated): 'Don't waste our national patrimony, the forest' and 'If we degrade the soil, we will perish'. The message was ignored.

The people of Cambodia

According to Cambodia's National Institute of Statistics, there are today over 13 million people living within the frontiers of the Kingdom of Cambodia. Some hundreds of thousands of other ethnic Khmers live outside of the country in the Vietnamese-administered lower Mekong delta, and in Thailand, particularly to the north of the Dangrek Mountains but even to the west of Bangkok. The overwhelming majority of the population is rural and the only real city is the capital, Phnom Penh, which is home to over one million people and is more than eight times the size of the largest town, Battambang, which has around 125 000 inhabitants.

Phnom Penh is a sprawling tropical city running along the Tonlé Sap and Bassac rivers and contains an intriguing mix of architectural styles, from the crassly modern and the jerry-built to the elegant cream and lemon-painted French colonial buildings. The central market is a fine example of Art Deco architecture, although its lines are partially obscured by the tarpaulin-draped stalls of the traders outside. The city took its name from the Khmer word for hill, *phnom*, and the hill in question, which is surmounted by a large bell-shaped stone *stupa*, is situated in the northern outskirts of the central city. Although Phnom Penh is over 500 years old, until the coming of the French in 1863 it was little more than a collection of ramshackle brick and wooden shops and houses close to the river. By the early 20th century, their efforts had transformed it into what the French writer Rose Quaintenne described as 'a very picturesque town . . . [which was] very pretty and seductive'.

Alongside the dominant Khmers, there are large minorities of

Chams, Vietnamese, Chinese and hill peoples. The Chinese, who have been present in the country since pre-Angkorean times, are primarily city dwellers, as are many Vietnamese, although the latter also make their living as fishermen on the Tonlé Sap, the Great Lake of central Cambodia. The Chinese and Vietnamese have provided a disproportionate number of the country's traders, businessmen and skilled workers. The Chams, who speak their own language and practise the Sunni variant of Islam, are the descendents of the once mighty empire of Champa, sacked by the Vietnamese in 1471, mixed with more recent Muslim Malay immigrants. They have been renowned as cartwrights and woodworkers. Although their number fell by around 36 per cent under Pol Pot, there are today about half a million Chams in Cambodia. They live in their own villages, replete with mosques, to which they are summoned to prayer not by the cries of a *muezzin* as elsewhere in *Darul Islam*, but by drums and gongs.

The hill peoples (known politely as *Khmer Loeu* by the Cambodians, but more generally by the derogatory *Phnong*, meaning 'savage' or 'slave') generally live in the remote uplands around the perimeter of the country and speak a variety of dialects and languages, some of which are related to Khmer. Many are animist and traditionally they have been non-state peoples who have paid little regard to frontiers. Traditionally they have practised swidden or slash-and-burn agriculture and live a semi-nomadic communal life. There are also smaller minorities of Lao, Thais and Shans, the latter once well known as workers on the Pailin gem fields near the Thai border. With the probable exception of the hill peoples, all of the minorities suffered cruel discrimination during the Pol Pot period (the Cham mosques were defiled as pigsties) and there is still widespread animosity towards the Vietnamese.

Most Khmers are peasants, steeped in traditional ways of life, and it is arguably this tenacity of tradition that has enabled them to survive their country's appalling catastrophes. In many respects, the countryside has not changed much since ancient times. The wooden buffalo carts and ploughs are timeless, sugar palms still dot the landscape above the intense green of the ripening rice in paddy fields that are too irregular in shape and size to belong to the more orderly Vietnamese countryside. This contrast hints at what is one of the sharpest cultural divides in Asia, between Indianised Cambodia and Sinitic Vietnam. Many rural Khmers live in the same kinds of houses as their remote ancestors: palm thatch huts with bamboo frames raised on stilts against floods and reptiles, with a few modest possessions and frugal diets based on rice, fruit, vegetables and *prahoc* (a pungent, fermented fish paste that provides the bulk of their protein). Many still wear the dress of their ancestors, simple black garments enlivened by the colourful checked scarf known as the *krama*, and at times the ornate *sampot*, the ankle-length skirt of the women. The rural folk are mostly burned almost black by the sun, but the better-off urban dwellers, particularly the women, are often of a lighter complexion.

Khmers are devoutly religious, practising the Theravada strain of Buddhism, mixed with elements of folk religion, superstition and remnants of Hinduism, or more accurately Sivaism (see Chapter 3). The central focus of village life is always the Buddhist temple, or *wat*, and the saffron-clad monks beg for alms as they have done for many hundreds of years. For many Khmers, religion and life are inseparable and one of the greatest horrors of the Pol Pot period was the government's attempt to stamp religion out. Theravadism is so closely interwoven with Khmer life that 600 years of Christian missionary activity has been a dismal failure, unlike in some neighbouring countries. Iberian Catholic priests lamented the hold of Buddhist 'wizards' over the people and subsequent American Protestant missions secured few converts despite vigorous proselytism. What remains a mystery is why the Khmers rejected their earlier Sivaism and Mahayana Buddhism and embraced the Theravada doctrines with such fervour in the 13th century, although scholars such as George Coedès have made educated guesses, as is discussed in the chapter on Angkor. Whatever the reason, it has been a lasting element of Khmer culture, and has enabled them to endure what has too often been a melancholy history.

2
CAMBODIA
BEFORE ANGKOR

For most people, the ancient city of Angkor is synonymous with Cambodia, but the Angkorean Empire dates only from 802 AD, when King Jayavarman II moved upstream from the Mekong Valley to found a new capital on higher ground near the north-western tip of the Great Lake, the Tonlé Sap. The country, however, was inhabited long before that. Stone Age remains indicate human presence in what we now call Cambodia for tens, perhaps hundreds, of thousands of years. We cannot say if these people were the distant ancestors of the present-day Khmers, but it does seem that the Khmer–Mon people settled in the area between Burma and the South China Sea some time before the third millennium BC, after migrating from the north. For most of this gulf of unrecorded time, the inhabitants were hunter-gatherers, nomads who roamed the forests and marshlands in search of game and vegetable foods. It is likely also that others practised swidden, or slash-and-burn farming, much as the Khmer Loeu tribes or hill peoples still do today, cutting and burning clearings in the forest and growing crops for a year or so before moving on when the soil is exhausted.

There is archaeological evidence to show that some of these nomads began a more settled, agriculturally based existence around

3000 BC, particularly east of the Mekong near the present-day settlements of Chup and Snuol. At some stage during this process, rudimentary state societies must have replaced the 'primitive communism' of these people's ancestors, which if like the simple societies of the hill peoples today, was based around a collective, non-state way of life. The early sedentary people used copper and bronze tools from at least 1500 BC. One thousand years later, these people—or others like them—lived in fortified settlements, using iron tools, in sophisticated social systems made possible by the creation of a social surplus product based on efficient agriculture and animal husbandry.

It is highly unlikely that there was any single unified state during this period; probably there were numerous petty principalities, ruled over by local chieftains, or *pons*. It might be tempting to impose the idea of 'Cambodia' on to the distant past, but all the evidence indicates that there was no unitary Cambodian state until after the foundation of Angkor at the beginning of the ninth century AD. Moreover, there is no hard evidence to prove that these early inhabitants were Khmers at all—it is not until the seventh century AD that stone inscriptions in the Khmer language began to occur. It is entirely possible that the inhabitants of the early settlements were ancestors of the modern Chams, or of some other people who might have died out or been pushed out by later settlers. After all, by way of comparison, until the fifth century AD, with the onset of the Dark Ages and the Saxon invasions, the inhabitants of what is today England were Romanised Celts, the ancestors not of the modern English but of the Welsh and the Cornish.

Ancient Funan

Whoever they were, by the beginning of the first century AD the inhabitants of Cambodia had achieved a high level of civilisation, influenced by the culture of India. One polity (or perhaps group of polities), known to us as Funan, has left an extensive record of its existence and way of life. The pre-Angkor scholar Michael Vickery has warned against assuming that Funan was a unified state—it is possible that it was a loose alliance of port towns in the lower Mekong delta. However, the existence of large canals suggests a strong state power capable of planning and managing the large numbers of labourers required for such projects. Such workforces would have depended on regular food supplies, produced by efficient agriculture and with an efficient tax collection system. On the other hand, we know that the city-states of Ancient Greece and Renaissance Italy were capable of building public works and large monuments without direction by overarching 'national' or supra-national polities, so Vickery is probably right about pre-Angkorean Cambodia.

The Chinese chroniclers claim that the first king of Funan was a man called Fan Shih-Man, but we have no way of telling whether that was his real name, or if indeed he was the first king, or if he ruled over a much greater territory than the other *pons* or petty chieftains of the time. The name Fan Shih-Man bears no relation to any of the Southeast Asian languages; it is a Chinese corruption of an indigenous name, but the question is, a corruption of what? The American scholar Lawrence Palmer Briggs believed that 'Fan' might have been a corruption of the Sanskrit suffix 'varman', which means protector, and which was appended to the names of many subsequent kings and petty kings in Cambodia. Michael Vickery argues more plausibly that 'Fan' is a corruption of the Khmer–Mon *pon*, which died out before Angkor.

Again, we have no way of knowing the ethnicity of the inhabitants of Funan, although if Vickery is right in his speculation about the origins of words such as *pon*, perhaps we might call them proto-Khmers. What language they spoke in everyday life we do not know. Although Funan was a literate, Indianised society, all trace of the books in what the Chinese described as impressive libraries have disappeared in the heat and humidity, and all stone inscriptions from before the seventh century are in Sanskrit. Indeed, we have no way of knowing even what the Funanese called themselves: Funan itself is a Chinese word, and although scholars have suggested it might be a corruption of the Khmer word *phnom*, this will remain speculation unless further evidence comes to light. On the other hand, Khmer folklore has it that the Cambodian people built a town at Angkor Borei, in the Mekong delta, around the time of Funan. However, folklore cannot put precise dates on places and events and there is no evidence to support the existence of Khmer speakers in the lower delta until the seventh century (although this does not mean that they did *not* exist).

What we do know of Funan comes from three sources: Chinese dynastic chronicles, Sanskrit stone inscriptions and the archaeological record. The earliest account of the kingdom is contained in the 'Chinshu', or the history of the Chin Dynasty, from 265–419 AD. Its reliability is a matter of debate, given that the writers often wrote hundreds of years after the events they were describing and on the basis of hearsay and second-hand reports. Nevertheless, the chronicles do give us some tantalising details of a long-gone civilisation. They tell us that the common people originally went naked, even in the streets of their towns, and that they were 'ugly, black and fuzzy haired'—a common (and unfair) criticism by the ethnocentric Chinese, who valued light skin colouring and spurned the 'barbarians' of the tropical lands. Puzzlingly, the Funanese are also described as being peaceful yet warlike, honest yet cunning. Probably, like human beings in general, they were a mixture of traits, although the discrepancies perhaps point to multiple authors, poor editing or muddled data available to the writers.

The Funanese, unlike the later Khmers, appear to have been keen seafarers, trading with India and China and sending tribute to the Chinese emperors. If Funan were a unitary state its capital is not known, with conflicting claims made by modern writers for Vyadhapura, Angkor Borei, Banteay Prei Nokor and even Prey Veng, all situated in the Mekong delta or reasonably close to it. Another Funanese centre, the port town of Oc Eo in what is today called the Camau peninsula, was excavated by the French archaeologist Louis Malleret before World War II.

Oc Eo was laid out geometrically, which suggests that it was planned—again by a strong state power, however geographically limited the extent of its authority might have been. The ruins of some brick buildings remain; stone is rarely found in the alluvium of the delta and the wooden or bamboo houses of the common people have long since disappeared. The brick buildings were probably temples and/or mausoleums, but they are of a simple design and do not appear to have housed bas-reliefs (stone friezes) as in the later temples of Angkor. One intriguing building at Oc Eo was a square brick structure, called 'Edifice A' by Malleret. He speculated that perhaps it was a 'tower of silence' similar to the raised platforms on which the Parsees of India to this day leave out their dead for consumption by vultures. Other writers have disputed this, noting Chinese accounts that the Funanese dead were cast into the delta waters and presumably eaten by the crocodiles.

As elsewhere in Cambodia, further exploration of archaeological sites was interrupted by the subsequent decades of war, domestic upheaval and international isolation. It is likely that what we know of Funan will be greatly enhanced by the current work of the Lower Mekong Archaeological Project (LOMAP), coordinated by the University of Hawaii.

Water was a significant element of life for the Funanese. Rainfall averages 2540 millimetres per year in the delta, and immense quantities of water pour through the network of distributaries of the Mekong. Although some writers concluded that the canals of Funan were the model for the presumed 'hydraulic city' of Angkor, based on irrigation, in fact Funan had too much water, rather than seasonally too little like its illustrious successor. In order to farm the low-lying, swampy delta lands, excess water had to be drained off into the Mekong's distributaries and provision made to prevent flooding. Essentially, the canals were for drainage. It is possible, too, that they served also as communication routes, linking Oc Eo with Angkor Borei and other centres for trade purposes. Oc Eo itself seems to have been, like Venice, built on canals, which the Chinese tell us were swarming with crocodiles.

The Chinese have left us fascinating details of the customs of the people. Like the modern Khmers, the Funanese lived in simple houses made of wood or bamboo, with palm thatch roofs and elevated on stilts. Their staple foods were, as today, rice and fish, the latter being plentiful in the streams and marshes. They also cultivated and ate fruits such as oranges and pomegranates, and grew sugar cane, perhaps fermenting the juice for alcoholic drinks. The French scholar Paul Pelliot tells us that they shaved their heads to mourn the dead, that at some stage they adopted loincloths to cover their nakedness, perhaps on the orders of their ruler, and that they watched cock and hog fights for diversion. The Funanese also had advanced metallurgical technology. They used bronze and iron tools and were capable of designing and smelting intricate bronze ornaments, some of which have survived and are housed in museums. Slavery was an integral part of what must have been a highly stratified society. Justice was rudimentary, but a legal code probably existed and like that of India (and that of Angkor and post-Angkorean Cambodia) included trial by ordeal. Innocence might be decided if a suspect was not eaten after being thrown to the ubiquitous crocodiles.

Although there is no evidence to suggest, as some writers have done, that the civilisations of the region were built by waves of immigrants from India, Indian cultural influences were crucial in shaping societies such as Funan. Indian traders arrived in the region in at least the first century AD and Funan became linked to a system of trade routes stretching as far away as Persia and Europe to the west and China to the north. According to the Chinese chronicles, the Funanese also had a powerful navy, which suggests that they themselves ventured onto the seas to trade. Excavations of Funanese sites have unearthed Roman coins, although it is unlikely that any Funanese sailors travelled as far as Europe and the coins probably changed hands many times across the continents and oceans before they arrived in Funan.

Indian influence was above all religious and cultural, but this would have had political ramifications, too. The Funanese adopted Sanskrit in the same way that European societies later used Latin for liturgical and intellectual purposes. Chinese visitors in the third century AD saw large libraries, with extensive collections of Sanskrit books. None of these have survived the insects and humidity, but it is probable that they resembled the religious books still in use in 19th century Cambodia, which were made of palm leaves stitched or glued together. Perhaps too, like the books the Chinese traveller Zhou Daguan later observed at Angkor, the pages were dyed black and written on (or scratched) with a sharp stylus. The Indians most certainly brought the Hindu religion, with the worship of Siva, Brahma and Vishnu and the Hindu world view, with the idea of Mount Meru as the centre of the world, surrounded by oceans, to be replicated in the erection of temples on hilltops, with water around the perimeters of the sites. There are also examples of early Buddhist art in Cambodia from this period. It is likely that in those days, as is the case with Buddhism in Cambodia today, Indian religion was blended with earlier folk religions and superstitions.

The decline of Funan

According to the Chinese accounts, the last king of Funan was called Rudravarman and he was chiefly distinguished in their eyes because he offered the gift of a live rhinoceros to the Emperor at Beijing in 539 AD. After this, the historical record becomes somewhat blurred. For many years, it was believed that Funan declined or disappeared because it was threatened by the rise of another, more powerful state called Chenla or Zhenla to the north. Again, Chenla, like Funan, is a Chinese corruption of an indigenous word, but we do not know what. There is a Chinese account of seventh century Cambodia, but it was written by Ma Touan-Lin in the 13th century, many hundreds of years after the events it describes. Although it contains many details, one is inclined to be sceptical given that the author believed Funan was an island. (It is, however, possible that Ma Touan-Lin believed this because one or more of the Funanese towns might have been built on islands in the delta.) Chinese sources also mention a King Bhavavarman, who lived during the late sixth century, and whom the scholar George Coedès believed might have been descended from Funanese royalty and married into a Khmer family from further inland.

Some authors even claimed that there were two Chenlas—one dubbed Chenla-of-the-Land, and the other Chenla-of-the-Water. This is possibly an echo of the confusion of a time in which the Cambodian lands were divided into a number of principalities. There is not even agreement about where Chenla might have been, or hard evidence to back up claim and counterclaim. Some accounts place Chenla in the Champassak region of what is today southern Laos. However, Michael Vickery points out that the inscriptions left by the chieftains of the adjoining Dangrek region make no reference to Chenla, and that it is most likely that Chenla existed within the boundaries of the modern Cambodian state, somewhere between the Great Lake to the west and Kampot, Takeo or Kompong Speu to the east, and within the Mekong Valley. The question is whether Chenla was a unified state, or whether Cambodia was divided into a number of principalities in the sixth, seventh and eighth centuries; probably the latter is the case. As Vickery points out, there was an 'explosion' of Khmer epigraphy from the seventh century, with the earliest recorded Khmer stone inscription dating from 612 AD at Angkor Borei. None of this refers to what the Chinese called Chenla. Probably, the decline of Funan was relative, with power devolving to a multiplicity of petty kingdoms along the Mekong.

What is at least clear is that the people who lived in the lower Mekong Valley and delta in this period were the ancestors of the modern Khmers, speaking an archaic form of the Cambodian language. The last years of the pre-Angkorean period appear to have been a dark era for the Khmers. It is probable that the Javanese invaded Cambodia during the eighth century and enforced vassal status on to the Khmer kings. A travelling Arab merchant, Suleyman, has recorded how a disgruntled Cambodian monarch, perhaps King Mahipativarman, expressed the wish to have the head of Saliendra, the Sultan of Zabag (Java), handed to him on a platter. Saliendra heard of this, and resolved to punish his unruly vassal. He dispatched troops, who put the Khmers to flight, decapitated the unhappy Khmer king and placed his head on a platter for Saliendra.

Jayavarman II moves his capital to the Great Lake region

Out of adversity, however, came triumph. In the last years of the eighth century, a restless Khmer king, Jayavarman II, resolved to move his capital from the lower Mekong to what is today the Siem Reap region north of the Great Lake. Vickery believes it likely that Jayavarman II came from eastern Cambodia, close to the Cham lands. In all probability, when he reached adulthood he would have been one petty Khmer kinglet among many. Yet he was to achieve extraordinary things. He was to reign for 48 years, to unite and pacify the multifarious statelets of the Khmer lands and to throw off the Javanese yoke.

Curiously, given his pivotal importance in Cambodian history, we know relatively little of Jayavarman II's reign. The surviving stone inscriptions don't reveal much and the Chinese chronicles are silent. Yet in 802 AD, according to the inscriptions, this man was to found the Angkorean Empire and establish a line of *devarajas*, or god-kings, that was to last for over 600 years and establish a mighty civilisation that could rival any of the other states of antiquity. His reign marks a sharp punctuation in the relative equilibrium of Khmer politics and society.

3
THE ANCIENT ANGKOREAN CIVILISATION

The world loves a good mystery, especially if it is an ancient one. Ancient Egypt provided the 'riddle of the Sphinx'. Religious zealots have claimed the antique cities of the Americas were the work of extra-terrestrials. The temples of Ancient Angkor—the largest ruins in the world and the only archaeological site visible from outer space—have presented their own share of riddles and these have prompted fanciful explanations for generations of visitors and readers.[1] The novelist Pierre Loti wrote in the first decade of the 20th century of Angkor as a remote place steeped in impenetrable mystery: nothing could be known about the purposes of the ruins, a brooding, unfathomable Other. Even the age of the city was exaggerated in many accounts.

The French naturalist Henri Mouhot is supposed to have 'discovered' Angkor by accident, allegedly whilst chasing butterflies in the jungle—a claim he himself never made as he was guided there by a French priest, Father Sylvestre. Another French missionary, Father Bouillevaux, had left an account of an earlier visit and Mouhot was aware of this. When questioned about Angkor's origins, Khmer peasants said giants built it. Europeans commonly believed that the builders belonged to a 'vanished race'. Others claimed that the city was of Indian, Roman, or even Italian origin, alleging common features with Mediterranean architecture. Victorian etchings depict intrepid Frenchmen in tropical whites and sola topees treading resolutely amidst broken masonry festooned with the roots of giant trees. So potent was the image that people reacted with horror when archaeologists of the École Française d'Extrême-Orient began to clear the forest and restore the temples. Even today, the root-bound ruins of Ta Prohm pander to this taste for the 'exotic'.

The truth about Angkor is rather more prosaic and yet, on another plane, more fascinating, because it is a story not of giants or extra-terrestrials, but of people just like us. The ancestors of today's Khmers built Angkor and the temple complex of the Heritage Area as the centre of a powerful empire and of a dispersed city with between 700 000 and one million inhabitants; it was the most populous city of antiquity, sprawling over an area of 1000 square kilometres or more. Today, in the elegant words of George Coedès, we see only 'the religious skeleton of the city', for the humble peasant dwellings and the richly decorated pavilions of the kings have long since rotted into the earth. The city was abandoned rather later than the romantics would have us believe and there is firm epigraphic and bibliographic evidence that it was still inhabited in the 16th century when Iberian monks first visited Cambodia. Although there is lively debate about a number of features of Angkorean civilisation, recent technological advances have enabled archaeologists to provide plausible answers to the puzzle of why the city was deserted. Although it is likely that a number of interlinked causes contributed to the collapse of this great civilisation, perhaps the most important was ecological degradation of the forests, water and soil. The fate of Angkor is a warning to the modern world that we are part of nature and must live within natural laws or face our ecological nemesis. If I have mentioned crocodiles more than once in this book, it is because I am aware of the ecological changes that

have greatly reduced the numbers of this awesome, yet vulnerable, creature in Cambodia.

Sources of information

Thanks to the painstaking work of generations of archaeologists, philol-
ogists and other scholars, we now know a great deal about the society
that built Angkor and the other architectural marvels of Cambodia.
The ruins themselves are the most obvious record of Khmer material
culture, and the bas-reliefs of the Bayon and Angkor Wat provide an
extensive pictorial record of Khmer society. These illustrate the everyday lives of the people and the deeds of the rulers. They show how the
inhabitants made war, fished, farmed, sold their merchandise, played
games and erected the great monuments.

One problem has been that, unlike other ancient civilisations, the
Khmers have left us no books. When H.G. Wells' fictional time traveller ventured far into the future, he found the ragged remnants of the
books of a long-dead civilisation within the solid walls of an ancient
library. The ancient Khmers had libraries, but the books have vanished.
The Chinese chronicles provide a record of the world's longest civilisation and the ghosts of the Romans, Greeks and Indians speak to us
through the pages of their books. The Irish have the splendidly illustrated *Book of Kells*, which dates almost exactly from the time at which
Jayavarman II founded Angkor. The Dead Sea scrolls are even older,
dating from the first century AD, a time when thousands of miles away
on the other side of Asia, the Funanese had begun construction of
their towns and libraries and canals. The soft Irish climate and the dry
desert air have been kinder to paper and papyrus than the tropical heat,
humidity and voracious insects have been to the palm leaf books of
the ancient Khmers.

There is only one written eyewitness record of Angkor, *The
Customs of Cambodia*, written during the late 13th century by the

Chinese traveller Zhou Daguan (Chou Ta-Kwan), who spent a year in the capital shortly after the death of King Jayavarman VIII, the last great builder of Angkor. The country appears to have been completely unknown to Europeans. The great Venetian traveller Marco Polo visited neighbouring Champa in 1288, and the peripatetic Italian friar Odoric of Pordenone wandered through Indochina in the 14th century, but neither mentioned Cambodia in their accounts of their travels. When Iberian travellers arrived in Cambodia roughly two centuries after Odoric's visit to Champa, Angkor's glory days were past, and the city was menaced by its powerful neighbours, Siam and Vietnam.

The Khmers of course did leave a written record, but it was carved in stone rather than written on paper. There are around 1200 stone inscriptions in the Angkor region, written in either Sanskrit, Khmer or, from the 13th century, in Pali, the sacred language of the Theravada Buddhists. Most of the Sanskrit inscriptions are prayers to the gods or to Buddha, or tell us the genealogies of the kings, ruling families and Brahman priests, together with praise of their putative good works and military and civic virtues.

While the Sanskrit inscriptions are an invaluable record of the religious life of Angkor, the Khmer epigraphy tells us much more about the everyday lives, customs and occupations of the people. The epigraphs tell us a great deal about the earthly city, the empire and the complex and hierarchical system of administration. They show that Angkor was a highly literate society, at least among the elites, and that those who wrote the inscriptions had a lively sense of style, with a love of puns and figures of speech and an appreciation of tragedy and comedy.

However, much of the literary treasures of Angkor perished when the frail materials on which they were written rotted to dust after the city was abandoned. Between them, the sources allow us to understand much about a society that was once held to be impossibly mysterious. Yet the sharp edges are blurred, the voices are muted, and we see this civilisation through a glass darkly. There are murky lacunae in our knowledge and perhaps our explanations of Khmer society might still come under challenge in the future as fresh evidence emerges with the new archaeological tools of aerial and satellite photography, radar imaging and radiometric dating. There are some heated debates about Angkor, particularly around the archaeologist Bernard-Philippe Groslier's 'hydraulic city' hypothesis, yet as another French archaeologist Christophe Pottier has cautioned, we should 'put aside theoretical dogmatism' until more facts are in.

Why was the capital moved?

The founder of Angkor, King Jayavarman II, is a shadowy figure and we still have no entirely satisfactory explanation as to why he moved his capital from the Mekong Valley to the drier region at the north-west tip of the Great Lake. He left no inscriptions that we know of. We know that he established his court in the region in 802 AD and that he reigned for almost 50 years before his death at Roluos, south-east of the main complex at Angkor.

The Angkor region was not virgin land when Jayavarman II arrived. Archaeological evidence shows that the land between the Great Lake and the sandstone hills to the north was inhabited at least as far back as 1200 BC, with Iron Age remains at Phnom Bakheng. Probably, there were small farming settlements in the region ruled over by petty kinglets. Jayavarman II's arrival was to transform the region. From his base at Angkor the king was able to unify the petty Khmer principalities into the single polity that was to become the centre of one of the most powerful, wealthy and populous civilisations in ancient history. At its zenith, Angkor was to control an empire that stretched from the South China Sea to the Isthmus of Kra and the Andaman Sea, and northwards into what is today Laos. As historians Ian Mabbett and David Chandler have pointed out, many of the subjects of this vast empire lived at remote distances to the capital city; even if they had obtained permission to travel, an elephant journey of only 50 miles from Battambang to Angkor would have taken five days, as it still did in the 19th century. This was no nation-state, but a multi-ethnic empire in which one ethnic group, the Khmers, was dominant. The core of the kingdom was the dispersed metropolis of Angkor—larger than Rome or any of the ancient Chinese cities, if we are to believe the most recent archaeological evidence—and Angkor was a Khmer city.

King Jayavarman II's restlessness did not end when he moved his court to the Great Lake region. During his reign he would build three capitals, abandoning each before he made his final choice at Roluos. Regarding his move to Angkor, Michael Vickery has suggested that it resulted from military and political pressure from the hostile kingdom of Champa. Angkor was also remote from the coast of the South China Sea—and seaborne enemies such as the Javanese—with access hindered by the numerous sandbars and treacherous currents of the Mekong delta. At that time, too, the Siamese threat to the west did not exist. Other writers have suggested that the lake region was the 'natural centre' of the Cambodian state, at the junction of roads linking the valleys of the Mekong and Menam, at the highest point of navigation upstream from the Mekong delta, with ample supplies of sandstone for building, rich in natural resources such as timber and fish, and with fertile soil to grow rice to feed a growing population.

Yet although Cham, and perhaps Javanese, hostility might well have contributed to Jayavarman's decision to move his capital to a more defensible site, the other explanations noted above are not very convincing.[2] The English writer Christopher Pym argues in his excellent book on Angkor that the current capital, Phnom Penh, lies at a more commanding site, the Quatre Bras. Moreover, it is likely that the land routes were only developed *after* the foundation of Angkor, and the most direct route between the Mekong and Menam valleys follows the path of the French-built railway through Battambang, to the south-west of the Great Lake. Nor is sandstone as close by as some writers claim. The Phnom Kulen quarries lie some 40 kilometres to the north of the centre of Angkor and the soils are not as naturally fertile as those in the Mekong Valley, although they are probably more fertile and less sodic and saline than those in many other parts of Cambodia. It is true that the Great Lake is an almost boundless source of the fish that, along with rice, is the staple of the Khmer diet, but fish are just as plentiful elsewhere in the lake and especially around the entrance to the Tonlé Sap River that drains it via the Plain of Mud into the Mekong at the eastern end. It is also true that there was ample timber close to Angkor for domestic buildings, scaffolding for construction of the temples and for fuel but, then again, much of Cambodia is equally well endowed with forest.

The relative paucity of inscriptions from the reigns of Jayavarman II and his son of the same name do not help us explain the move. Perhaps, as Pym sensibly argues, the move was sparked by Jayavarman's desire to get out of the 'centre of things' in Southeast Asia by relocating to a remote site. However, one intriguing suggestion is that climate change might have contributed to the move. James Goodman, an engineer with an interest in archaeology, argued at a recent convention of Angkorean scholars in Japan that the move 'coincided with a series of remarkable changes in global climate patterns' associated with the Southern Oscillation Index (ENSO). The late eighth century saw the onset of the 'medieval warm period', with a 'wet anomaly' in Cambodia and 'dry anomalies' elsewhere on the Pacific Rim, including Java. The wet anomaly might have caused increased flooding in the lower Mekong Valley and delta, but would also have meant more humid, favourable conditions for agriculture in the seasonally drier regions to the north of the Great Lake. Angkor also lies on higher ground, normally beyond the reach of flooding. Goodman also speculated that the relative decline of the power of Java, Cambodia's former suzerain, might have been due to the onset of the dry anomaly, which would have unfavourably affected Javanese riziculture, as it did other civilisations around the Pacific Rim. That such climate change did occur is attested to by analysis of the pollen record, but more research needs to be done to ascertain its contribution to Jayavarman II's move.

The move did not mean emigration to a land of milk and honey. Settlement near the tip of the lake required strenuous labour before the virgin lands could become productive. Marshes needed to be drained, embankments built to stop floods and—as Bernard-Philippe Groslier argues—an intricate system of canals built for irrigation purposes, for if the climate were anything like that of the Siem Reap area today, it would have been one of six months' rain and six months' drought. The hydraulic system, however, was not started until after Jayavarman II's death, when in 877 AD King Indravarman I ordered construction of the Indratataka, the 'sacred pool of Indra', a large *baray* or reservoir measuring 3.6 kilometres by 800 metres.

As we shall see, the question of whether Angkor depended on highly developed irrigation is a moot point. It seems likely, therefore, that the shift to the Great Lake region would have been due at least in part to religious imperatives; Cambodia was, and still is, an intensely religious society. As the Japanese scholar Yoshiaki Ishizawa has argued, the choice of site has religious symbolism for the Khmers, who took their cosmology from the Indians who believed that at the centre of the world was Mount Meru, surrounded by oceans and seas and walled off by the Himalayas. Khmers tend to build their temples on hills to reflect this belief; Angkor stood on higher ground and just as India has the sacred Ganges and the sacred mountains, so Cambodia had the Siem Reap River and the Great Lake, with Phnom Kulen and the Dangreks to the north. The decision to shift the Khmer capital to Angkor was probably caused by a variety of overlapping political, economic, religious and perhaps ecological factors. Short of raising Jayavarman II from the grave, we will probably never know for sure.

The kings, their temples and monuments

A passion for grand monuments marks the greater part of the six or seven centuries of Angkorean civilisation and this only abated with the

Angkor Wat showing the five towers. (Author's collection)

spread of Theravada Buddhism, which spurned vanity and megalomania. Slaves, serfs and artisans expended the sweat of centuries on the sandstone mausoleums-cum-temples of the *kamrateng jagat*, the 'lords of the universe', who ruled over them. Scholars disputed the purpose of the temples for many years until in 1933 Jean Przyluski formulated his thesis, daring for the time, that Angkor Wat was both a temple and the tomb of Suryavarman II, and thus both a sepulchre and the centre of a funerary cult. The grand buildings of Angkor are at one and the same time funerary temples, mausoleums and tombs, the 'distinctive glory of the Khmer Empire' in the words of the celebrated French epigrapher George Coedès. Although those who ordered their construction have long since rotted into the soil, their monuments still bid us to 'look upon my works, ye mighty, and tremble', for the kings assigned to themselves the title of gods—*devarajas*—though they were 'creatures of clay' like the meanest of their subjects.

Marvellous though they are as architecture and works of art, the temples of Angkor are the reflection of the overweening egotism and peculiar religiosity of the hereditary rulers, for whom no sacrifice was great enough provided it was made by their slaves and willing subjects, whose warm blood and sweat could not outlive the cold stone they placed block on block in the exquisite confections of Angkor. Perhaps, when we gaze on these stupendous monuments, we should muse over their human cost. That said we should be wary of extrapolating modern attitudes and ideologies into the remote Cambodian past. For many free men—serfs at least—it was probably an honour to toil on the monuments for the glory of the god-kings; for many slaves, their condition was one legitimised by age-old custom, as natural as the setting of the sun. They had no words for freedom and liberty.

The purpose of these immense buildings had nothing in common with the great cathedrals of Europe or the grand mosques of the Muslim world. Nor were they like the modern pagodas of the Theravada Buddhists of Cambodia and neighbouring countries. Angkor Wat is, on the face of it, a temple dedicated to Vishnu, but the deity worshipped here is not the same as the ancient god of the Hindu triumvirate. Rather it is King Suryavarman II, the temple's inspirer, who was seen in life as the incarnation of Vishnu. Hence, as eminent French scholar Paul Mus wrote, these buildings are not so much shelters for the dead 'as a kind of new architectural body—a house of the dead but only in the same way that his body lived in it while still alive'. Even the numerous statues of Vishnu and Siva are dissimilar to most of their kind in India, for they have the features of the kings who were the earthly incarnations of the gods. The temples are the houses of the god-kings, the lords of the universe, immortalised in solid rock. They were not like pagodas, churches or mosques where the common people might come to pray. If they were ever admitted, it would only be to grovel at the feet of the mighty *devarajas*.

The monument building obsession began some years after the death of Jayavarman II's son and successor, Jayavarman III; although these first two kings did leave some hilltop shrines and smaller monuments, they were dwarfed by later developments. A new king,

Indravarman I, ordered the previously mentioned *baray* and also the Preah Ko and Bakong temples. Indravarman was succeeded in 889 AD by Yasovarman I, who built a new reservoir, the Yasodharatataka, with the Lolei temple on an artificial island in the lake. Yasovarman also ordered construction of the temple mountain of Phnom Bakheng, excavating the slopes of a hill to form a pyramidal structure surmounted by five central towers and 104 smaller ones. The 13th century Chinese chronicler Zhou Daguan says that a Khmer king is buried at Phnom Bakheng, and if this is the case it was both a temple and a mausoleum, as Przyluski speculated. During Yasovarman's reign, engineers appear to have diverted the course of the Siem Reap River and built the large Eastern Baray, the latter fact attested to in an inscription in its northeast corner.

Subsequent kings continued the program of temple building and waterworks. In the tenth century, King Rajendravarman ordered the construction of a series of monuments, including the Pre Rup temple. The temple of Takeo dates from the reign of Jayavarman V in the final years of the tenth century. Suryavarman I, who reigned from 1002 until 1049, was responsible for the construction of the huge West Baray and a number of temples including Preah Vihar in the Dangrek Mountains. Suryavarman II, who reigned in the early part of the 12th century, ordered the construction of what is arguably the most famous of the Angkorean temples, Angkor Wat, the name of which is often confused with the city of Angkor itself because of its imposing beauty and scale. Suryavarman II's successor, Yasovarman II, had the temple of Bakong built. Jayavarman VII, a Buddhist king who reigned during the last decades of the 12th century and the first two of the 13th, ordered construction of the temple of Ta Prohm and the first stages of the Terrace of the Elephants, along with the impressive Angkor Thom, dedicated to Buddha (not Siva or Vishnu as is commonly supposed) and extensive waterworks including the Jayatataka *baray*.

These public works—if such is the name for private edification at public expense—were augmented by more utilitarian infrastructure,

footways, bridges, rest houses, hospitals, canals, reservoirs and embankments. The empire was administered and policed via a network of
well-maintained roads, which also served for trade purposes. These roads
often ran on stone causeways or earthen embankments, high above
the floodplains of lakes and rivers, and well-engineered bridges spanned
the rivers. Although the network fell into disrepair after the decline of
the empire, some of it was re-opened by the French and is still in use
today. One particularly imposing bridge, the Spean Praptos, crosses
the ravine of the Stung Chikreng and is still open to traffic. Guest-
houses were built at regular intervals along the major roads—22 between
Angkor and Kompong Thom alone—for shelter and security against
bandits who preyed on travellers. The wealthy rode in palanquins
(hammocks slung between Y-shaped poles and carried by muscular
servants), or astride horses or aboard tented structures on the backs of
elephants. But the poor travelled in buffalo carts, much the same as
they do today, or else they walked. During the six-month rainy season,
boats were used for some journeys, as they were all year round on the
Great Lake which lay to the south of Angkor, and along which Zhou
Daguan travelled on his way up from the far-away delta of the Mekong.

The climax of empire

Jayavarman VII's reign, between the late 12th and early 13th centuries,
is regarded as the climax of the empire. Angkor stood at the centre
of a vast realm that extended from the Andaman Sea in modern
Myanmar to the South China Sea in today's Vietnam, and far north-
wards into what is now Laos. Although it might have been ultimately
constrained by what modern historians call 'imperial overstretch',
Angkor's expansion was checked by natural, rather than human
barriers—seas, mountain ranges and impassable jungles. However, as
George Coedès has written, the huge effort needed to carry out Jayavarman VII's building program was an ultimately unsustainable drain on
the resources of the empire. The empire also sustained vast numbers
of unproductive people, including aristocrats and Brahman priests,

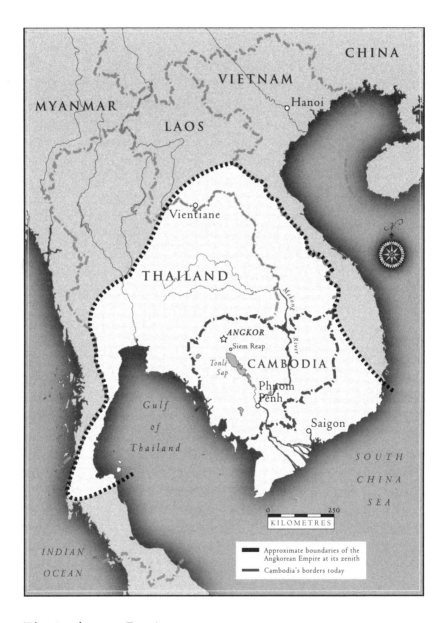

The Angkorean Empire

members of the religious orders and the royal family itself. An inscription translated by George Coedès recorded that the *devaraja* cult necessitated 306 372 'servitors', who lived in 13 500 villages and ate 38 000 tons of rice every year. This does not take into account the immense amount of riches in the form of silver, gold, bronze and stone appropriated by the cult.

This empire was maintained by force of arms, often clashing with neighbouring peoples such as the Chams and later the Thais, both of whom were formidable opponents. In contradiction to the modern European stereotype of Cambodia as 'the gentle land', the Angkor bas-reliefs depict a warlike society. Men march in formation, armed with a variety of weapons including swords, lances, bows and arrows and clubs. Catapults are mounted on carts or the backs of elephants. Commanders canter on horseback while their men march past resolutely in grim processions. Elephants were also employed for cavalry purposes, their foreheads anointed with human gall which, as Zhou tells us, was drained from the bodies of hapless passers-by by men armed with special knives. Other scenes show naval battles, with unfortunates falling overboard into the jaws of the lurking crocodiles. On the other hand, an inscription at Ta Prohm extols Jayavarman VII as a 'provident and compassionate ruler' and perhaps not without cause. Although he was determined to bend the population to his will to make his mark on posterity in the form of huge temples and monuments, he also built 102 hospitals during his reign.

The last great spurt of building activity occurred during the reign of Jayavarman VII (1181–1219). These works included the construction of Ta Prohm, Banteay Kdei, Preah Khan, Banteay Chhmar and the magnificent Bayon. However, during the 16th century, when the first Europeans visited Cambodia, King Satha I carried out extensive renovations to monuments and the hydraulic system.

Building the temples

Visitors to the ruins often wonder how they were built and where the immense blocks of stone used in their construction came from. The Khmers certainly were ingenious engineers, but the construction program relied on the muscle power of tens of thousands of labourers. The temples are built of an assortment of materials—laterite, three different types of sandstone, and brick, some of which was rendered with stucco. The laterite was obtainable locally, but the sandstone was brought considerable distances from the Phnom Kulen quarries, where men cut it from the living rock with crowbars, chisels and fire. Many of the blocks weigh up to five tonnes, and the very largest include one of eight tonnes at Angkor Wat and another of almost ten tonnes at Preah Vihar.

In the past, observers have speculated that the blocks were dragged by elephants, loaded on ox carts, floated down the Siem Reap River from Phnom Kulen, or sometimes taken on rafts down other tributaries then across the lake and up the Siem Reap River to Angkor. While these methods are possibilities for the smaller pieces of stone, it seems unlikely they were used for the bigger blocks. Ox carts could not support the weight and elephants probably lacked the stamina needed to transport the blocks from the Kulen Hills, which stand approximately 40 kilometres from the temple sites. In 1999, an attempt was made to float stone down the river from the ancient quarries. It was concluded that this was an unlikely method; to move a five-tonne block would require an enormous raft built of 1000 pieces of ten-centimetre diameter bamboo. It is more likely that human muscle power was employed, with the largest blocks requiring the strength of up to 160 men, their task only made slightly less onerous by the use of wooden rollers, crowbars and rattan ropes. (Even today, heavy machinery is sometimes rolled into position using similar techniques, but for a fraction of the distance.) There is some evidence to suggest this on the Bayon bas-reliefs (upper gallery, east side), which appear to depict men hauling stone blocks with the assistance of rollers, although there is some damage to the bottom of the frieze, which leaves this interpretation open to question. This gruelling work in the tropical heat and humidity was more than likely allocated to the lowest grades of slaves. There was probably a more complex division of labour at the actual construction sites: general labourers to supply raw muscle power; skilled masons and bricklayers, carpenters, scaffolders and riggers, perhaps; metalworkers, who gilded many of the domes; and finally, the most skilled artisans of all, those who carved the statues and the exquisite and complicated bas-reliefs in the corridors of Angkor Wat and the Bayon.

When the blocks were on site, the construction workers would take over and the exhausted transport crews would perhaps be allowed to rest a while before returning to Phnom Kulen for more stone. The blocks were dressed on site and a close fit was achieved by grinding the blocks against each other; joints are rarely at right angles and there are rarely perfectly flat planes. After this, the blocks would be rolled to the base of the worksite, ready to be lifted into position to where the masons toiled high above on wooden or bamboo scaffolding probably very similar to that which is still widely used in Asia today, as is shown on the Bayon friezes.

The builders probably used a variety of lifting gear to assist in their work. There is some evidence of the use of metal lifting dogs and clamps and it is highly likely that blocks were also lifted on rope slings, which were attached to wooden pegs inserted into holes drilled in the stone. Afterwards, the pegs were removed and the holes filled with mortar, as we can see on many of the monuments today. We also know from the Bayon bas-reliefs that Khmer sailors used windlasses and pulleys, so it is probable that similar lifting gear was used at Angkor, logically in conjunction with gin poles, sheerlegs, gallows frames, whip hoists and rudimentary cranes. Perhaps other stones were winched up temporary inclines of compacted earth. One can imagine the scene high above the ground atop the scaffolding—workers spreading mortar compounded of powdered limestone, vegetable juice and palm sugar, in the shadow of a huge block of stone swinging above, the labourers inching it down into position, their muscles aching from the effort. Construction work is dangerous even today with vastly superior technology, so the death toll must have been colossal with such enormous pieces of stone, dizzying heights and rattan ropes. We will never know how many workers plunged to their doom or were crushed to death by falling masonry.

One of the most curious facts about Khmer building techniques is that they never discovered the secret of the true arch, which employs a keystone to prevent it from falling down. Instead, the Khmer builders used the more rudimentary method of corbelling—gradually bringing in two facing edges of wall until they touch—giving an almost gothic appearance to the edifices. This technique can only be used with massive stone or brick walls, not for lighter domestic architecture. It can be seen on many of the ancient temples, and even on those Angkorean bridges that are still in use today. Another curiosity is that the columns of the temples are almost always square or rectangular in cross-section, probably because the Khmers were afraid that the natural round shape of trees was the abode of spirits. Where columns are round in section, this is because the Khmers wished to bring spirits into the building.

What kind of civilisation built the monuments?

Today, natural decay and the ravages of vandals and thieves (including the French novelist André Malraux, it might be said) have left their mark, but no one who visits Angkor can fail to be stirred by its grandeur. Yet, although the spectacular stone and brick ruins the kings left behind are the most visible reminders of Angkor's past glories, they tell us only part of the story and this chapter does not purport to be a guide to the ancient remains. What is perhaps even more intriguing is the question of what kind of civilisation was able to devote so much labour and so many resources to such gigantic projects. We actually know a surprising amount about the lives of the common people of Angkor. It is now clear that the temple complex was the centre of an enormous dispersed city, home to up to one million inhabitants, making it the largest city of antiquity. The empire itself comprised some 90 provinces at the time of Zhou Daguan's visit.

Zhou Daguan, who visited Angkor the year after Jayavarman VIII's death in 1295, has left us fascinating details of what the city was like during its period of human occupation, and although the decline had already set in by then, Angkor was still an impressive place. Zhou tells of a 'walled city' with five gates and lines of statues 'brilliant with gold'. Many of the buildings were gilded; Zhou describes a 'square tower of gold' (Neak Pean) at the centre of a lake, the 'Golden Tower' of the Bayon, and another of bronze. North of the Golden Tower was the royal palace, an opulent wooden structure with long colonnades and floors of yellow pottery and lead tiles. The immense lintels and columns of the palace were richly carved and there was a frieze of elephants in the chamber of state, lit by a golden window. In this setting, the king (Srindravarman at that time) moved around in sumptuous garments bedecked with pearls and precious stones. Although he had five official wives, he also kept a huge harem, with 'three to five thousand' concubines and 'palace girls' who seldom set foot outside the palace. The parents of noble families thought it an honour for their daughters to be accepted. Anyone wishing an audience with the king had to abase themselves, crawling across the floor, forbidden to actually look at this exalted personage or, more strictly, god-king.

The king never left the palace except as part of a grand procession of soldiers, palace girls, royal ministers and princes, many of them in palanquins and chariots or astride elephants with 'flags, banners and music' and hundreds of golden parasols held aloft. The king himself stood 'erect on an elephant and holding in his hand the sacred sword'. The royal elephant's tusks were 'sheathed in gold' and around the royal beast were the massed ranks of the king's bodyguard. Any passers-by who caught sight of the king 'were expected to kneel and touch the earth with their brows'. Marshals seized anyone who failed to comply, and placed him or her under arrest.

The Angkorean social system

In total, 28 kings ruled over this vast and powerful empire for over 600 years. Although in theory kingship was hereditary and monarchs were *devarajas*, or god-kings, in practice usurpers were common enough, the qualification being that they had to prove they were blood descendents of Jayavarman II, the founder of Angkor. It was for this reason that dignitaries and military leaders were required to swear an oath of loyalty to the reigning king, on pain of horrible punishments. One such oath is recorded in an inscription translated by Coedès, and promises eternal punishment in hell if it is broken. As the writers Mabbett and Chandler remarked, although Angkorean society was hierarchical, the fact of usurpation indicates that the rulers were not 'worshipped as gods and given unquestioning obedience by all their subjects'. The extraordinary security measures described by Zhou Daguan above attest to this.

Nevertheless, although they feared usurpation, these kings were absolute rulers in every sense of the term. As *devarajas*, their power surpassed even that of the European monarchs who claimed to rule by divine right. The inscriptions indicate that they were seen as incapable of breaking religious laws, and they were the source of all legal power in the empire. The law itself was administered via a hierarchy of courts and legal officials. The lower courts dealt with routine matters, but the royal court itself could deal with even the pettiest of matters. Zhou Daguan records that every day the king held two audiences, for which no agenda was provided and which could be attended by both 'functionaries and ordinary people' for the adjudication of disputes. The inscriptions show that commoners could bring lawsuits against one another and a common method of ascertaining who was in the wrong was to place the plaintiff and the accused in stone towers for a period of three to four days. It was held that the person in the wrong would always develop an illness, such as catarrh, fever or ulcers. The penalties for convicted malefactors were often draconian. For the gravest crimes the punishment was death, possibly by decapitation with a sharp sword, as in the 19th century, but it was possible for felons to be buried alive.

Five of the worst crimes are mentioned in the inscriptions: murder of a priest, theft, drunkenness, and adultery, or complicity in any of these. (The tradition persisted: during the reign of King Norodom under the French Protectorate, a young Vietnamese servant girl was put to death for knowledge of the adultery of her mistress, a wife in the king's harem.) It is also very likely that the Cambodian kings sponsored human sacrifice and that the custom predated Angkor and persisted into the 19th century. A Chinese account of a visit in 616 AD claims that the victims were dispatched during the night at a ceremony attended by the king at a hilltop temple called 'Ling-kia-po-pho'. David Chandler believes that human sacrifice in post-Angkorean Cambodia was reserved for those found guilty of serious crimes. The unfortunates were decapitated as part of the *loen nak ta* ceremony during rice planting as an offering to the consort of Siva.

The inscriptions also record a range of cruel punishments for lesser crimes, including punches to the face, flogging, amputation of the hands and lips, and squeezing of the feet or head in a vice. An inscription from the 11th century records that one wretch had both his hands and feet amputated. The methods of ascertaining guilt were no less cruel and included, as in China and Europe, trial by ordeal. Zhou relates that the accused might have his hand thrust into boiling water and would be deemed innocent if the skin did not flake into ribbons.

Angkor, in common with most state societies throughout recorded history, was never a democracy and although social stratification in Cambodia has never been as rigid as the caste system of India, there was little social mobility. The ruling elites owed their position to birthright and the lower orders by and large accepted their status as natural, particularly as it was closely bound up with the religious idea of one's station in this life being a reward or punishment for deeds in past lives. Liberty was an alien condition beyond the social imagination, without words to express it, although some 'plebeian' revolts do appear to have broken out before being brutally suppressed. The doctrine of reincarnation at least held out the promise of better luck next time, if one had lived an honest, obedient and virtuous life. As we shall see, life for the common people and slaves was onerous indeed and legends such as the Churning of the Sea of Milk gave hope to the downtrodden. This legend, depicted on the bas-reliefs of Angkor Wat, shows lines of people pulling a rope backwards and forwards, looped around a pole which is resting on the back of Kurma the tortoise. The aim of the exercise was to recover lost objects from the sea, foremost of which was ambrosia, the gift of immortality. Ambrosia also meant prosperous times, ample food, and well-deserved rest after the rigours of labour in the fields or construction sites.

The strict stratification of Khmer society was reflected in the division of the common people themselves into different categories; the *knum* who were bound to the monasteries, temples and religious orders; the peasants or the soldier-builder-farmer class; and slaves. The Angkorean civilisation supported a number of large religious foundations and monasteries, which had great influence in Khmer society and whose activities are recorded in some detail in the inscriptions. These orders controlled vast tracts of land and employed large numbers of workers. There is surprisingly little in the inscriptions about the monks and abbots of these orders, but a great deal about those who did the work, the *knum*, who appear to have been bound to the land in a condition akin to serfdom or perhaps slavery, although perhaps this condition was mitigated by the belief that they carried out the 'work of the gods'. Some of the *knum* appear to have been slaves in the strict sense of the word; they could be bought and sold and were often prisoners of war or captured hill tribesmen from beyond the settled lands. Others seem to have been villagers from the vicinity of the monasteries and foundations. The inscriptions are explicit on the division of labour, with field hands, herdsmen who looked after the herds of sacred cows, fruit pickers, guards and other outdoor workers. There were also weavers and clothing workers, secretaries, kitchen hands and cooks, even *parfumiers* and 'guards of the holy perfume'. Still others were employed as singers, dancers and musicians within the temples.

The most numerous class were the peasants, who also served as labourers on the temple construction sites, and who were liable to be mobilised into the army in time of war. These appear to have been a different category to the *knum*, for they were able to keep slaves themselves; Zhou Daguan records that only the very poorest peasants did not keep at least one slave. In many respects, the lives of this peasant class appear to have been similar to those of the modern Khmer peasants, who were until recently liable to serve as *corvée* labourers on the roads and other public works, or work free of charge for the benefit of rural notables. The men dressed in loincloths, the women wore a longer garment much like the *sampot* of today and both went naked to the waist. These garments were of simple design for, as Zhou tells us, the poor were forbidden to mimic the sumptuous garments of their 'betters', even if they could have afforded to do so.

Clothing reflected rank in this rigidly stratified society and only the king was allowed to wear clothing with an overall design. Whereas the common folk dressed in material of coarse fustian weave, the nobles were clad in silk, which most likely came from abroad (as did wool). Rank was also reflected in physical complexion, particularly for women. The women of the upper class prided themselves, as they do today, in their light complexions. They did not work outdoors and took parasols when they ventured outside. The skin of the women of the poorer classes was burned dark by the sun.

The soldier-builder-farmer class also included those who made their living by petty trade. The Bayon bas-reliefs depict market scenes, in which many of the traders were women, selling farm produce and other goods—or rather bartering them, for the Khmers had no currency. In addition, there were better-off Chinese merchants and a long history of Chinese settlement and intermarriage in Cambodia. Zhou records that Khmer wives were keenly sought after by Chinese settlers, who valued their business acumen.

Perhaps different from the *knum* were the slaves-proper, who must have been very numerous in Angkor. We do not know what proportion of the population were slaves, but if the evidence supplied by European observers in the 19th century is anything to go by their numbers must have been considerable—perhaps hundreds of thousands across the empire. The evidence from inscriptions, such as that at Preah Khan, suggests that slaves included debtors, hill tribesmen and prisoners of war. Slavery was hereditary, although they could in exceptional circumstances be emancipated by the king.

We do not know how much of the work was carried out by slaves, but it is likely that the Angkorean economy and public works schemes relied upon them to a large degree, although according to inscriptions they did *not* form the majority of the labour force. Most likely, they were put to the hardest physical labour, including tasks such as canal building and maintenance, and quarrying and transporting the enormous blocks of stone for the construction of the temples. However, other slaves did higher or less onerous grades of work, employed for example as clerks or scribes, domestic servants and musicians. Some were known by titles such as *ku*—or 'born for loving'—suggesting compulsory employment as prostitutes. Probably the worst treatment was meted out to hill tribespeople who, even up until the abolition of slavery by the French in the 19th century, were viewed with contempt. This is reflected in their names, one of which was recorded as 'Stinking'.

The price of slaves varied depending on individual age, strength and skill. Inscriptions from religious orders indicate that female slaves might be bought for twenty measures of unhusked rice. Another inscription records that a particular slave was exchanged for a metal spittoon. Yet another slave was bartered for a buffalo which itself was valued at five ounces of silver. Runaways were savagely punished; the milder retributions included slicing off the ears.

The religion of Angkor

Life for all except the Brahmans and the aristocracy must have been hard in Angkor, yet suffering was mitigated by the consolations of religion. Angkor, like modern Cambodia, was an intensely religious society, with all aspects of life inextricably bound up with faith. The religion of Angkor, as with Funan and the other Khmer principalities earlier, was imported from India, but was modified by local tradition. There was a caste of hereditary priests (a remnant of the broader Indian caste system, perhaps) who purported to trace their ancestry back to those who had served Jayavarman II. For most of the 600 years of Angkor, Hinduism cohabited fairly comfortably with Mahayana (Greater Vehicle) Buddhism, albeit mixed with Khmer folk beliefs and superstitions. At times the pattern was broken by periods of religious iconoclasm, during which partisans of the different sides damaged religious statues in sectarian frenzies much as the early Christians defaced the works of pagans in the Roman Empire. A number of Buddhist statues in the Bayon, for instance, were damaged—perhaps by Brahmans, as statues of Siva and Vishnu were not damaged.

The Cambodian variety of Hinduism differed in some ways from that in India. In India, Brahma was the chief god of the Hindu trinity; in Cambodia, Siva and Vishnu shared first place. During the 13th century, however, a new religion, or perhaps a variant of an older one, appeared. This was Theravada Buddhism, or the Lesser Vehicle. Although it shared many of the beliefs of the older Buddhist sect, Theravada Buddhism taught that one would arrive at nirvana via a saintly and ascetic life, during which one should be resigned to suffering. Quite simply, good karma was determined by doing good works. The Greater Vehicle held, in contrast, that one could achieve nirvana via appeals to incarnations of Buddha, or *bodhisattvas*. The two older religions had also merged with the *devaraja* cult, whereas Theravadism tended to undermine it. Some writers, George Coedès notable among them, have pointed to the possible role of this gentle religion in the decline

Apsara, celestial nymphs and dancers, were represented at the beautiful Banteay Srei.
(Author's collection)

of the empire. Yet it brought solace for the common people, on whom the demands of their rulers for labour on the temple construction sites had become an intolerable burden.

The idea of reincarnation was prominent in all of these religions, yet the very wicked and disobedient could suffer eternal damnation. The hell scenes on the Angkor Wat friezes show that blasphemers and those who destroyed religious artefacts, along with those who bore false witness and gluttons, adulterers, arsonists, liars, poisoners and thieves could expect to go to hell. Interestingly, given that hell in the western tradition is a place of perpetual fire, the Khmer version is one of eternal, bone-chilling cold. One frieze shows another Khmer vision of hell, with sinners climbing thorn trees as punishment for their wicked ways. Life and religion were inseparable; indeed, life without religion would have been unthinkable. And although the Khmer religion, particularly in its Theravada form, is in line with Marx's characterisation of religion as 'the sigh of an oppressed creature in a heartless world', the Hindu and Mahayana priests were an integral part of the ruling class and the caste system.

Everyday life in Angkor

Zhou has left an account of the houses of the common people, which were remarkably similar to those of the peasants today; built of wood or bamboo and standing on stilts, and thatched with woven sugar palm fronds, for they dared not imitate their social superiors who were allowed to put tiles on their roofs and live in larger dwellings of more intricate design, built of more durable woods such as *koki*. (Pieces of this tropical hardwood, richly decorated, have survived at Angkor Wat.) The interiors of the houses of the poor were much as found today in rural Cambodia: simple places, spread with palm mats and without tables or chairs. The common people had few possessions apart from some ceramic pots and other basic kitchen utensils.

Although they do not seem to have been a particularly sybaritic people, sexual morality was somewhat more liberal than in many other societies. Khmer mores allowed a wife or husband to have another sexual partner if a partner was absent for more than ten nights, although this could be dangerous as a husband could have a man who cuckolded him put in the stocks. Khmers married in their teenage years and once a couple were betrothed, premarital intercourse was accepted. A major rite of passage for girls was the custom Zhou Daguan has recorded as the *chen-t'en*, which tends to shock modern readers. Following lavish celebrations, a priest would deflower the girl with his hand, for which he would be rewarded with gifts of alcohol, rice, cloth, silver, betel and silk. In wealthier families, the ceremony happened when the girl was aged between seven and nine years old, in poorer, when she was 11. Some slave women appear to have been made to work as prostitutes, and male prostitution and homosexuality existed.

Although some Khmer customs, such as women urinating while standing up, struck Zhou as 'absurd', the Khmers for their part were equally shocked or amused by the behaviour of the Chinese, particularly by the latters' habit of cleaning themselves with paper instead of water after defecation. The Chinese custom of using human manure to fertilise the fields also shocked the Khmers, who abhorred it as bodily pollution, a belief probably inherited from India. These attitudes have continued to the present. More puzzling is the matter of how the ancient Khmers disposed of their dead. Zhou Daguan claims that corpses were either left outside the city for wild animals to dispose of, or were buried or cremated. (Earlier, in Funan, cadavers were cast into the rivers.) Zhou's belief that cremation of the dead was a new practice when he visited in the 13th century is contradicted by another Chinese account, which records that the custom was already established in the early seventh century. Although the Khmers believed in reincarnation, death was nevertheless an occasion for grief, and the mourners would shave their heads as a mark of respect and loss.

The staples of their diet were rice and fish, which was plentiful in the artificial and natural watercourses of Angkor, and which was cooked fresh or added to other dishes in the form of the pungent fermented paste, *prahoc*, as it is today. These staples were supplemented with fruit, particularly oranges and bananas, of which there were numerous kinds, but also tamarind, edible flowers (from the dipterocarp hardwoods, for example), coconut milk and flesh, mangoes and mulberries. A number of varieties of beans, along with sorghum millet and sesame, were also cultivated. Fermented alcoholic beverages were made from sugar cane and perhaps rice and honey. We know from the inscriptions that the Khmers ate venison and pork, but these meats were perhaps beyond the reach of the poorer members of society. They drank milk, but this, along with meat, was largely proscribed when Theravada Buddhism arrived. Although the fiery chillies with which Southeast Asians love to flavour their food were imported into the region by the Portuguese after the demise of Angkor, the ancient Khmers spiced up their food with a variety of condiments including cardamom, turmeric and black pepper (all of which are still grown in Cambodia today) and salt, which was brought by boat from the Kampot district adjacent to the Gulf of Siam.

There is a wealth of detail about the customs and amusements in Angkor. From these we know that the Khmers had a variety of musical instruments, including percussion (drums, cymbals, tambourines and bells) and stringed instruments resembling harps and guitars, or perhaps mandolins. Rockets and firecrackers were set off during major festivals, as Zhou observed. The bas-reliefs also depict: elephant, pig and cock fights; snake charmers, raconteurs and strolling minstrels; pugilistic games and archery contests; and team games, one of which resembled polo and which is depicted at the Terrace of the Elephants at Angkor Thom.

The hydraulic city debate

It is something of an understatement to say that water was important to the ancient Khmers. Angkor is situated in a region that is subjected to six months of drought and six months of rain every year, unlike the delta, where Funan was, which has high, year-round rainfall and a surfeit of river water. The early archaeologists quickly became aware that the ancient Khmers had built three enormous barays, or artificial lakes, the largest of which, the West Baray, measures some 8 kilometres by 3 kilometres. More recently, satellite imagery has revealed that there was a fourth baray, long since drained. The West Baray, started between c.975 and 1020 and completed in 1050, was formed by throwing up 10-metre high earthen ramparts, which extended for over 20 kilometres: a project that took colossal amounts of man-hours and human sweat to build. The first *baray*, the Indratataka, had been built earlier, in 877 AD, during the reign of Indravarman. Yasovarman I, who succeeded him to the throne, built a new reservoir, the Yasodharatataka, in 889 AD.

In 1961, the archaeologist Jacques Dumarçay found a length of copper pipe on the artificial island in the centre of the lake and this, together with other evidence, led him to surmise that the king would regularly visit and use the pipe to measure water levels to ascertain whether rice planting could begin. Dumarçay, like others before him, assumed that the purpose of the *barays* was at least partly to do with irrigation. This idea found its fullest expression in the work of the celebrated French archaeologist Bernard-Philippe Groslier, who developed his controversial 'hydraulic city' hypothesis in two articles published in 1974 and 1979. According to Groslier, a vast irrigation system of canals, tanks and larger reservoirs, of which the *barays* were part, had allowed the Khmers to plant two, and even three rice crops per year instead of one (Zhou Daguan claimed three or four crops annually). This highly efficient agricultural system had enabled the Khmers to provide for a huge city population of perhaps close to two million. The social surplus product also enabled the leisure time needed for the creation of sophisticated high culture, including the 'plastic arts' and literature. It also provided stockpiles of food to feed the enormous numbers of labourers and artisans necessary for the construction of the monumental temples of Angkor.

Although it is likely that Groslier's original population estimate was too high, Angkor was probably the largest pre-industrial city in the world. The most recent archaeological work indicates that one million is a reasonable estimate of the city's size. Groslier's hypothesis was important because it represented a shift in focus *away* from the monuments themselves to an investigation of the society that had produced them. This does not mean that scholars such as George Coedès had ignored the social dimensions of Angkor, but the emphasis did begin to swing to a more anthropological approach.

The hydraulic city debate soon came under fierce attack and the debate still rages, often with more heat than light. In 1980 and 1982, the distinguished writer W.J. van Lière published two articles in which he wrote that 'not a drop of water from . . . the temple ponds was used for agriculture'. Van Lière claimed that there was no evidence of the existence of a network of irrigation canals, or of intake or outfall structures at the *barays*. The ancient Khmer rice crop, he insisted, had depended on bunded fields and flood retreat agriculture, much as today. (The former refers to the practice of erecting low dikes around paddy fields to trap rainwater, the latter to a system of embankments to trap retreating floodwaters to irrigate crops.)

More recently, the American geographer Robert Acker has disputed Groslier's estimates of the size of Angkor's population, at the same time accepting van Lière's claims that there is no evidence to suggest the existence of irrigation works. James Goodman argues that the key to understanding the extraordinary productivity of Angkorean riziculture lies in the salient natural feature of the region—the Great Lake. Every year, during the monsoon and after the spring thaw in distant Yunnan, the volume of water in the Mekong is so great that it cannot drain away quickly enough through the delta to the sea. Immense quantities of water build up on the flat lands at Phnom Penh and, with nowhere else to go, flood upstream into the Tonlé Sap River, reversing the normal direction of flow and pouring into the Great Lake. As a result, the level of the lake rises by between 7 and 9 metres and floods an area of over 13 000 square kilometres. This, argues Goodman, made food production 'virtually climate proof'. Goodman also argues that the main settlement pattern of the Angkorean civilisation followed the flood line on the fertile lacustrine plain, with dense settlements between Angkor and Banteay Chhmar, rather than in the immediate environs of the temple complex adjacent to the modern town of Siem Reap. Goodman also points out that the soil in the vicinity of the monuments is poor and that it would have required heavy manuring to maintain any fertility. Although human manure has been used as fertiliser for many centuries in Vietnam and China, the practice, as noted previously, is abhorrent to the Khmers. Goodman asks why, if irrigation were the preferred method in ancient Angkor, it accounts for less than one per cent of rice produced in the Siem Reap region today. Finally, in the view of these critics of Groslier's original thesis, the *barays* and smaller artificial lakes had a purely religious purpose.

It is unfortunate that the debate has become so polarised, with supporters of the hydraulic city thesis dismissed as dogmatic Wittfogelians (see Glossary). Groslier never doubted that the *barays* and canals had a 'dual function', both for utilitarian and religious purposes, and argued that the Khmers would have made no distinction between the two. The Japanese scholar Yoshiaki Ishizawa maintains that 'in reality, it is impossible to separate the everyday lives of the Cambodian people from ponds and water'. The utilitarian purposes of the waterways (for example bathing, fishing, irrigation, flood control and drainage) were inseparable from the Khmers' religious faith. Many ponds are associated with temples and often the *barays* and smaller lakes have a religious shrine in the centre. It is very likely that the moats were originally dug to provide landfill for the temple mounds and that they served thereafter for drainage purposes. It is also clear from the inscriptions that the waterways served for purposes of religious purification and that the temple mounds and moats and *barays* were a symbolic representation of Khmer cosmology. The temple represents Mount Meru, at the centre of the world; the city walls represent the sacred Himalayas; the moats and *barays* represent the oceans and seas. The Siem Reap River, too, was the Khmer version of the sacred Ganges. So too were the drops of water with which the Khmers bathed their bodies or watered their crops seen as part of the sacred order of the world.

W.J. van Lière's assertion that not a drop of water from the *barays* and canals was used for irrigation has been repeated by Groslier's opponents without them checking the known facts. The evidence—much of it new—suggests strongly that the waterways *did* have a dual function. Many inscriptions refer directly to the waterways and although the majority of these do refer to their religious functions, some explicitly mention irrigation. One inscription in particular refers to *canhvar*, which means a waterway used for irrigation purposes. It should also be remembered that a number of Iberian travellers who visited Cambodia during the 16th century, when Angkor was still inhabited, remarked that the prosperity of the kingdom relied on irrigation.

This does not mean that the Khmers did not employ other methods for growing crops. It is altogether likely that they practised dry rice farming in remote areas and that they built dikes around other paddy fields to capture rainwater in other areas distant from the canals. They probably also carried out flood retreat farming in the fertile areas subject to inundation along the Great Lake. Indeed, if the estimates of the population of the ancient city are correct and over one million people lived there, it is altogether likely that they had to employ multiple methods of farming. However, the latest archaeological evidence indicates that a vast system of irrigation canals and reservoirs was at the centre of the Angkorean economy. W.J. van Lière claimed that as he had not seen any intake or outlet structures at the *barays*, or any distribution systems, these did not exist. The latest evidence from aerial photography and radar imaging indicates that Groslier's critics were quite wrong to assert that there were no canals at Angkor.

The Australian archaeologist Roland Fletcher insists that Angkor was a 'gigantic, low density, dispersed urban complex' sprawling over at least 1000 square kilometres between the Great Lake and the Kulen Hills to the north, and that the irrigation system was vital to the city's survival. Some of the larger canals still exist, for instance at Beng Melea, east of Angkor, where they took water from the temple moat to the rice fields. Remote sensing also shows the existence of a network of distributor channels, and larger canals of up to 40 metres in width are visible from the air with the naked eye, leading from the East and West barays and the Angkor Wat moat. Although W.J. van Lière categorically ruled out the possibility of the ancient Khmers creating temporary breaches in the *baray* embankments to drain off water for irrigation purposes during the dry season, this still remains a distinct possibility. In 1935, M. Trouvé of the Hydraulic Service of Indochina conducted an experiment at the West Baray. A breach was made in the embankment, a pipe inserted and the earth replaced around it. Shortly afterwards the dike broke, but was repaired more carefully and remained intact thereafter. It is possible that the ancient Khmers inserted laterite pipes through the embankments and remote sensing shows possible breaches. It is also now known that the *barays* had permanent outlet/inlets in their eastern walls.

Even more importantly, the latest evidence shows the existence of a large feeder canal, perhaps 20 metres in width, which ran north-wards for some 40 kilometres from Angkor Thom to the hills. This trunk canal fed a fine network of distributors and embankments, which covered a large area to the north of the central city. This area, which naturally was rather dry for six months of the year, was converted by the Khmers into what Roland Fletcher describes as 'a highly structured anthropogenic wetland', criss-crossed with canals and embankment-cum-roads and capable of supporting the largest concentration of people in the pre-industrial world. These people lived in a dispersed pattern, strung out along the canals and embankments, ringing the paddy fields, or clustered around the numerous smaller reservoirs. The slope of the land is gentle, so erosion would not have been a major problem except in the foothills of Phnom Kulen.

Fletcher also suggests that the *barays* could have functioned as 'complementary opposites'—both as reservoirs and as settling ponds for silt brought through the canal system to the north from the hills. It is probable that the city was able to function in a state of 'dynamic equilibrium' for many centuries before increased population pressure caused the people to seek additional land to settle on and cultivate. It was then, argues Fletcher, that the fine ecological balance of the city began to break down and the city and its empire went into decline.

The decline of Angkor

That empires rise and fall is a cliché of history and Victorian melo-drama. What are more difficult to establish are the specific reasons for their decline. The puzzle of the Angkorean decline has taken a long time to unravel and we still don't have all the answers. It is likely that the city's decline resulted from a combination of political, social, religious and ecological factors. The conventional explanation held that collapse came suddenly, around 1431, when the Siamese King Paramaraja II sacked the city. Christopher Pym believed that the cause was 'the empire's dismemberment from without and a loss of religious equilibrium within'. The Siamese (or Thais), who had moved into the Menam basin from Yunnan, were originally under Khmer suzerainty, but after the death of Jayavarman VII they established their own sovereignty and began to challenge Khmer hegemony. Zhou Daguan records that there were devastating wars between the Siamese and the Khmers in the mid-13th century, with great loss of life and destruction of property in the outlying areas of the empire. Even before they sacked Angkor in 1431, the Siamese had occupied large parts of the empire, carrying off Khmers as slaves and possibly sabotaging the irrigation system according to some writers.

While the incessant Siamese incursions undoubtedly weakened Angkor politically, it is unlikely that they caused the empire's collapse. Although the Khmers shifted their capital to the Quatre Bras region after the Thais sacked Angkor in 1431, the city was not completely abandoned. When the Iberian missionaries Diego do Couto and Gabriel Quiroga de San Antonio visited the city in 1550 and 1570 respectively, it was still a going concern, the latter noting that the kingdom was still densely populated. (Do Couto's account of Angkor was lost for centuries until re-discovered by the celebrated English historian C.R. Boxer in Lisbon in 1954.) King Satha I carried out extensive rebuilding work on the temples and the irrigation system during the same period and an inscription from 1587 records restoration work on Angkor Wat. Angkor Thom seems only to have been abandoned in 1629, but other parts of the city were refurbished during the reign of King Ponhea Sor in 1747. Tragically, a description of the city written by a European traveller in the 1780s has been lost. When the French came in the 19th century, there were still Buddhist monks at Angkor. The city, however, was in ruins, with much of it lost to the rapacious advance of the jungle. Something had happened, but at a later date than the Siamese attacks, which suggests that although these might well have weakened the empire, they are not the sole explanation for its decline.

George Coedès believed that the mania for temple building placed an immense burden on the people, and was a huge drain on the resources of the empire. (If the excesses of Louis XIV, the Sun King, absorbed no less than 50 per cent of the wealth of 17th-century France, one wonders at the exorbitant cost of the much larger building programs and other demands of the Angkorean kings.) The excessive demands wore the people down, drained their vitality and perhaps even led to rebellions, although there is no real, hard evidence of this, just tantalising hints in inscriptions. After the frenzy of temple building during the reign of King Jayavarman VIII in the 13th century, during which monuments were thrown up at feverish speed, the program ran out of steam. British historian Arnold Toynbee might be guilty of hyperbole when he writes, 'The Khmer civilization, like so many civilizations before and after it, wrecked itself by indulging in these mad crimes', but there is an element of truth here. This great coda of temple building also coincided with the arrival of the new religion, Theravada Buddhism, via a Burmese monk called Shin Tamalinda, whose standing was no doubt enhanced by his claim to be the son of a Khmer king.

The common people took to the new religious doctrines with great enthusiasm. By the mid-14th century the country had converted to the new creed and Sivaism and Mahayana Buddhism were displaced. (Elements of Hinduism persist to this day in Cambodia, however, and include aspects of royal court ritual, art and literature, and the recognition of Indian gods.) Khmers even travelled to Laos to proselytise for Theravadism. The new religion was 'democratic' in that there were no hereditary priests, such as the Brahmans—anyone might don the saffron robes and become a monk, and even a king who converted might beg for alms in the street. The new religion made a huge impact on those exhausted by the worldly demands of their sybaritic rulers. The material world was one full of vanity and one's best chance of a better reincarnation and eventual ascendance to nirvana lay not with the accumulation of power and wealth, but in renouncing it and dedicating one's life to good works. And what were the temples but monuments to the monstrous vanity of men who presumed to be gods when, according to the Theravadins, not even Buddha himself was a god?

One can only speculate what effects the new religion might have had on the economy. Pym says that because of Theravada Buddhism's spurning of the material world, the irrigation system fell into disrepair. Again, there might be an element of truth in this. Although the modern Khmer peasants are often scorned as being lazy, particularly in comparison with their industrious Vietnamese neighbours and by the yardstick of the European Protestant ethic, this really is a misunderstanding. For the Khmer peasants, like their Irish counterparts, 'contentment is wealth'. The purpose of life is not the accumulation of material goods, but to live a good life, which includes the renunciation of earthly desires in order to accrue merit. As the historians Chandler and Mabbett have observed, the 'indolence' of the Cambodian peasants is 'a form of wisdom'. It is quite possible that the new religion did, as Coedès argues, sap at the foundations of a society that was predicated on the existence of strong, centralised state power. Marx's theory of the Asiatic Mode of Production (AMP) has fallen somewhat into disrepute, not the least because it is often confounded with Karl Wittfogel's dogmatic generalisations about 'oriental despotism'. However, while the theory of AMP does not fit with many of the diverse societies of Asia, it does measure up remarkably well to Angkorean civilisation, a hierarchical society based on a strong state, without landed property and with a heavy emphasis on government public works schemes. If Groslier's hydraulic city thesis is established it is very possible that Theravada Buddhism might have acted as a subtle yet powerful agent subversive of Angkorean state power. This might also help explain why irrigation is not widely used in modern Cambodia.

The new religion also forbade the taking of life, and although this has not prevented subsequent generations of Cambodians from warlike behaviour, it might have dampened the imperial ambitions of the kings. It is not unknown for Khmer peasants to spurn other Khmers who have taken human life. Anthropologist May Ebihara has recorded that some villagers disdained those who had taken human life during the Khmer Issarak insurrection of the 1940s and 1950s against France.

The legend of the kingfishers

The eccentric English writer Osbert Sitwell recorded a charming Khmer tale which held that Angkor fell into decline because the supply of kingfisher feathers, which were exported to China, ran out. On one level the tale is absurd, yet read as a parable it perhaps contains the key to the decline of a great empire. Bernard-Philippe Groslier drew attention to the possibility of ecological damage as a factor in the decline of Angkor, and the thesis has been fleshed out by the more recent work of Roland Fletcher. Groslier believed that there was probably extensive environmental damage in Angkor, with deforestation of the slopes north of the city leading to leaching, soil compaction, sheet and gully erosion and the silting of watercourses on the flatter lands. It is likely too that deforestation caused a decline in the amount of water available from convectional rainfall. The conventional wisdom that silt is immediately fertile is in fact untrue. Soil is a complex biosystem and to become fertile it needs the addition of humus from plant material along with the actions of worms, insects and microscopic organisms. While the *barays* might well have functioned as a dialectical balance between storing water and as sediment traps, deforestation of the watersheds could have drowned the canals in silt faster than it could be cleared. It is also possible that rotting waterweeds depleted the amount of oxygen in the canals and moats, a process known as eutrophication. This most certainly is a problem in modern Cambodia, with a plentiful supply of water-borne nutrients providing ideal conditions for the rapid growth of plants such as hyacinth and lotus. Rapid growth and decay seriously depletes the amount of oxygen in the water and reduces its value for irrigation and smothers fish life.

Groslier also speculates that the large quantities of slow-moving water would have provided a breeding ground for malarial mosquitoes. In fact, there is evidence that irrigation systems in British India *did* increase malarial infection rates, and it is well known that Mussolini's actions in draining the Pontine marshes near Rome led to a decrease in infection rates. Within a decade of the opening of the Sarda Canal in India in 1928, the irrigated areas suffered problems of evaporation and seepage, but also 'waterlogging, salinity and malaria'. Earlier British attempts to use the waters of the Cauvery and Coloroon for irrigation purposes largely failed because of silting. Salting might have been a problem in Angkor too: many Cambodian soils have problems with salt and sodicity; for instance, 50 per cent of the soils of modern Kompong Speu province are sodic at a depth of 30 centimetres.

In the language of systems-theory, the Angkorean irrigation system was a delicate balance of human and natural inputs and outputs—a dynamic equilibrium—which was capable of sustaining a population that was huge by the standards of antiquity. The system was thrown out of ecological balance by the cutting of large areas of forest, particularly on the watersheds in the Kulen Hills. Roland Fletcher believes that the trees were cut down to provide more farmland for an expanding population and that there was 'a vast consumption of timber . . . for the scaffolding of the temples [and] for building the palaces and houses . . .'. Timber would also have been used for cooking and 'industrial' purposes, both in the peasants' houses and on the monastic estates. Put in this context, the legend of the kingfishers is not so far-fetched after all. Damage to the ecosystem of Angkor might well have first manifested itself in the disappearance of the birds. With no scientific explanation for this, the Khmers might well have regarded the disappearance of the birds as a harbinger of doom.

If Fletcher is right, the fate of Angkor is a lesson for modern Cambodia and the rest of the world. There is mounting evidence that

Cambodia is suffering an accelerating environmental crisis that could mimic the calamities of the ancient Khmers. Logging—much of it illegal—is widespread on the hills and ridges. As a consequence, sheet and ravine erosion is increasing, with silting of land and watercourses downstream. The results of such recklessness are compounded with the effects of the current Chinese dam-building program in Yunnan, which has led to record low water levels in Mekong and the Great Lake in Cambodia. The loss of habitat, which has seen a marked decline in the numbers of wild animals including tigers and crocodiles, might well be a re-run of the habitat loss that ended the trade in kingfisher feathers with China and heralded the decline of Angkor. As Jean Lacoursière, the former head of the Mekong River Commission's environmental unit, put it: 'Today we have the technology to repeat, on a larger scale, what happened at Angkor . . . The principles are the same: reduction of habitat, and changes in the overall ecology of Tonlé Sap.'

4
FROM ANGKOR'S END TO THE FRENCH PROTECTORATE

Although the Angkorean system was in decline some centuries before 1431, when the Siamese burned the city, the sack was probably a turning point in Cambodia's history. There was a sharp discontinuity between the civilisation of Angkor and that of its successor state, when a different kind of economic and social order evolved in the country. According to the 16th century Iberian visitor Diego do Couto, the Khmers had forgotten Angkor's existence, although we should be cautious about accepting such evidence. The pre-Angkorean scholar Michael Vickery argues that the decision to shift the capital to the Quatre Bras region was prompted by an expansion of Cambodia's trading relationship with China rather than because of Angkor's collapse. Other writers assert that the country was plunged into a downward spiral and transformed seamlessly from a mighty empire into a vassal state. On the other hand, David Chandler has claimed that Cambodia's misfortunes during this period were episodic rather than perpetual. The evidence for either side is tantalisingly thin, but what is clear is that Cambodia *did* suffer a long-term decline relative to its own former power, and to the growing strength of its rivals. From the 17th century, internal political strife often weakened the vitality of the kingdom, and external enemies were quick to take advantage. The French had their own motives when they set up their Cambodian protectorate in 1863, but there can be little doubt that they prevented the final absorption of the kingdom by its neighbours.

By the 15th century the Siamese, former vassals of the Angkorean kings, had become deadly rivals, and another menace was growing as the Vietnamese were slowly but inexorably drawn southwards down the coast of Annam. Between them, these neighbours would come to so dominate Cambodia's fortunes that by the late 18th century the Khmers would dub them the Tiger and the Crocodile. At times, Cambodia almost ceased to exist and for much of the time it was a tributary state of one or another of its powerful neighbours.

Ironically, Cambodia's long-time Cham rivals were the first to suffer from Vietnamese expansionism. The Cham kingdom extended between what is today northern Cochin-China and the Danang region of Annam, and when Marco Polo visited in 1288 it was still powerful. While Champa held out, the Khmers were reasonably safe from Vietnamese incursions. In 1471, however, the Vietnamese sacked the Cham capital and reduced the kingdom to a tiny rump vassal state before they destroyed it entirely in 1693. Over 70 years earlier, the Vietnamese had moved into the adjacent Khmer littoral and in the process had begun to strangle Cambodia's maritime trade. By 1780, they had expanded more or less to the current border between the two states and turned the Khmer population of the region into a minority in their own country. By the late 18th century, a terrible Dark Age had descended on the country.

The coming of the Europeans

When the first Europeans came to Cambodia in the early 16th century, they could have had no inkling that they were walking on the soil of what had once been the most powerful empire in Southeast Asia, centred on the largest city of antiquity. The ruins of Angkor, while impressive, were only the 'skeleton' of the former city. Cambodia had also been territorially truncated, stripped of her outer provinces, which had once stretched clear to the Andaman Sea and the boundaries of Burma, and northwards into what is now Laos. The Siamese had occupied much of the western part of the Khmer *srok* (see Glossary) including Angkor, and the Vietnamese would soon nibble at its eastern flank.

Yet, if the sack and occupation of Angkor in 1431 had bloodied the nose of the Khmer king, it did not signify the total collapse of his kingdom. The Cambodians fought back fiercely against the Siamese occupiers. When the Siamese king Paramaraja II put his own son, Indra-path, on the Khmer throne in 1431, the Khmers assassinated the young man. In 1432 the new Khmer king, Ponhea Yat, moved his capital first to Srei Santhor and then to Phnom Penh. There are a number of hypotheses to explain the move: perhaps it occurred because Srei Santhor was less accessible to raiding Siamese forces; perhaps it was to take advantage of burgeoning trade links with China; perhaps it was to escape the effects of the ecological degradation of the Angkor region. It is possible that the Siamese attacks only sped up the implementation of a decision that would have been taken regardless. Ironically, over 600 years earlier another Khmer king, Jayavarman II, had moved his capital in the opposite direction, in part to escape pressure from hostile Champa.

The wars continued and by the early 16th century the Khmers had managed to expel the Siamese from much of the older Khmer heartlands occupied around 1430. Around 1510, the Khmer king, Ang Chan, regained control of the province of Angkor. Fifty years later, after a confused period of attacks and counterattacks by Siamese and Khmer forces about which we have only sketchy information, Chan's son, Barom Rachea I, made the region a springboard for an invasion of Siam. According to an inscription at Angkor, Barom Rachea's own son, King Satha, partially rebuilt the capital after he came to the throne in 1576. It was still a bustling society when the Iberian friar, Gabriel de Quiroga, visited in 1570 and found it to be 'very densely populated'. In contrast, later travellers would comment on the melancholy vistas of a sparsely populated land. One can only wonder at what had become of the million or so people who had inhabited the city.

Increasing numbers of Europeans arrived in Southeast Asia by sea following the voyages of Diaz and Vasco da Gama round the Cape of Good Hope in the late 15th century. The Spanish and Portuguese, it is often said, came with a sword in one hand and a crucifix in the other. In 1511, the Portuguese annexed the strategic Straits seaport of Malacca, and the Spanish conquered the Philippines after 1565. Covetous of souls and gold, they cast their eyes to the mainland and Cambodia did not escape their notice. In a letter published in 1513, the Spanish King Manuel informed Pope Leo X that Cambodia was a strategically important and powerful kingdom in the Far East. The first European account of Cambodia, the *Suma Oriental* of the Portuguese apothecary Tomé Pires, dates from the years between 1512 and 1515, although it was based on hearsay. Pires' book casts doubt on the idea that Cambodia had collapsed as a military power, and perhaps it helped restrain his countrymen from precipitate imperialist action against the kingdom. Pires noted that the Khmers were a warlike people and none more so than the king, who was 'a heathen and knightly' and who was 'at war with the people of Burma and with Siam, and sometimes with Champa, and he does not obey anyone'. Cambodia had not yet been reduced to vassal status.

Nevertheless, by the last decades of the 16th century (during the period of the Iberian dual monarchy over Spain and Portugal between 1580 and 1640) the Spanish had pacified most of the Philippines and had converted much of the population to Christianity. Fired by religious zeal and the baser passions of greed, they turned their eyes to the Asian mainland. Tomé Pires had already noted Cambodia's riches, remarking that the Khmers produced large quantities of rice, meat and 'wines of their own kind', together with gold, sticklack (see Glossary), ivory and large quantities of dried fish. In 1584, the Catholic bishop of Malacca produced detailed plans for the invasion of the Southeast Asian mainland, after which the conquistadors would turn their attentions to the glittering prize of China. In the event, King Philip II refused to endorse the bishop's plans, viewing them as a distraction from his own designs for the sea-borne invasion of England (the doomed Spanish Armada).

In any case, Iberian missionaries were disheartened by the indifference of most Cambodians to the gospels, an attitude the wandering Portuguese friar Gaspar da Cruz put down to the malevolent influence of the Buddhist monks, whom he described as 'wizards'. Nevertheless, Lisbon and Madrid were a long way from Goa and Manila, and the local authorities had a great deal of autonomy. They were perhaps also worried about the possible designs of their archrivals, the Dutch and the English, on the Southeast Asian mainland. Indeed, the English queen, Elizabeth I, authorised the setting up of the East India Company in 1600, and shortly afterwards the directors petitioned her to allow them to trade with, among other places, 'the Kingdome of Camboia'. For his part, the Dutch adventurer Jan van Linschoten displayed a keen interest in the possibilities of trade with Southeast Asia in his book *Voyages into Ye Easte and Weste Indies*, which included an account of his visit to Cambodia, Siam and Champa in the 1570s. Soon afterwards, the Dutch East India Company was set up in Amsterdam with a charter for trade and conquest in the Far East. European imperialist rivalry had begun in earnest.

Conquistadors in Cambodia

As it turned out, the Iberians were never to gain more than the most precarious of toeholds in Cambodia. Although today in Cambodia there are still a number of influential families of Portuguese descent, Iberian imperial ambitions for direct conquest were to founder during an invasion by a handful of desperadoes and religious fanatics in the closing years of the 16th century. This curious affair began in 1593, when King Satha of Cambodia dispatched an embassy to Manila, with promises of friendship and trade if the Spanish would send military forces to help fight off an impending Siamese invasion. Satha had gained a high opinion of the Iberians because of his friendship with Diogo Veloso, a Portuguese adventurer who had settled in the country in 1583, learned the language and married a Khmer princess. The Governor of Manila was politely non-committal and in the meantime the Siamese invaded Cambodia and occupied the capital at Lovek. Satha fled into exile in Laos, never, it seems, to return. The Jesuits in Manila were righteously indignant. Satha had a reputation for friendliness towards Christians, so the priests declared that the Spanish should send soldiers to throw back the Siamese in what would be a 'just war'. They proposed that in effect, Cambodia would become an Iberian protectorate, and vowed that her rivals, including Champa and Siam, would be put down in 'a war of fire and blood' as part of the wider conquest of all of Indochina. The French would act on a similar pretext some two and a half centuries later, when they subjugated Vietnam and set up a protectorate in Cambodia. History repeated itself, but the first time as farce, as it turned out.

Although the Governor of Manila was reluctant to dispatch a large force to Cambodia (there being no more than 1500 Spaniards in the Philippines, exclusive of priests and monks at the end of the 16th century), he sent what the historian C.R. Boxer described as a 'motley group of soldiers, vagabonds, Filipinos and Japanese' under the command of the Portuguese swashbucklers Diogo Veloso and Blaz Ruiz. The little army sailed away in a fleet of ill-matched ships, ostensibly to assist Satha, but with the desire for colonial conquest in their hearts. After a number of setbacks, including the dispersal of the fleet in a typhoon and Veloso's temporary capture by the Siamese, the expedition managed to drive out the Siamese, suppress an uprising by a Khmer usurper named Chung Prei, and clamp down on anti-Iberian intrigues at the royal court. They were able to do all this because of their superior weaponry, which included muskets and cannon. Forgetting their earlier pledges of friendship to Satha, Ruiz and Veloso placed the king's youngest son on the throne, perhaps believing he would be pliable, for Ruiz declared that the young man was 'a child and addicted to drink more than was his father . . . he thinks only of sport and hunting and cares nothing for the kingdom', although he worried that the young man 'fears the Spanish even while he loves them, for he dreads lest they deprive him of his kingdom'. (French officials were to make similar estimates of their royal protégés in 19th and 20th century Cambodia.)

In the end the arrogance, greed and general bad behaviour of the conquistadors led to their deaths in a massacre at Phnom Penh in 1599 at the hands of an outraged mob stiffened by *Tagals*, the Cham and Malay palace guards, who would have been equipped with firearms. Ruiz and Veloso died with their dubious cohort and with them perished Spanish hopes of carving out God's Empire in Indochina. Afterwards, French missionaries took over the work the Iberian Church Militant had initiated, albeit with no greater success, at least in Cambodia. But for their avarice, incompetence and casual brutality, Veloso's conquistadors might well have established a European colony in Indochina and changed the course of history. We should not jump to the conclusion, however, that Cambodia was weaker than it was because a small number of Europeans almost managed to annex it to their empire. Small numbers of determined men could defeat much larger numbers of soldiers because of cannon and gunpowder, as the Aztecs and Incas learned to their cost.

The post-Angkorean social and economic system

It is impossible to say how the Iberians might have fared against Angkor at the apogee of its power, for it seems that a different kind of social and economic system had supplanted the old model. Political power was less centralised, the old political and religious institutions were waning, and perhaps this less organised society was less capable of responding swiftly to the Iberian threat than Angkor might have been.

There were many similarities between late and post-Angkorean Cambodia, but several key differences. Theravada Buddhism had already implanted itself firmly before the fall of Angkor, and the monument mania had ebbed. The people spoke the same language and had many of the customs and beliefs of their Angkorean ancestors. Yet even in the domain of language there were some big changes, in part because of cultural cross-fertilisation with Siam. This led to Angkorean syntax being supplanted by that of Siamese. This shift paralleled the emergence of a different kind of economy and society in Cambodia from the 15th century onwards.

If the economic base of a society helps shape its political and social system, then the decision to shift the capital from Angkor to the Quatre Bras region must have led to, or been accompanied by, huge social changes. If, as was argued in the last chapter, Angkorean Cambodia exemplified some aspects of Marx's so-called Asiatic Mode of Production, with large state-directed public works and dependence on an elaborate hydraulic system for food production, then the shift would have meant an enormous break with the past. Irrigation plays only a minor part in modern Cambodian food production and although European visitors commented on the continuing existence of hydraulic agriculture in the 16th century, it must have fallen into decline. If, as the archaeologists believe, Angkor's population was over one million, it is puzzling to consider where they went. Were there mass migrations? Perhaps as the hydraulic system fell into disrepair as a result of the ecological crisis and possible sabotage by the Siamese, the population would have had to relocate as a matter of survival. How many perished during the Siamese invasions? Did the apparent ecological crisis lead to famine and disease? Or did the population decline more gradually? Cambodia twice suffered demographic catastrophe during the 19th century—during the incessant wars of the 'Dark Age' and after the Great

Rebellion of the 1880s—so perhaps something similar happened in the 15th century. Unless fresh archaeological or documentary evidence emerges, we may never know.

Not all Khmers had lived in the enormous dispersed city of Angkor. Large tracts of the countryside were owned and worked by the religious orders, with both free and slave labour. Many other Khmers lived in villages distant from the city, growing rain-fed rice. This lifestyle, or something like it, became the norm for most of Cambodia's post-Angkorean population and perhaps they also found a less regimented existence more congenial and more in conformity with Theravadist exhortations to spurn worldly vanity and greed. King Satha refurbished the city in the late 16th century, but he abandoned it again shortly afterwards. Angkor Thom was deserted in the mid-17th century and although King Ponhea Sor partly rebuilt the city in 1747 this did not arrest the general decline of state power, and the centre of gravity of Cambodian political life and population had shifted downstream to the lower Mekong Valley. Angkor was to remain crucial to Khmer identity, and was emblazoned on the country's currrency, but it belonged to the past.

The era of gigantic monument building had ceased forever. The irrigation channels were blocked with silt. At least one of the massive *barays* disappeared from sight and the advancing jungle overwhelmed the mighty feeder canal that had carried water from the mountains. Roland Fletcher's 'gigantic, low density, dispersed urban complex' had vanished. The Angkorean road system gradually fell into disrepair, so that by the time the French came, large tracts of the countryside were linked only by dusty tracks that became impassable in the wet season. The centralised, bureaucratic state gradually withered away. In some ways, the changes were probably so slow as to be imperceptible. In the words of J.A. Spender, 'All that the historians give us are little oases in the desert of time, forgetting the vast tracts between one and another that were trodden by the weary generations of men.'

At Angkor, people had lived in 'a highly structured anthropogenic wetland', criss-crossed with canals and embankment-cum-roads and capable of supporting the largest concentration of people in the pre-industrial world. After Angkor, the Khmers lived an altogether different style of life which, by the 16th and 17th centuries, had crystallised into a pattern still seen today outside the major towns and cities of Cambodia. Cambodia became an overwhelmingly rural country, very different from the dispersed city of Angkor.

The Khmers now lived in small villages, of which David Chandler describes three broad types. The largest, the kompongs (from the Malay *kampong*), stood on navigable waterways and were sometimes home to a few hundred inhabitants, including local officials known as *chauvai srok*. They might be enclosed behind a palisade for defence against bandits, the armed followers of millenarian rebels or foreign marauders. The second type were the rice-growing villages, which were less permanent than the kompongs, although they might contain a Buddhist *wat* and perhaps some government officials if they were large enough. Lastly, there were remote villages located on the ambiguous margins; maybe many days' travel from the rice-growing villages and sometimes with no organic links to the Khmer state, and perhaps inhabited by ethnic minorities practising animist rites.

Unlike the Vietnamese villages, the Khmer villages lacked formal authority structures; disputes were settled informally and the remoter the village, the more inwards looking and tradition-bound its inhabitants became. Perhaps an analogy might be made between post-Angkorean rural society and that of 19th century Haiti. After the French were driven out of their West Indian slave colony of Sainte-Domingue, the plantation system was replaced by private peasant agriculture. The revolted slaves spontaneously reincarnated a society, based on the traditional African village, on the ruins of the hated plantations. In both cases there was a change from highly efficient, large-scale, directed agriculture to small-scale subsistence farming, mirroring a privatisation of life. Cambodia had no civil society, with no stable groups between the family and the state, which was often remote from the agglomerations of families that made up the villages. As David Chandler has observed, such non-state and non-family organisations as existed tended to be of a temporary nature, as when villagers would band together to fight off the ubiquitous bandits or to organise festivals. This is not to say that the villages were anarchic. Religion acted as a social glue; as the American-Asian scholar Theodore De Bary noted,

> The [Buddhist] ideal is a society in which each individual respects the other's personality, an intricate network of warm and happy human relationships: mutual respect and affection between parent and child, teacher and student, husband and wife, master and servant, friend and friend, each helping each other upwards in the scale of being.

There were also patronage networks, in which the powerless would attach themselves to local notables and others with more power. Indeed, the anthropologist May Ebihara claims that at the time 'All free men had to be registered as clients of a particular patron', who could be an official, royal family member or local grandee. Slavery, too, persisted as an integral part of Khmer society and was not eliminated until the time of the French Protectorate.

Death and taxes were as certain in Cambodia as Benjamin Franklin later observed of human life in general. Taxation was paid on demand and in kind, generally one-tenth of the rice crop, give or take what the peasants could conceal from the eyes of the tax gatherers. The peasants were also liable for conscription into the army in times of war and the state bureaucrats could call upon them to perform unpaid labour, or *corvée*, on 'official' projects. There was little expectation that government officials would be anything other than corrupt and brutal, nor that they would organise much for 'the general good', although it is doubtful that any such concept existed in the peculiarly Cambodian variant of feudalism that replaced the Angkorean system. Many officials abused their power to enrich themselves and Cambodian proverbs exhort the peasants to be wary of the officials, who are portrayed as wild beasts and venomous snakes. The proverbs also preach the wisdom of resignation to one's lot in life, although some peasants took to a life of banditry, some of it perhaps of a 'social' nature, to survive. (Social banditry, a term coined by the British Marxist historian Eric Hobsbawm in his classic book *Bandits*, suggests a quasi-political dimension of resistance against tyrannical rule.) The peasants had also inherited the religiosity of their Angkorean forebears and it gave them consolation in an often harsh and unjust world. The head of state, the king, was venerated and seen as occupying a special place above the hierarchy of officials. Nor was he held accountable for their misdeeds. Most villagers stayed close to their homes and fields and never saw him in their lives. He was, as Chandler puts it, 'at once as real (and as unreal) as the Lord Buddha', an unearthly being with supernatural powers.

The shift of the capital to the Quatre Bras region had freed up Cambodia's sea-borne trade with the outside world, particularly China, and indeed as Vickery argues this might have been a reason for the move. By the first half of the 17th century, Cambodia was conducting a thriving trade with China via ports on the lower Mekong. In the 16th century, King Satha told the Spanish in Manila that he was keen to trade with them. In 1702, another king permitted Allan Ketchpole to set up a trading post for the English East India Company on the island of Poulo Condore (then part of Cambodia), although it did not prosper. Shortly afterwards, the Scottish sea captain Alexander Hamilton published an account of two Cambodian seaports on the Gulf littoral. He described the town of 'Cupangsoap' (Kompong Som, or today's Sihanoukville) as a place that 'affords elephants teeth, sticklack and the gum Cambouge or Cambodia . . .' and its neighbour 'Ponteamass' (Banteay Meas) as being located on 'a pretty deep but narrow river, which, in the rainy seasons of the Southwest Monsoons, has communication with [the] Bansack [Bassac] or Cambodia River . . .'. Other products traded with the outside world included 21 carat gold, and 'raw silk at 120 dollars per Pecul' (see Glossary), 'elephant's teeth at 50 to 55 dollars', sandalwood, agala-wood 'and many sorts of physical drugs, and Lack for japanning'. Despite widespread subsistence agri-culture, we know that Cambodia exported a variety of other products, including rice, cotton, hemp, probably fish and fish products, also pepper and cardamom. There was also a big enough social surplus product to feed not only the thousands of state officials, but also a startling number of Buddhist monks. Gaspar da Cruz claimed that at the time of his visit in the 16th century a third of the population were monks, and that there were 1500 of them in Phnom Penh alone. The gradual settlement of the lower Mekong delta by Vietnamese did, however, block a major trading artery and this contributed to Cambodia's later decline.

Between tiger and crocodile

In his account of his visit to Cambodia, Captain Alexander Hamilton remarked that the seaport of Banteay Meas had 'flourished' until it was burned by a Siamese fleet in 1717 and that he had also gazed upon the burnt ruins of 'Cupangsoap'. The two towns had suffered what was all too common a fate for Cambodian settlements from the 17th century. The Siamese, perennial enemies of the Khmers, had emerged as a formidable, rich and martial people. Jean-Baptiste Tavernier, a French Huguenot who visited Siam sometime during the 1640s, recorded that there were 'masses of gold' at the royal court and that the king travelled between gilded pagodas in an enormous boat propelled by 400 oarsmen. A century later, Captain Hamilton described the Siam-ese capital as a fine city built of stone and brick, with many canals, and about 16 kilometres in circumference. There were 'steeples gilded in gold' which, 'at two or three miles distance . . . disturb the eye when look'd upon'. The captain also wrote of Vietnam as 'a country far larger than Cambodia, and much richer, and the inhabitants [are] more couragious [sic] and hardier . . . than the Cambodians, but are not so conversable and civil to strangers'. The Italian Christoforo Borri, who visited Vietnam during the first decades of the 17th century, had a high regard for the Vietnamese, whose culture he adjudged to be little different to that of China. The people were strong, agile and brave, with 'good intelligence' and open to foreign ideas. Technologically they were on a far higher plane than the Khmers and their system of government was much more centralised, with government power operating down to village level.

The first independent Vietnamese state had been established in 939 AD and afterwards their expansion southwards was inexorable. They began to annex the Cham lands as early as 1069, and after sacking the Cham capital in 1471 they forcibly assimilated their new subjects. The road was also clear for them to begin to move into Cambodian territory. In the 1620s, they began to move into the Khmer lands adjacent to Champa north of the Mekong delta. Their task was made easier by the disarray of the Cambodian government, which one historian has described as 'faction-ridden and under Siamese influence'. Vietnamese influence at the Cambodian court was also growing during this period. Borri mentions that in 1620 the 'king of Cambogia' (Jayajetta II) married a Vietnamese princess in order to cement an alliance against the Siamese. Jayajetta's marriage was part of what was to become an ongoing process in which the Cambodian state sought to play off its powerful neighbours against one another in order to maintain some measure of sovereignty; King Sihanouk would play a similar game during the 1950s and 1960s. Given Cambodia's increasing weakness *vis-à-vis* its neighbours, it was probably the best diplomatic option down through the centuries to the international *Realpolitik* of the 20th century.

In 1623, King Jayajetta II granted Vietnamese traders and settlers permission to live and work near the Khmer town of Prey Nokor, situated on a distributary of the Mekong delta, and the largest town in that sparsely settled region of Cambodia. This was probably part of the price of the king's marriage to the Nguyen princess. The settlers' numbers steadily increased and in 1698 they set up a Vietnamese vice-royalty in the district and renamed the town Saigon. Earlier, in 1658, a Vietnamese army had penetrated deep into Cambodia-proper, only withdrawing the following year. By 1780, the Vietnamese controlled almost the whole of the lower delta region and the Camau Peninsula. In the delta, the Vietnamese had carried out a process similar to that of the Israelis in the present-day Occupied Territories of Palestine, of 'creating political facts on the ground' by populating the region with settlers. It was a slow-motion annexation in which the hapless Khmers were pushed over the de facto border, or onto marginal lands. The 19th century French historian Adhémard Leclère claimed that the Vietnamese settlers provoked border incidents so as to be able to demand indemnities in land from the Khmers.

Although almost half a million *Khmer Krom* still live in the Vietnamese lower delta today, it is probable, as the distinguished archaeologist and writer Louis Malleret has argued, that only the coming of the French saved them from assimilation or extinction. The Khmers' religion taught them resignation in the face of seemingly inevitable misfortune and they would need every ounce of faith in a 'historical amphitheatre' that, as Albert Camus reminds us, 'has always contained the martyr and the lion' and where the 'former relied on eternal consolation and the latter on raw historical meat'. For their part, metaphorically speaking, the Siamese tiger and the Vietnamese crocodile had voracious appetites for Cambodian flesh. However, the designs of Cambodia's external enemies were assisted by periodic bouts of dynastic feuding within the country itself and by the late 1770s, during which decade the Siamese burned Phnom Penh, the country's fortunes were at their lowest ebb.

From the 18th century onwards, Cambodia became a tributary state of its neighbours, a common form of foreign relations in Southeast Asia and one originally developed by the Chinese. The Cambodian kings were expected to pay annual tribute in ritual ceremonies in Hué or Bangkok. Gifts and letters would be exchanged, underlining the dependent status of the vassal monarch at Phnom Penh. In its turn, Vietnam was expected to acknowledge its own tributary status with regard to China. There were differences in the relationships between

Cambodia and its neighbours. There was a sharp cultural divide between Cambodia and Vietnam; although both countries were based economically on wet rice cultivation, Vietnam was a Sinitic society and shared much of its powerful northern neighbour's cultural, social and political institutions. Vietnam, like China, based its system of government and administration on the principles of Confucius. The Vietnamese also shared the cult of ancestor worship, Chinese calligraphy and many aspects of family life. Like China, Vietnam was a bureaucratised state with a high degree of centralisation and social stratification. Its people generally ascribed to the tenets of Mahayana Buddhism, although French missionaries had been rather more successful in Vietnam than in Cambodia.

Cambodia, on the other hand, shared an Indianised cultural tradition with its other neighbour, Siam, and both countries practised the Theravada brand of Buddhism, leavened with residual Hindu and animist influences. Government and administration was looser and these dissimilarities were reflected in the differences in relations between the three countries. For the Vietnamese, the Khmers were by definition barbarians to be punished, patronised or civilised, depending on the situation. The Siamese, who shared much of the culture of Cambodia, were often more tolerant and tended to view the Khmers as children, albeit unruly and disobedient ones. This would explain the frequent resort to stern measures, as for instance when they burned down Phnom Penh in 1772, and invaded the country in 1811, 1833 and again in the 1840s. However, it is clear they also felt some sense of responsibility for the fate of their Theravadist neighbour, whose capital lay much closer to Vietnam than to Siam.

Until the 19th century the actions of Siam and Vietnam in Cambodia were usually constrained by the desire on both sides to avoid an all-out military collision with each other. Although they continually intrigued and jockeyed for power and influence in the kingdom, they both understood that it was in their interests to allow Cambodia to exist as a semi-independent buffer state. This did not stop them from pushing home the advantage when the other was preoccupied with other problems, as when the Nguyen dynasty was confronted with the Tay Son rebellion in Vietnam, or when the Siamese were distracted by wars with Burma. The situation changed in the early 19th century when the Vietnamese decided on a policy of territorial and cultural assimilation. The resulting chaos and instability almost destroyed Cambodia.

The Cambodian Dark Age

Norodom Sihanouk, king of Cambodia until his retirement in 2004, has described the history of Cambodia in the 17th, 18th and 19th centuries as 'an immense, painful tragedy'. Most painful of all were the years between the 1780s and the coronation of Ang Duang in 1848, during which time the Khmer monarchy and national sovereignty almost vanished. Perhaps the only darker period for Khmers was during the 1970s, the decade of civil war, carpet-bombing and genocide. As David Chandler reminds us, the Siamese burned down the Khmer capital three times in the first half of the 19th century and the Cambodian Royal Chronicles lament a succession of plagues, famines, floods and other natural and man-made calamities. It was a grim era in which rival states fought over the carcass of Cambodia and in which peace was only a time of recuperation from the last war and preparation for the next.

The Dark Age began around 1778, when the Siamese invaded Cambodia only six years after an earlier incursion. When the Siamese withdrew, the country exploded into a civil war that pitted rival bureaucratic factions and court intriguers against one another, while behind the scenes Vietnamese agents plotted in the murk. A rebellion in southern Vietnam had spilled over the border into Cambodia and at the other end of the country, in the vicinity of the Angkor ruins, a local Cambodian official, or *oknya*, called Ben or Baen, of the Apheuvongs family, suppressed dissidents and carved out a power base for himself in the north-west provinces. Later, Ben set himself up as a kind of viceroy, under Siamese patronage at the royal capital of Udong. Still later, he retreated to his north-west bastion and, with Siamese blessing, set up what amounted to a breakaway Khmer state—a de facto partition of Cambodia that was to last until 1908 when the French negotiated the return of Battambang and Angkor provinces from Siam.

During the course of these disturbances, the Cambodian king Ang Non was killed and in 1783 his nine-year-old son, Prince Eng, sought sanctuary at the court of King Rama I in Bangkok. It was a fateful flight, for it was to re-establish Siamese suzerainty over Cambodia after it had lapsed following a Burmese military victory over Bangkok in 1767. For over a decade following Non's death, the Cambodian throne was vacant, with power in the hands of a pro-Siamese regent. Ang Eng came of age and was crowned in a ceremony in Bangkok, but he died shortly there-after, in 1797 at the age of 23 years, possibly as a baptised Catholic. His eldest son, Prince Chan, was only six years old at the time and the country was placed once again into the hands of a regent.

The Siamese king, Rama I, allowed Chan to ascend to the Khmer throne in 1803, at the age of 16 years. Although Rama might have considered the new king's youth would make him tractable, he was more independent minded than his father and seems to have brooded on slights and to have resented Siamese domination. Intrigues broke out again at court between pro-Siamese and pro-Vietnamese factions, with Chan's own brothers aligning themselves with the former. Ang Chan's writ did not run far into the provinces, and not at all into Ben's juris-tiction around Battambang and Angkor. When Ben died, the Siamese appointed his nephew to succeed him and the districts became a semi-independent part of Siam, under a family of hereditary viceroys. Chan was so angry that he refused to travel to Bangkok for Rama's funeral. Meanwhile, the internal intrigues had escalated so far that there was danger of civil war. Perhaps sensing that the Siamese might intervene to aid his enemies, Chan appealed to the Vietnamese for help and they responded by sending ships and troops up the Mekong to guard his palace at Udong. Whether he acted out of pique or calculation is difficult to say, but the results were disastrous for Cambodia. The Vietnamese were to stay for over thirty years and almost succeeded in turning the country into a province of Vietnam.

The Siamese had not forgotten Chan's calculated snub to the memory of their ruler, which in their opinion transgressed the rules of the client–tributary relationship. The Siamese invaded, perhaps with the design of planting Chan's brother Snguon on the throne, and Chan fled into exile at Saigon. Ominously, his two other brothers, Im and Duang, sided with Siam. Neither Vietnam nor Siam were prepared to risk open war at this stage, as the former was weakened by internal revolt and the latter was waging war against their Burmese neighbour. In 1813 the Siamese withdrew, taking Snguon, Im and Duang into exile at Bangkok after burning the citadels of Udong and Phnom Penh. Chan returned with a permanent garrison of Vietnamese troops and shifted his capital downstream from Udong to Phnom Penh, presumably as it was closer to his patrons. Cambodia had become a vassal of Vietnam, although large parts of the west of the country remained within the Siamese sphere of influence. Weakened by their wars with Burma, the Siamese bided their time, grooming Im and Duang at Bangkok and waiting for better days.

Vietnam, the only Sinitic state in Southeast Asia, always regarded the Khmers as barbarians. When Chan died in 1835 they adopted the policy of 'civilising' the barbarians, attempting to introduce a Vietnamese-style taxation system and bullying the Khmer mandarins to wear Vietnamese-style bureaucratic dress. Later, they attempted to make the general population wear Vietnamese clothing and hairstyles. They also conscripted Khmer peasants to dig a canal from the Gulf of Siam to the Mekong delta, and behaved with great brutality. In 1820, the Khmers rose in revolt but it was a futile gesture in the face of a powerful occupier. The rising was put down with torture, public executions and the burning of villages in a grim fore-echo of what would be done to the Vietnamese themselves by the French colonialists.

In 1834, towards the end of Chan's reign, the Siamese had

recuperated enough from the Burmese wars to send an invading force deep into Cambodia via Pursat, one of the 'four gates of Cambodia', which lies to the south of the Great Lake. The exiled Khmer Princes Im and Duang rode with them. One can only wonder at what the pair thought of the behaviour of their patrons, who burned down Phnom Penh and looted it so systematically that 'even the dogs were loaded onto wagons', according to French missionaries. When they retreated after a Vietnamese counteroffensive, the Siamese troops forced thousands of peasants to accompany them into exile. So many others fled into the forests that the region south of the Great Lake, severely depopulated, became a melancholy wasteland.

The Vietnamese reinstalled Chan on the throne, but they were contemptuous of his ineffectuality in the face of the invasion and dismissive of Cambodia's quasi-sovereignty. The gloom hanging over the kingdom deepened after Chan's sudden death in 1835, at the age of 44. The Vietnamese pondered who would replace him. Chan had not left any sons, and the Vietnamese made a sharp break with tradition by putting his daughter, Mei, on the throne. The ill-starred Mei was the first and the last Cambodian queen. Even more than Chan, Mei was a puppet, dancing for her life to tunes sung by Vietnamese 'advisors'. Meanwhile, the Siamese king, Rama III, was becoming more belligerent. In a chilling phrase, he threatened to 'turn Cambodia into a forest' if the Khmers resisted him when he launched a fresh invasion.

Rama III planned his new invasion for 1836. Im and Duang were to play starring roles, and one of them was to be placed on the throne if and when the Vietnamese were expelled. The Vietnamese responded by sending an envoy to meet with Duang, asking him to come to Phnom Penh to discuss his future. Duang declined, but Rama III got wind of the plot and imprisoned him at Bangkok, despite Duang's protestations of loyalty. The invasion was postponed and in the meantime the Vietnamese *mission civilisatrice* proceeded apace. As David Chandler has observed, Queen Mei was 'demoted to the status of a salaried Vietnamese civil servant' and the Vietnamese replaced the Khmer seals of office with their own. The Phnom Penh region was given a Vietnamese administrative name and the aspect of the city became increasingly Sinitic, just as Prey Nokor had become Saigon. The region looked set for absorption into Vietnam, just as the lower delta or *Kampuchea Krom* had been during the previous century.

However, in 1840–41 the Khmers once again rose up in rebellion against the foreigners, this time with more effect. The revolt lasted for six months and although it was suppressed it did ensure the continued existence of the Khmer state. Seizing the opportunity, the Siamese assembled an army of over 50 000 men and prepared to invade. The Vietnamese deported Queen Mei to Vietnam, probably to a life of concubinage, and executed her pro-Siamese sister Baen for treason. On the Siamese side, Prince Duang swore an oath of loyalty to Rama, after which he was released from prison and travelled to Battambang, which was under the control of the Apheuvongs viceroy.

Siam and Vietnam were pretty evenly matched and the situation bogged down into a military stalemate that lasted until 1845. For the Khmers, there was no respite from the horrors of war. Both sides inflicted mass deportations and public executions on the populace. Farmland was laid waste and towns and villages razed as the rival armies attacked and counterattacked, looting, raping and burning their way across the countryside. The population fell dramatically to somewhere around half a million, according to the accounts of foreign visitors such as Sir John Bowring. Phnom Penh's population was no more than 25 000 and that of Udong perhaps half as large. Famine and epidemics of disease stalked the land. Trade had almost completely dried up and literacy rates had fallen. The towns and villages were depopulated and much of the agricultural land had reverted to nature.

The suffering ended only when the Vietnamese withdrew from Phnom Penh and sued for negotiations with Siam. Both sides were weary after years of war and the Vietnamese were increasingly worried—not without foundation—about the designs of France on their kingdom. They agreed to allow Duang to stay in the capital and eventually they returned the royal regalia, without which the Khmers would not consider him a legitimate ruler. In effect, both sides agreed that Cambodia would become a neutral state, albeit a client of its neighbours. Both sides withdrew their troops (with the exception of the Siamese in the north-west provinces) after more than three decades of occupation.

Relative peace and stability under Ang Duang

Duang was finally crowned in 1848 and became the first king to sit on the Khmer throne since Chan had died in 1835. The unfortunate Mei had died in exile in Vietnam and had never been accepted as a legitimate monarch by the majority of Khmers. For the common people it was a time of celebration. The coronation was also a much-needed confirmation of the proverb 'the Cambodian *srok* will never die', because for much of the past period the country's sovereignty and territorial integrity had hung by the slimmest of threads.

Duang's reign, in comparison with those before him and the interregnums between them, was peaceful and secure, and two revolts that flared were crushed with relative ease. He introduced some administrative reforms, replaced certain grades of officials (*chau muong*) with centrally appointed ones with the generic title of *chauvai srok*, and amalgamated some of the smaller provinces into larger units. Although it would take decades for the damage of war to heal, towns were gradually rebuilt, old wats refurbished and new ones built. The people who had fled to the forests returned and trade was revived to some degree. When the British diplomat Sir John Bowring visited in 1855, he reported that only one Cambodian seaport remained, the estuarine town of Kampot, but that it carried on a 'considerable trade'. Square-rigged vessels regularly sailed to the Straits Settlements with cargoes of rice, gamboge, pepper and dyewoods. They brought back cotton goods, hardware and, less happily, opium from British India. The French missionary Monsignor Pallegoix described Kampot as a flourishing little town of 3000 people, with never less than 60 junks in the harbour.

Much of the king's activities during this period consisted of giving out titles and seals of office to ministers and government officials, together with uniforms coloured according to rank. It would be easy to dismiss this as mere bureaucratic protocol or ritual hocus-pocus, but David Chandler has argued that it was in fact an essential part of the reconstitution of the Cambodian state. The king needed the royal regalia to confer legitimacy on his reign, and he also needed to dole out the symbols of office to confer legitimacy on Cambodian officials. It was also a purging of the alien bureaucratic customs that had been enforced by the Vietnamese during the dark decades. Cambodia was reborn as an Indianised, Buddhist state and the king acted as his subjects believed he ought to do.

However, the degree of independence Duang enjoyed during his reign should not be overstated. He reigned by courtesy of his powerful neighbours and he was crowned by both Khmer and Siamese Brahmans. The north-west provinces—which contained the great national symbol of the ruins of Angkor—had been severed from Cambodia, seemingly forever, and the boundary between the kingdom and Vietnam must have been a source of private grief for the new king. Siamese influence remained strong, although the soldiers were gone, and Duang's sons lived as guests-cum-hostages at Bangkok to ensure their father's good behaviour. An officer from the British Indian Army who spent some time in the country during Duang's reign remarked that the king was a 'vassal of the King of Siam, being not able to bring above thirty five thousand men into the field'.

On another level, lest we risk romanticising this king, the account of the 'Madras Officer', who was a guest at Duang's court, should be considered. The king's palace was a rambling wooden structure at Udong which he shared with 300 dancers or concubines and four 'married wives', wrote the officer. The shaven-headed sixty-year-old himself was 'enormously fat', reported the British officer, and 'his appearance is not at all King-like or imposing, being dull-looking, with a heavy, stolid air about him, and his face and breast much pitted with small-pox'. He was arthritic and short-tempered; in one incident he struck

CAMBODGE : Le palais du roi d'Oudon.

The Royal Palace at Udong, circa 1863.
(Courtesy of Cambodian National Archives, Phnom Penh)

one of his wives or concubines with a cane in the presence of guests because he thought she had taken some gold jewellery from him, although it was lesser stuff that the visitors had electroplated for her. Despite his age and ugliness, his women included 'the best-looking girls we had seen in the country'. Most of them were the daughters of ministers and other dignitaries 'who vie with each other for the honour of furnishing a fresh inmate for the royal harem'.

The Madras Officer had also brought intriguing examples of European technology to the royal court, including the electroplating equipment and batteries, and the king asked him to repair his coining machine, which was malfunctioning. Duang was an intelligent man and would have had an appreciation of European power relative to that of his Asian neighbours. Just as the British officer was scrutinising him, he was no doubt shrewdly sizing up his guest and he would have known that British influence was growing in Siam. Behind what the officer considered a bovine appearance lurked an agile mind. In 1853, Duang made diplomatic overtures to the French emperor, eager to find a patron to counterbalance the power of Hué and Bangkok, and possibly that of the British. However, other matters preoccupied Napoleon III, and two years elapsed before he sent the Montigny diplomatic mission to discuss Duang's overtures. By this time, the Siamese had sniffed out what was happening and brought pressure to bear on Duang to let the matter drop.

Duang died in 1860, apparently depressed, leaving instructions that his body be left for the wild beasts to devour. (This somewhat bizarre order—which, however, followed a custom common in Cambodia up to Angkorean times—was not obeyed and Duang's body was cremated.) Perhaps the old king despaired that he had been able to do no more for his kingdom, but if so he underestimated himself, for he had brought some stability and warded off chaos and disintegration. His death was followed by another depressing interregnum of court intrigues, dynastic squabbling, revolts and foreign meddling. Duang's oldest son, Prince Norodom, turned to the French for support, and this time the French were quick to accept. During the monsoon of 1863, a bluff middle-aged French admiral sailed up the Mekong to Udong by gunboat to sign a treaty with this prince. A new era in Cambodian history was about to begin.

5
THE FRENCH PROTECTORATE, 1863–1953

French colonialism arrived in Indochina in 1858, four centuries after the Iberian conquistadors set sail from Manila on a doomed mission to carve out an empire on the Southeast Asian mainland. This time, the Europeans would succeed. French marines landed from warships anchored off Saigon after a pogrom had broken out against Catholic missionaries and their Vietnamese converts. What was ostensibly a 'protective mission' became a permanent occupation force. The Vietnamese troops were no match for French marines armed with breech-loading rifles and naval guns. Blocked from expansion in India and kept out of the rest of Southeast Asia by the Dutch, the Spanish and the British, the French were eager to plant the tricolour in Indochina.

Once the French naval officers had established a beachhead at Saigon, they gradually wrested control of the surrounding districts from the Vietnamese authorities. In 1863, they set up a protectorate in neighbouring Cambodia. By 1893, after a bloody war of conquest, they would control all of the Vietnamese territories from the Chinese border in the north to the tip of the Cape of Camau in the south, along with Laos and Cambodia upstream on the Mekong. They partitioned Vietnam into the protectorates of Tonkin and Annam, along with the direct colony of Cochin-China in the south, and gradually tightened control over the protectorates of Laos and Cambodia. The word 'protectorate' was a euphemism. After the conquest of Tonkin, French governors-general administered Indochina as a federated colonial unit from Hanoi. Under these republican 'viceroys', power was deputised to the *Résidents Supérieurs* in the four protectorates and the governor at Saigon. The French would stay in Indochina until 1954, when a peace conference in Geneva brokered a settlement to the anti-colonial war that raged in the region after World War II. Cambodia secured its own independence the year earlier following King Sihanouk's 'royal crusade', although this must be seen in the context of France's reversals in Indochina as a whole, which culminated in catastrophe at the Battle of Dien Bien Phu in 1954.

The tricolour comes to Cambodia

The first administrators at Saigon were naval officers, brisk, efficient and patriotic men who were determined to carve out a place for the Fatherland in the tropical sun. Their behaviour suggests that they had entertained designs on Cambodia some years before the establishment of the protectorate. French missionaries had proselytised in the kingdom since the 17th century, and although they made few converts, they had won the trust of King Duang and several of his predecessors. There had also been a tremendous spurt of popular interest in the kingdom following the posthumous publication of the diaries of the French traveller Henri Mouhot. These contained a description of the ruins of Angkor, which the popular imagination saw as an Eldorado in the East. To acquire them would bring glory to *la belle France*.

There had been sporadic diplomatic contact with the Cambodian court since 1853, when Ang Duang had sought French protection on the advice of Catholic priests based at Udong. In 1855, the Montigny mission arrived to discuss the request, but Duang, under Siamese duress, declined to pursue the matter. Ang Duang died in 1860 and the following year a French gunboat steamed up the Mekong to the royal capital at Udong, ostensibly to protect Christians from persecution but more likely to 'case the joint' as American gangsters might say, with a view to annexation. Around the same time, the Viscount de Castelnau attempted unsuccessfully to reach an understanding with the Siamese about the future of their Cambodian vassal state, and the following year Admiral Bonard made a preliminary survey of the country and its resources. These were tempting prizes in themselves, but the French had two other compelling reasons for their interest. Their old rivals, the British, had an eye on Siam and a friendly Cambodia might act as a buffer against the uncomfortable proximity of 'perfidious Albion' (a traditional French appellation for Britain). Secondly, the Mekong was one of the world's great rivers, running down from distant Yunnan, and the French were interested in its potential as a trading and military artery; what the Australian historian Milton Osborne has called a 'river road to China'.

The treaty of 1863

When King Duang died in 1860, Cambodian fell into a familiar pattern of instability. Duang's three older sons, Ang Vodey, Sisowath and Si Votha, jockeyed for the throne, and Cham insurgents marched on the capital. Ang Vodey, the Siamese nominee for the Cambodian throne, no longer had to fear Vietnamese designs on the kingdom, but the Siamese now had a freer hand to meddle and they were jealous lest France supplant them as 'protector' of the Khmers. Ang Vodey, who was to reign as King Norodom after his coronation in 1864, sought talks with France on the advice of French missionaries, and this time the response came quickly. On 11 August 1863, Norodom signed a 'treaty of friendship, commerce and French protection' with the Breton sailor

Admiral Pierre de La Grandière, whose gunboat was moored on the river nearby.

Norodom signed under the muzzles of de La Grandière's naval cannon, and although the threat was implicit rather than open, the French were determined to bring the country into their orbit. In the circumstances, Norodom probably thought he had made the best of the situation, for the terms of the treaty were apparently innocuous. France was to have the right to station warships and soldiers at the Quatre Bras. The Catholic Church was to receive special privileges and the French could trade freely throughout the kingdom. A French *Résident* would advise the king. On the other hand, the Cambodians could maintain a representative at Saigon and could trade freely with the French, and the special place of Buddhism as a state religion was ensured. After centuries as a tributary state of Vietnam and Siam, Norodom perhaps figured that he could have made a worse bargain.

Unsurprisingly, King Mongkut of Siam was furious at what he saw as his vassal's ingratitude. Norodom tried to placate Mongkut by arguing that de La Grandière had bullied him into signing the treaty before he had time to read the Khmer text. In December 1863, Norodom signed a secret treaty with the Siamese king, which ran counter to his pledges to France. His behaviour seems erratic, but perhaps he was uncertain of France's willingness and ability to defend him against the angry Siamese. The French were busy fighting Vietnamese insurgents at the time and, perhaps more importantly, Emperor Napoleon III had yet to ratify the treaty; indeed there is some evidence to show that the Saigon admirals had acted with considerable autonomy in the matter and in the context of factionalised politics at the imperial court. In fact, Napoleon did not ratify the treaty until April 1864.

It seems that Norodom's demeanour at the time did not inspire the confidence of the Saigon admirals. Their misgivings intensified when, in March 1864, they caught him trying secretly to slip out of Udong for his coronation at Bangkok. A few salvos from a gunboat convinced Norodom that he should abandon the plan. Instead, he was crowned at Udong the following June in a ceremony presided over jointly by the French and Siamese. The story did not end there, however, for two months later the French learned (via a report in the Singapore newspaper the *Straits Times*) of his secret treaty with King Mongkut, the terms of which gave the Siamese the right to appoint 'the kings or viceroys' of Cambodia and gave further slices of Cambodian territory to Siam. Under French pressure (and on the advice of the British), the Siamese formally agreed that their treaty was null and void.

For the first six or seven years of the protectorate, the colonial hand lay relatively lightly on Norodom, whom the French shored up against a series of rebellions, the most celebrated of which was led by the pretender Pou Kombo. While they were privately dismayed by the misrule of the Khmer administration and by the king's indifference to the welfare of his subjects, the French naval officers remained aloof so long as they could guide Cambodia's foreign affairs and their missionary and trading activities were unimpaired. During this period, they were preoccupied with the pacification of the Vietnamese resistance to the piecemeal annexation their country. Besides, France was itself a monarchy at this stage and Napoleon III was no model of probity. This brief pragmatic hiatus ended when the Second Empire collapsed as a result of Napoleon III's disastrous war against Prussia in 1870. With the new Third Republic came a reforming zeal that coincided with a more vigorous style of imperialism by the European powers. The inefficient and corrupt Khmer state would have to be replaced with government and administration based on European ideas of fiscal prudence, and legal–rational principles. Cambodia, which had been a drain on the French exchequer, would pay its way.

The French reform program

Implementing the *mission civilisatrice* would prove harder than the French realised. For the next thirty-odd years, the French *Résidents* would wage a constant battle against Norodom and his ministers and provincial officials. Too weak to actively oppose the French, Norodom's preferred

*Jean Moura, French Resident in the 1870s. He was also a naval officer,
a scholar and the author of a history of Cambodia.
(Courtesy of Cambodian National Archives, Phnom Penh)*

method was passive resistance. To mounting French disbelief and irritation, he would agree with their proposals for reform and then passively sabotage them. The main planks of the reform program included: the creation of private property in land, the abolition of slavery, legal and administrative restructure, and cuts to royal spending and sinecures. Although they might not have realised it, the French were following in the footsteps of the earlier 19th century Vietnamese occupiers, who had also grown frustrated by their fruitless attempts to reform the Khmer bureaucracy (see Chapter 3).

Cambodia had no private landed property in the normally accepted sense of the word. All land was crown land, the property of the king, who was indistinguishable from the state. The French saw this as a barrier to material progress. They believed it encouraged sloth and passivity on the part of the peasants, who made up the overwhelming majority of the Cambodian population. There was no doubt that it prevented the establishment of a stable taxation base for state revenues. Under the Cambodian system, which was a form of usufruct, anyone could work the land with the king's blessing. However, should the occupants leave the land fallow for three years, anyone else was free to take it over. In return for the right to use the land, the peasants had to hand over one-tenth of their income, in kind, to the state. They were also expected to perform *corvée* labour, in theory for a stipulated number of days per year but in practice often at the whim of local officials, who often put the peasants to work on private projects. The system entrenched subsistence agriculture and discouraged private enterprise. The tax-in-kind system also fostered corruption because tax collectors could understate the amount of taxable farm produce in any particular year. On the other hand, the peasants could understate their actual production to avoid tax. By privatising land, the French reasoned, they could introduce fixed land taxes, which would generate a stable source of state revenue and which would be less prone to pilferage by dishonest officials.

The second aim was to abolish slavery, on both moral and pragmatic grounds. France had itself only finally abolished slavery a few decades before, but the custom flew in the face of the (in theory) cherished Rights of Man and it was also economically inefficient (as Marx had noted in Volume I of *Capital*, for instance). According to one estimate, 150 000 people out of a total Cambodian population of 900 000 in the 1880s were slaves. Those in bondage fell into two broad categories, hereditary slaves and debt slaves, but there were also slaves at the royal court and even in the Buddhist temples. However repugnant to modern eyes, slavery had been part of life in Cambodia since pre-Angkorean times, and Khmers—including the slaves themselves—saw it as a natural part of life, and there was no indigenous emancipation movement. Its eradication therefore proved extremely difficult.

The third major aim of the French reform program was the overhaul of the Khmer legal and administrative apparatus—later described by French administrator Gustave Janneau as 'worm-eaten debris'. Creaking, inefficient and corrupt, the French saw it as a system of licensed robbery in which the main purpose of officials seemed to be personal enrichment at public expense. The French believed that of a potential revenue base of five million francs, two million francs either disappeared into the pockets of shady officials, or were not collected. The country was divided into 57 provinces, each of which was administered by a member of the royal family or a high mandarin, and with considerable duplication of functions between the provinces and the central government. Worse still, there was little comprehension of any difference between private and public wealth, and this attitude became more pronounced the further one scaled the ladder of status and privilege. There were no public works schemes of any consequence, with Norodom himself once questioning the need for the construction of a road because he never went to the road's proposed destination. There was no system of education apart from limited instruction given to boys by monks at the pagodas, and no institutions of social welfare or health (in contrast to what had existed at Angkor). The legal system was often irrational, cruel and unjust. The towns were ramshackle places, little more than extended villages; the most imposing edifices in Phnom Penh, apart from Buddhist *wats*, were a few jerry-built brick shop houses along the riverfront.

At the top of the ramshackle social pile sat the considerable figure of the king himself. He had proven himself to be an incompetent military commander during the Pou Kombo revolt of 1866 and the French viewed him as greedy and vain. He smoked prodigious quantities of opium, downed vast quantities of wines and spirits, and concerned himself little with administrative affairs. Then there was the matter of the royal harem, which *Résident* Étienne Aymonier claimed consumed the 'greatest part of the country's revenues'. The harem was a town within a town, inhabited by Norodom's 400–500 wives and concubines, with a total population of up to 1500 women and children, plus the palace guards and other staff. A French report of 1894 estimated the cost of maintaining Norodom at some 800 000 piastres per annum. (The piastre, issued by the private Banque de l'Indochine at Hanoi, was worth five French metropolitan francs.) We should also consider the numerous members of the royal family, each of whom was an idle belly kept full at public expense. The French were intent on drastic cuts to the royal expenditure and the introduction of a civil list.

The cost of administering Cambodia was a steady drain on the French public purse. In 1881, a French official complained that the 'situation in Cambodia is still the worst . . . The financial disorder surpasses all bounds and the King takes all revenues for his personal use'. The Colonial Minister at Paris ordered the French authorities to take over Cambodia's financial affairs and ensure that the king regularly put back a proportion of taxes into the costs of running the country. Norodom played for time in his usual fashion, but French patience was at an end. In March 1884, they insisted on a thoroughgoing revision of the 1863 treaty. Three months later, after further procrastination by Norodom, Governor Charles Thomson's gunboat churned up the Mekong from Saigon with a small army of French marines and Vietnamese riflemen aboard. Thomson hauled Norodom out of bed in the predawn darkness and forced him to sign the new treaty, the first article of which committed the king to accept 'all the administrative, judicial, financial and commercial reforms that the government of France deems useful in future'. Thomson gave Norodom a clear choice: sign or abdicate and, under *force majeure*, he signed.

The Great Rebellion of 1885–86

An eerie calm fell over the country. Thomson was so flushed with success that he floated the idea of annexing Cambodia outright and French officials moved confidently to introduce the program of reforms. It was a profound miscalculation. Forty years earlier, a heavy-handed campaign by the Vietnamese to 'civilise' the Khmer 'barbarians' and force them to adopt Vietnamese styles of government and administration had triggered off a desperate insurrection. Thomson's forced *mission civilisatrice* was to do just the same.

In early January 1885, Khmer rebels attacked a number of isolated French military posts, heralding a general insurrection that was to embroil almost all of the country. The central figure in the revolt was Norodom's half-brother Prince Si Votha, a seasoned guerrilla and royal pretender who had already spent many years in the forests. The revolt united the disparate factions of the Khmer aristocracy in the common cause of driving the French back down the Mekong and won the support of the common people, tacit or otherwise. Norodom himself stayed out of the fighting, but others of his immediate family actively supported the rebels. There is also evidence that elements of the Chinese and Vietnamese minorities joined the fight against France, despite ethnic animosities between them and the Khmers. As I have written elsewhere,

> For the French, it was a costly lesson in the futility of waging war against guerrillas operating on their own terrain, with natural refuge provided by forest, marsh and mountain ... Not even 4000 heavily-armed French troops, equipped with artillery, gunboats and quick-firing guns, could quell the rebellion.

Many French soldiers fell victim to disease, while others fell under the bullets of the rebels who eluded them in the forests and fields. Stung, the French responded as many others would do in colonial wars, burning villages and terrorising the peasants whom they suspected of secretly aiding the rebels or of taking up arms themselves. By the middle of 1886, it had become clear to the French Colonial Ministry that there would have to be a negotiated solution to the conflict and that this would involve backing away from the terms imposed upon Norodom in the 1884 treaty. Moreover, the French would have to solicit the king's support to end the uprising.

In return for a promise from the French that they would not try to impose total control over the Khmer administration, Norodom agreed to issue a proclamation for peace and to travel the country to ask the rebels to lay down their arms. Within six weeks, he had achieved what had proved impossible for the French. Resistance tapered off dramatically, although Si Votha held out intransigently in the forests until his death in 1890.

The country was largely at peace, but it was the peace of an exhausted and devastated land. The French estimated that 10 000 people had died during the revolt, but other statistics show that the Cambodian population fell from 945 000 in 1879 to 750 000 in 1888: a net loss of 195 000 people. Many of these must have died, but tens of thousands of peasants had also fled to Battambang and Siam proper, or else sought refuge in the jungle. Once again, famine and disease broke out as farmland was abandoned or devastated. It was yet another immense tragedy for a land that had never recovered from the wars, famines, deportations and insurrections earlier in the century.

France's strategic retreat

The French had been forced to back off from their reform program, but later developments make it clear that they regarded this as a strategic retreat and not a permanent defeat. Before the insurrection they had toyed with the idea of putting Norodom's more pliable half-brother Sisowath on the throne. Sisowath had signed a secret agreement with the French, promising his full cooperation if he were to be crowned king. Norodom had, however, proved indispensable in ending the revolt. For most Khmers he was the legitimate sovereign and the French realised that to depose him would be to overplay their hand. In any case, they reasoned, his life of excess meant that he would not live long. They would bide their time, gradually tightening the screws on the Khmer administration, careful not to force the pace lest it trigger a repeat of 1885. They also rebuilt parts of the capital, and many of its handsome colonial buildings date from the 1890s.

The main street in Phnom Penh, 1894, prior to the demolition of shop houses.
(Courtesy of Cambodian National Archives, Phnom Penh)

As it turned out, Norodom's constitution was more robust than
the French had hoped, and he resumed the old game of passive resistance to reform. He agreed a number of times, for instance, to abolish
slavery yet the practice continued as before. By the 1890s, French anger
was simmering afresh and the increasingly infirm Norodom lacked the
stamina to resist. He was brow beaten by officials and one *Résident
Supérieur* appears to have threatened him with death for recalcitrance.
The French forced him to disown two of his favourite sons, one of them,
Prince Yukanthor, for acting as a go-between in an ill-fated attempt to
complain to the French government over his father's treatment. The
other son, Duong Chakr, had died in exile in a dusty Algerian town on
the edge of the Sahara Desert. For some time before his death in 1904,
Norodom was a shell of a man, kept a virtual prisoner in his palace at
Phnom Penh, his health sapped by drink and opium. Perhaps he brooded

on the wrongs he had done his sons and regretted his role in ending the Great Rebellion. Perhaps he even repented bringing the French to his kingdom in the first place.

Sisowath and the Franco–Khmer accord

Norodom's successor's loyalties were never in doubt. Succession to the Khmer throne has never been governed by strict primogeniture and for a long period before the arrival of the French, Cambodia's kings had been chosen by Siam and/or Vietnam. The French had chosen the new king, the *Obbareach*, Prince Sisowath, many years previously when he had agreed to support their reform program. Shortly before his half-brother's cremation, the 64-year-old Sisowath was crowned king (by Governor-General Paul Beau in the name of the French Republic) in a ceremony at Udong.

The French were eager to accelerate their reform program. Although stymied by what they saw as the laziness and incompetence of Khmer officialdom, the French were to achieve more in the first few years of Sisowath's reign than they had managed in the 40 years under Norodom. Slavery was abolished, the Khmer legal code overhauled, and a system of competitive entry to the civil service introduced. The institution of private property in land, long a key plank of the reform plan, began with the introduction of a cadastral program and the distribution of title deeds. Steps were taken to root out corruption, particularly in the collection of taxes, and there was some expansion of public works schemes such as roads and bridges, government buildings and dredging of the port of Phnom Penh. A limited civil list was introduced to curb spending on minor royalty. The system of apanage, under which district administration was farmed out to members of the royal family and high mandarins, almost as individual fiefdoms, was abolished. Most importantly, a new three-tier system of local government bodies was set up under the supervision of French *Résidents*.

The extent of the reforms should not be overstated, however. In most respects, the French were content for Cambodia to remain an

A fine example of French colonial architecture, the former French Residence at Battambang. (Author's collection)

economic backwater, as they had done for most of the 40 years since the creation of the protectorate. So long as Cambodia paid its way, and public funds were used for public purposes instead of personal enrichment, they would be reasonably content. In the colonial banquet, Cambodia was a side dish compared with the Vietnamese main course.

Sisowath's coronation in 1904, however, marked the beginning of a new stage in Franco–Khmer relations. Sisowath was a docile supporter of France, although he had proved himself a competent and physically courageous military commander during the Pou Kombo insurrection. His pliability reflected a pragmatic mix of self-interest, resignation to the facts of *Realpolitik*, a genuine respect for French culture, and faith in the ability of France to protect his kingdom. His reign, and that of his son Monivong (who succeeded Sisowath after his death in 1927) was one of Franco–Khmer accord, marked by social peace and stability—a break from the more turbulent Norodom years. The palace

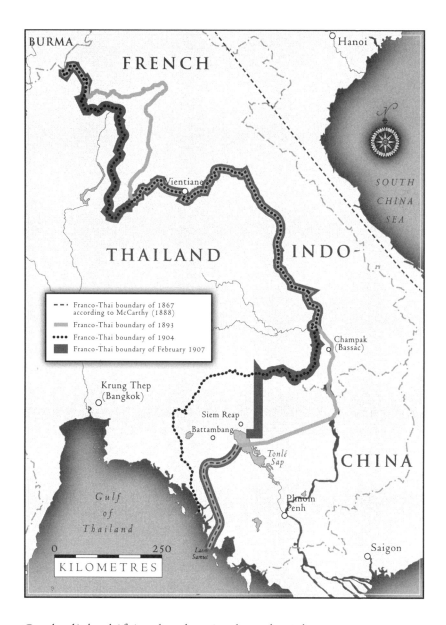

BURMA

FRENCH

Hanoi

THAILAND

INDO-

SOUTH
CHINA
SEA

Vientiane

- - - Franco-Thai boundary of 1867
according to McCarthy (1888)
Franco-Thai boundary of 1893
•••• Franco-Thai boundary of 1904
Franco-Thai boundary of February 1907

Champak
(Bassac)

Krung Thep
(Bangkok)

Siem Reap

Battambang

Tonlé
Sap

CHINA

Gulf
of
Thailand

Phnom
Penh

0   250

Laem
Samui

Saigon

KILOMETRES

Cambodia's shifting borders in the colonial era

intrigues of supporters of the Norodom wing of the royal family, who felt one of them should have inherited the throne, were ineffectual. Influential civil servants such as Thiounn were resolute Francophiles. Sisowath's loyalty to France was cemented early in his reign when in 1906 he undertook an extended tour of France, his first and last overseas journey apart from his youthful sojourn as a guest-hostage of the Siamese king at Bangkok. Sisowath was delighted by what he saw. Cheering crowds of ordinary French folk lined the roads to welcome him, there were dazzling displays of military power, and the President of the Republic received him in the Elysée Palace at Paris. Equally impressive were the civic and industrial wonders of the protector-nation. He committed a major diplomatic gaffe in France when he called publicly for the restoration of the lost provinces of Battambang and Angkor to Cambodia, but he was rewarded soon afterwards when in 1908, after delicate negotiations, Siam agreed to their return. Shortly afterwards—following an unsuccessful anti-French revolt by followers of the Apheuvongs family who had governed the provinces on behalf of Siam since 1795—a French archaeological team began the painstaking task of restoring the Angkor ruins. These had remained a symbol of *Khmerité*—'Khmerness'—since their loss over a century before, and with their return Cambodia was almost whole again.

Sisowath's gratitude showed in his wholehearted support for the French cause during the Great War of 1914–18. Some 2000 Cambodians served as *tirailleurs* (sharpshooters or light infantrymen) in French colonial regiments in Europe, while some hundreds of Khmers joined the hundreds of thousands of colonial workers in the munitions factories of France. Members of the Khmer Krom minority from Vietnam also served in other Indochinese regiments. A number of Khmers won medals for bravery in battles on the western front and in the Balkans. A number of members of the royal family served in the armed forces. These included Sisowath's eldest son, Prince Monivong, who trained at the Saint-Maixent military academy and rose to brigadier's rank. Another prince, Leng Sisowath, left his bones in a French military cemetery. However,

Young Khmers rally to the colours, Phnom Penh circa 1914. The statuary on the Wat Phnom behind them commemorates the return of the lost provinces from Siam in 1907. (Courtesy Archives d'Outre-Mer, Aix-en-Provence)

Monivong did not serve at the front because of the possibility that he might be needed to succeed his elderly father on the throne.

The 1916 Affair

The sacrifices of the Khmer *tirailleurs* should not blind us to the fact that the majority of the common people did not share Sisowath's enthusiasm for France's war. Recruitment fell short of targets and the authorities resorted to heavy-handed methods to meet quotas. The resulting resentment combined with long-brewing discontent over rising levels of taxation and abuse of the *corvée* regulations and sparked off an extraordinary movement of peasant protest that the French authorities dubbed the 1916 Affair. There is some evidence to suggest that dissident circles associated with the exiled Prince Yukanthor, the rebellious anti-French son of Norodom, had a hand in stirring up discontent, and the synchronicity of events and striking similarity of demands across the country suggests the existence of some kind of organisation or resistance network. Some 100 000 peasants flocked into the capital from the provinces, and although there were some instances of violence against Khmer bureaucrats and Chinese traders and one recorded assault on a French administrative office, in the main the demonstrations were peaceful.

What is striking about the Affair is that, on the whole, the tens of thousands of peasants involved ignored the French authorities and took their grievances directly to the king. The vast majority of them would never have seen Sisowath—he was as remote for them as the man in the moon—yet they trusted him because of their faith in the institution of kingship. The French were largely invisible, particularly in the countryside where most Khmers lived, and the peasants blamed the Khmer bureaucracy for the abuses they suffered, despite the efforts of more political elements to turn the protests into an anti-French crusade. The peasants saw the king as a *devaraja* with supernatural powers: a being quite disconnected from the state apparatchiks who collected the taxes, forced them to labour on the roads and often lined their own pockets in the process. In fact, the French administration had been increasing taxes for some years, but because Khmer officials collected these the peasants held them responsible.

The movement ebbed as swiftly as it had begun, after the king promised to investigate the peasants' grievances and the French authorities agreed to tax relief and to end some of the more egregious abuses of *corvée*. The Affair ended with tragedy, however. The authoritarian *Résident Supérieur* François Baudoin—perhaps fearing a repeat of the 1885 rebellion—ordered a crackdown. 'Agitators' were hunted down and many received long prison terms. There were reports of soldiers machine-gunning crowds and tossing the corpses into the river, although these were printed in anti-regime papers and should be taken with caution. We cannot say with certainty how many died: the lowest estimates claim half a dozen slain and Baudoin himself admitted 21 deaths. It is likely that scores or even hundreds perished.

French power was stretched thin during World War I, with many troops and officials called to the colours in Europe. Yet despite the spectre of 1885, France's grip was never seriously threatened during this period. A combination of repression and amelioration of the tax and *corvée* burden—which the peasants probably attributed to the king's good influence—put the lid on further large-scale manifestations of popular discontent. Nor were worries that returning soldiers and workers might act as a conduit for radical ideas borne out, although some Khmer soldiers did become moderate nationalist politicians in later decades. The Allied victory in Europe probably enhanced France's prestige among the general population, and further strengthened ties with the Khmer elite. The French built a huge commemorative monument in Phnom Penh (later demolished by the Pol Pot regime) and the war hero Marshal Joffe made a triumphal tour of the country, including to the Angkor ruins. It was the beginning of the zenith of French power in the kingdom, a period described by the Cambodian writer Huy Kanthoul as 'a kind of *belle époque*'.

By the 1920s the economic austerity of the war years had lifted and there was something of an economic boom, marked by increased spending on public works, health and education, and by the development of large-scale rubber plantations on the left bank of the Mekong, upstream from Phnom Penh. The Angkor restoration project had continued throughout the period, and under the able direction of French scholar and linguist Suzanne Karpelès a Buddhist Institute was set up to study and preserve Cambodian religious culture. There was also something of a revival of traditional Cambodian arts and crafts, many of which had been threatened with extinction by cheap mass-produced imports.

The relative prosperity and progress of the 1920s, however, came to a sharp end with the onset of the Great Depression. The economy stagnated, public expenditure was slashed to balance budgets and there

This French-built commemorative monument to the Allied victory in
World War I was later demolished by the Pol Pot regime.
(Courtesy David Chandler)

was great destitution among the Khmers. On the eve of World War II,
though, the economy was on the mend again and many colonial officials
and settlers must have believed that the *belle époque* would continue for
many years.

The Bokor and Bardez Affairs

But there was a dark downside to this period. The French *Résidents* gave
the police a free hand to use brutal methods against the Asian populations, and ratcheted up taxation levels in the 1920s to cancel out
the concessions granted as a result of the 1916 Affair. The French
authorities also encouraged increased Vietnamese immigration to
provide indentured labour for the plantations and construction projects.
Living and working conditions on the plantations were often appalling,

99

to judge by the French labour inspectors' reports and by the strikes and mass desertions that were commonplace. Not surprisingly, the Khmers tended to shun plantation work. Two incidents underline the arrogance and contempt of French officialdom for the common folk during this period, the Bardez Affair and the construction of the Bokor hill station.

After World War I, *Résident Supérieur* François Baudoin decided to build a French pleasure palace at Bokor atop a mountain overlooking the Gulf of Siam behind Kampot. It would rival the British efforts at Poona. There was to be a grand hotel, a casino, tennis courts, gardens and paths along which *colons* and their wives could take the cool mountain air. At an altitude of over 1000 metres, European fruits and vegetables thrived, to the delight of French palates. Baudoin ordered construction of a special bungalow for himself within the complex. The project consumed an enormous slice of government revenues and led to protests by the radical press at Saigon and in France at the excesses of Baudoin, whom they dubbed the 'tyrant of Cambodia'. The building of Bokor also claimed many lives, particularly on construction of the road, which snaked up through the jungle-clad mountainsides from Kampot. The authorities never published any figures of the death toll, but the French Saigon press claimed there were between 900 and 2000 dead and the novelist Marguerite Duras recalls her settler mother's horror at the brutality meted out to workers.

The French built Bokor to benefit themselves, but the peasants paid for it in blood and sweat, and in taxes. Taxation levels crept upwards again in the early 1920s and caused widespread discontent. This led to tragedy in 1925, when Baudoin dispatched a peppery 'trouble-shooter' called Félix Louis Bardez to the Khmer village of Kraang Leav, in the Kompong Chhnang district, to investigate complaints of excessive taxation. Bardez, a decorated former non-commissioned officer and long-serving colonial official, was not renowned for his tact. He summoned the villagers and, via his interpreter, subjected them to an insulting harangue. Later, when the sun rose high in the sky and after the consumption of quantities of palm wine, the peasants battered Bardez, his interpreter and a Khmer militiaman to death. Although the administration claimed that the murders were in no way political, dissident European elements in Saigon were able to turn the subsequent murder trials into an indictment of the Baudoin administration. Be that as it may, the assassination of *Résident* Bardez was the first overtly political murder of a French official for many years, and it was to be the last until the twilight days of the Protectorate after World War II. Discontent was more likely to be channelled into endemic banditry or into ethnic strife between Khmers and Vietnamese or Chinese. Indeed, anti-Vietnamese feeling has coloured Cambodian nationalism from its beginnings in the 1930s until the present day.

Cambodian nationalism's hesitant beginnings

By the 1920s, the political passions of their homelands had spread to the Chinese and Vietnamese minorities in Cambodia. These minorities were substantial, particularly in Phnom Penh where the population was fairly evenly divided between Khmers, Chinese and Vietnamese. After World War I, the tenor of the Chinese and Vietnamese political and quasi-political associations was distinctly anti-French and anti-colonial. Affiliates of the Chinese Nationalist Kuomintang took root in Phnom Penh after the war, and more militant, illegal Marxist-inspired tracts appeared among the city's Vietnamese population.

From the late 1920s, revolutionary cells were set up and attracted much police attention. There were strikes among building workers in the capital and persistent agitation against bad conditions on the rubber plantations. In general, the Khmers stood aloof from these developments, seemingly immune to the clarion calls of socialism and nationalism. However, there was a gradual change in consciousness, and although this was not always overtly political it arguably laid the groundwork for Khmer nationalism.

Sirowath's royal boat, Phnom Penh, in the 1920s was a showpiece for the revival of traditional Cambodian arts and crafts.
(Author's collection)

During the 1920s, a number of Khmer-language cultural magazines appeared. These were apolitical, but they did assist in the formation of a Cambodian cultural–ethnic–political identity. In 1936, a group of youngish Khmer intellectuals began publication of the Khmer-language magazine *Nagaravatta* (*Angkor Wat* in English) and a number of Cambodian novels and volumes of poetry appeared. This movement was ambivalent towards the French because, as Huy Kanthoul has pointed out, the Khmers had tended to look towards the French as protectors against their neighbours. The perceived enemy during this period was the Vietnamese, not the French, and what direct political comment we find in the pages of *Nagaravatta* and other publications is charged with the 'politics of envy' against the immigrants from down the Mekong.

While it would be drawing a long bow to claim that the French deliberately imported the Vietnamese in order to play a game of divide and rule, the presence of so large a minority led to ethnic friction, and the French made opportunistic use of it when it suited them (just as they played off the Khmer Krom minority against the Vietnamese in Cochin-China). Upon the outbreak of war in Europe in 1939, Khmer nationalism was weak and unfocused, with most Khmers either indifferent to the French or well disposed towards them. Even today there are some very old Khmers who look back with nostalgia to the colonial era. However, war and French humiliation at Asian hands during the Japanese occupation were to change the political situation forever, and trigger a qualitative leap in consciousness that was to lead to independence within less than a decade after 1945.

War, Japanese occupation and French humiliation

The fall of France came swiftly in June 1940. The victorious Germans partitioned the country into a nominally independent state with its capital at Vichy in the south and a directly occupied zone in the north. The authorities in some of France's overseas colonies heeded the call of General de Gaulle to continue resistance, but many others, including those in Indochina, declared their loyalty to the quasi-fascist pro-Axis regime at Vichy, led by the geriatric war hero Philippe Pétain.

In the case of the French Indochina Governor-General at Hanoi, Admiral Jean Decoux, it was perhaps a matter of discretion being the better part of valour to support Vichy. Battle-hardened Japanese armies were on the northern borders of Tonkin after fighting their way south through China, and the military forces at Decoux's disposal were at best mediocre in the case of his European troops, and downright untrustworthy in the case of his 'native' infantrymen. The Japanese, too, were

Members of the Yuvan youth organisation march in support of the Vichy government in France. (Author's collection)

Vichy's nominal allies, however terrifying they appeared to Decoux's ramshackle army. Decoux became a zealous Vichyite, enforcing Pétain's version of the racist Nuremberg Laws, setting up concentration camps and enforcing other tawdry symbols of European fascism in his tropical fiefdom: the goose-step, the fascist salute and ritualised chanting of Pétain's name. As if at a word of command, the French-language press in Indochina switched from pro-Allied propaganda to hate-filled invective against Jews and the English, and gloated over Allied reversals. This calls into question Decoux's later claims to have merely gone through the motions to placate the Japanese.

The Japanese aim was to strike southwards into Southeast Asia in order to gain control of the oil, tin and tropical commodities they required for the Home Islands and to run their war machine. The French government readily agreed to their request to station troops throughout Indochina, and also to provide them with rubber, coal and other products. They were scarcely in any position to refuse. For their part, the Japanese were content to leave the day-to-day administration of Indochina to the despised whites, so that they could concentrate on their war aims. It was a marriage of convenience that was to last until the dying days of the war.

The French capitulation was a devastating blow to French morale in the colony, and it must have given the Francophile Khmer elite cause for grave concern. Worse was to come in early 1941, when the Japanese brokered a humiliating agreement between France and Siam—by now renamed Thailand—following a short-lived war. The war had broken out in late 1940, with the Thais taking advantage of France's weakness to demand the handover of Cambodia's western provinces, which they had ceded in 1908. While the land war was inconclusive, the French had inflicted a stinging defeat on the Thai navy at the Battle of Koh Chang in the Gulf of Siam, and might have expected a more favourable outcome than that imposed by Japan. However, despite its nominal alliance with Vichy, Japan's underlying aim was to undermine western colonial power in Asia, regardless of its political complexion. They awarded Thailand almost all of the territories she had asked for, with the exception of the area around the Angkor ruins, which France argued bitterly to retain.

The Cambodians had tolerated the French and many, especially in the elite, had welcomed them, so long as they acted as protectors of *srok khmer*. Now, their protector's sword and shield were broken, and the ancient predators were at the gates of the kingdom. Perception of France's weakness led on one hand to profound disillusionment and depression, but on the other to the growth of nationalist sentiment and to a new confidence that Asians could defeat the almighty Europeans. The former effect was most pronounced in the case of King Monivong, who had succeeded his father to the throne in 1927. Monivong could pass as a 'brown Frenchman', for although he never lost his identity as a Khmer, he spoke fluent French and had adopted many western customs. He had risen to the rank of brigadier in the

French army and although he was a figurehead who played relatively little part in government affairs, he was intensely loyal to France. When the news came through of the forced cession of Battambang and Siem Reap provinces, Monivong was plunged into deep gloom and retired to his estates at Bokor where he refused to meet with French officials and even 'forgot' their language. He died soon afterwards in the company of his favourite concubine, Saloth Roeung, the sister of a man called Saloth Sar who was later known to the world as Pol Pot.

While Monivong died without hope, the French humiliation had electrified the young Cambodian intellectuals associated with the magazine *Nagaravatta*, and nationalist sentiment swept through some circles of the Buddhist *sangha*. *Nagaravatta* openly criticised the French authorities, who responded with heavy censorship before banning it outright in 1942. Monivong's successor to the throne, a baby-faced 19-year-old prince from the Norodom wing of the family, made little impression on politics at the time. The young Norodom Sihanouk, whom Decoux had installed on the throne in the belief that he would be a docile puppet, initially surpassed their best expectations, preferring to chase girls and watch films than worry himself with affairs of state or nationalist politics. Decoux was not the first person to underestimate him, but Sihanouk's nature had not formed and it is doubtful that he had a subversive thought in his head at the time, regardless of his later claims. Another young man called Son Ngoc Thanh, a Khmer Krom from the lower delta and a member of the *Nagaravatta* circle, came to symbolise Cambodian nationalism at this stage.

The Vichy regime in Indochina was viciously repressive. The police rounded up thousands of real and imagined opponents and interned them in prisons and concentration camps, including the Pich Nil camp in the coastal mountains south of Phnom Penh. It was also a period of mounting austerity with widespread shortages of food and clothing and, according to Cambodian nationalists, taxation grew steadily heavier. The Allied navies cut Indochina's overseas trade routes and the Japanese occupation forces requisitioned much of the country's food and

The young Norodom Sihanouk.
(Author's collection)

plantation products for their own consumption and for export to the Home Islands. This built up a head of resentment against the French, whom the Khmers held responsible for the shortages.

The Vichy political regime was also contradictory. While the French authorities were repressive and insensitive, they were also conscious of their extreme weakness, *vis-à-vis* both the Japanese and their colonial subjects. The Japanese had ousted the British and Dutch colonial authorities in Malaya and the East Indies and their rhetoric was stridently anti-European. The French must have been fearful of the longer-term intentions of their nominal allies. They responded by attempting to mobilise the Khmers behind their regime. They encouraged *Khmerité*, and while this was in the main cultural and meant to bolster French rule, it was to have unforeseen consequences. Vichy's quasi-fascist trappings were visible everywhere, at least in the towns, with huge portraits of Pétain on the façades of buildings and exhortations to uphold the imperatives of 'Work, Family and Fatherland'. Khmer boys were encouraged to join the scouting movement and a kind of mass youth militia, the Yuvan, was set up to mobilise young Cambodians behind the regime. However, these organisations brought young Khmers out of their families and villages and gave them an inkling of potential collective strength that would be turned against the colonialists.

The Revolt of the Parasols

Despite their promotion of *Khmerité* the French were inconsistent. In 1941, the French authorities decided to replace the ancient Khmer script (based on Sanskrit) with a new romanised script known as *quoc ngu khmer* after the reformed Vietnamese script.[3] The move caused widespread indignation, particularly in the Buddhist *sangha* and in the proto-nationalist circles around Son Ngoc Thanh and *Nagaravatta*. Son Ngoc Thanh secretly negotiated with the Japanese who, while they counselled prudence, did not discourage his nationalist ambitions. The *quoc ngu khmer* issue provided the Cambodian dissidents with a focus for popular discontent; on the one hand, the French encouraged *Khmerité*, yet on the other they threatened the age-old Khmer customs.

In July 1942, a nationalist monk called Hem Chieu delivered a vitriolic anti-French sermon to a group of Cambodian *tirailleurs* in a Phnom Penh *wat*. An informer tipped off the French police, who arrested Hem Chieu and a number of other monks and lay nationalists. In response, several thousand angry Khmers, including monks with their distinctive orange robes and parasols, marched on the *Résidence Supérieure* demanding the prisoners' release. A riot ensued, in which a number of police and demonstrators were injured and more arrests made. Further bloodshed was probably deterred by the presence of Japanese military police, the *Kempetei*, who stood by but did not intervene. The event entered Khmer political folklore as the Revolt of the Parasols, after the monks' sunshades. In another country, the incident might have been relatively unremarkable, but in hitherto docile Cambodia it was a significant milestone on the road to national independence. Afterwards, the colonial authorities launched a general crackdown, banned *Nagaravatta* and sentenced several of the perceived ringleaders to death. The French government commuted these terms to life imprisonment on the prison island of Poulo Condore in the South China Sea. There, tutored by Vietnamese nationalist prisoners, the Khmers gained an advanced anti-colonial political education. Son Ngoc Thanh, meanwhile, had sought sanctuary with the Japanese, who spirited him out of the country to Japan, where he was to remain until the last months of the war, remaining in postal contact with his supporters in Cambodia.

With hindsight, it is clear that the high tide of Japanese expansion in Southeast Asia and the Pacific came in the months immediately after the aerial attack on Pearl Harbor in December 1941 and the fall of Singapore in early 1942. Thereafter, with her supply lines dangerously over-extended, Japan was to face the full might of American military and industrial power, and soon suffered big defeats at the Battles of Midway and the Coral Sea. The D-day landings by the Allies in France in the summer of 1944 led rapidly to the liberation of Paris and the fall of Vichy. Governor-General Decoux decided it was time to indicate that he was prepared to change his political spots and made a secret agreement to back the Allies when the time came. Meanwhile, he dropped the fascist paraphernalia and pro-Axis rhetoric and although he was anxious not to provoke the Japanese these changes raised their suspicions. With Vichy dead and a new anti-Axis government at Paris, Decoux's usefulness to the Japanese was in question.

The Japanese coup and puppet independence

On 9 March 1945, the Japanese staged an Indochina-wide *coup de force* against the French, crushing feeble efforts at resistance with ease. The brutal military police of the *Kempetei* threw the French soldiers and civilians into concentration camps, treating them with neglect and great cruelty, and murdered some in the streets of Phnom Penh. The Japanese government also decided that the time had come for King Sihanouk to declare independence, as had already happened in Burma. They took this step both from political conviction and from the desire to focus their efforts on the military struggle, free of administrative distractions. Sihanouk recalls that he was greatly amazed when Kubota, the Japanese special advisor to Cambodia, directed him to declare his country's independence from France. This he did, in an unusually restrained broadcast; he must have been under no illusions about the coming Allied victory and couched his statement in guarded terms rather than a ringing declaration.

Sihanouk's new government trod warily, doing little beyond reversing the *quoc ngu khmer* decree and changing street names. He pointedly ignored the newly liberated Khmer prisoners when they arrived back from Poulo Condore, and offered them no posts in his government. Perhaps he saw them as a potential threat to his position, but it is also probable that he wished to distance himself from people whom the Allies would call traitors upon their inevitable return to Indochina. Later, seeking to cast himself as the sole architect of Cambodian independence, he attempted to write them out of history.

In May 1945, Son Ngoc Thanh returned from exile aboard a Japanese bomber and enormous crowds of supporters welcomed him at Pochentong airport. Such was Thanh's prestige among Khmers and standing with the Japanese that Sihanouk stifled his jealousy and appointed his rival as Foreign Minister. Nationalist firebrand or not, Thanh did little to change the timid course of the government at this stage, although he appears to have been an enthusiastic collaborator with the Japanese. He was instrumental, however, in setting up a nationalist militia, the Greenshirts, as the core of a projected national army.

When the first atomic bomb fell on Japan on 6 August, Thanh's supporters grew restless. Although the Japanese army in Indochina was intact, Germany had already capitulated. Two days later, the USSR entered the Pacific War. If the hard-line nationalists were to take control of government, they had to act soon before Japan's collapse. On 9 August, the day the second atomic bomb fell on Nagasaki, a group of militiamen burst into the royal palace, demanding the removal of old retainers and bureaucrats from the government and their replacement with nationalists. It amounted to a putsch. Some of the old guard ministers retained their posts, but Son Ngoc Thanh took up the post of prime minister and other nationalists took key positions.

The whole affair had strong comic opera overtones. Son Ngoc Thanh insisted on the centrality of the alliance with Japan even as Tokyo was on the brink of unconditional surrender and news of the horror of Nagasaki and Hiroshima spread round the world. It was only a matter of time before the French returned and they would not tolerate what they would see as a government of Japanese puppets and traitors. In the meantime, Thanh took few initiatives apart from organising a referendum on the question of independence and the legitimacy of his government. The vote was Stalinist style, with 99.999 per cent voting for Thanh, but it probably did reflect a genuine desire for independence. It was also the first time that a government had allowed the Khmers to vote for anything.

The return of the French and the fall of Son Ngoc Thanh

The end came inevitably for Thanh's government. An advance guard of British troops flew into Pochentong airport in early October, soon followed by General Jacques Leclerc, the French commander in Indochina. Leclerc arrested Thanh at gunpoint and dragged him off to prison in Saigon, to the slightly guilty bemusement of the British commander, who had regarded Thanh as a 'silly little man'. Sihanouk assured the Allies that 'the Cambodian people had always loved France'. The French, for their part, did not publicly hold Sihanouk's lapse against him. Most likely they were aware of the deep reverence with which the Khmers viewed the monarchy and were unwilling to stoke nationalist fires by moving against him.

The French government was aware that there had been a sea change in political consciousness in Southeast Asia. The hothouse of war and Japanese occupation had caused a flowering of nationalism across the region. The eternal colonial afternoon of the 1930s was over. The Cambodians had enjoyed a kind of independence and they saw no reason why colonialism should return. The British were already preparing to depart from Burma. The Roosevelt administration in the United States had been openly hostile to the reimposition of French colonial rule in Indochina and the Cold War had not yet undermined American sympathy for Asian peoples' national aspirations. President Harry Truman was committed to honour the US promise to quit the Philippines by 1946. The Viet Minh controlled much of neighbouring Vietnam and their uneasy truce with France would not last long.

In this atmosphere, it was prudent for France to make a number of reforms. In the balance of things, it was better for them to work with Sihanouk and to contain nationalist feeling by granting some autonomy to Cambodia. In early January 1946, Sihanouk's uncle Prince Monireth and Major-General Marcel Alessandri signed a provisional agreement that granted increased powers to the Cambodian government. The old colonial titles would be abolished and a high commissioner would be responsible for supervision of the Cambodian authorities. Plans were also made for an elected assembly as part of a constitutional monarchy. It was not real independence, though, as control over military affairs and foreign relations, finances, customs and excise, posts and telegraphs and railways remained in French hands, and French officials would supervise most aspects of the Khmer government, bureaucracy and the police.

The agreement meant that the future Cambodian government would have less power than the Japanese had allowed to Sihanouk and Son Ngoc Thanh, but it was an advance over what had existed until March 1945. The Khmers could look forward, perhaps, to the gradual extension of their government's powers. Cambodia's first ever elections were scheduled for April 1946 and a number of political parties emerged to contest them. Most of these parties represented the interests of factions, extended families, and cliques within the Khmer elite, and some of them existed for little more than the personal self-enrichment of their tiny memberships. Given that Cambodia had no experience of democracy, and that political parties had never existed before, this was not surprising. Such parties were fluid and transient and won few votes, despite financial backing from the French administration. In the lead-up to the 1946 elections, two major parties crystallised, the Liberals and the Democrats, and these became, roughly, the right and the left inside the national assembly and were to dominate parliamentary politics until Sihanouk amalgamated most of the parties after independence.

The Democrat ascendancy

Despite their name, the Liberals were conservatives, with strong ties to the monarchy, the Khmer elite and the French. Founded by Prince Norodom Norindeth, their most important supporter was King Sihanouk, who became a key political player during this period. However, despite their influential backers in the Khmer elite, the support of the king and the covert backing of the French administration, the Liberals and other rightist parties were perennial also-rans in all the elections in the period up to independence and were never a serious electoral threat to the Democrats. Eventually, frustrated by their inability to win government by democratic means, Sihanouk and his allies staged a coup to remove the Democrats from office—but this was some years in the future, and for the time being there was a flowering of relative democracy in the country. Before the war, the few publications that appeared were subject to approval by the French administration and could fall victim to the censor's blue pencil for trifling reasons. In the postwar years, France's new approach saw the appearance of numerous Khmer and French language newspapers.

The first leader of the Democrats, Prince Sisowath Yuthevong, was perhaps the ablest political figure during this period, with the possible exception of the wily Sihanouk. A genuine intellectual with postgraduate degrees in astronomy and mathematics from French universities, Yuthevong had a real commitment to the development of his country. Cursed with ill health, he died young, to the great misfortune of his country. Yuthevong's fledgling party soon attracted support from former members of the *Nagaravatta* circle, educated civil servants and intellectuals such as Huy Kanthoul, and from the peasants and town-dwellers.

Whereas the Liberals stood for the status quo, with all of its attendant privileges for their supporters, the Democrats adhered to many of the policies of the French Socialist Party. They stood, broadly, for a modernised and democratic Cambodia as an independent state and constitutional monarchy within the French Union. Concretely, this meant universal suffrage, a bicameral parliament and the gradual transfer of power from the French administration. Unlike the anti-French Khmer Issarak guerrillas, who were already ambushing French patrols in the countryside, the Democrats believed it was possible to win independence by peaceful and constitutional means.

The ideological differences between the Liberals and the Democrats also translated into a different style of political organising. For the first time in Cambodian history, a political organisation reached out to the common people and sought to enrol them in its ranks. This gave the Democrats the edge over the rightist parties, who believed in authoritarian government and the divine right of kings, and saw politics as a vehicle for self-enrichment. In the Liberals' elitist view, the people were a passive mass, not a power base. By contrast, right from their inception in early 1946, the Democrats began to build up a party organisation that stretched down to village level. Their message found ready listeners among the peasants and town poor who had been radicalised during the war and Japanese occupation.

The Democrats won a landslide victory in the April 1946 elections. With 50 seats, they dwarfed the 14 Liberals and the three independents in the National Assembly. Moreover, they had won despite a 'dirty tricks' campaign and shameless vote-buying by their opponents. This was to be the pattern up until Cambodia's last relatively free election in 1951. Even before the newly elected members took their seats in this first Cambodian parliament, the king's uncle, Prince Monireth, had written the draft of a constitution for the country. The first task of the newly elected national assembly was to ratify the draft, but if the Khmer elite and the French administration had expected it to be rubber stamped they were mistaken. Prince Monireth was an austere individual who had moved away from youthful liberalism to a more traditional view of authority, and this was reflected in his draft. After stormy debates, the Democrats made major revisions to the document and produced something more in keeping with their ideals. Sihanouk, who was in a somewhat democratic mood at the time, ratified the constitution in May 1947. The constitution enshrined the rule of law, guaranteed basic rights and liberties, and placed limits on the powers of the monarchy. It was not a revolutionary document, but it was nevertheless a significant departure from absolute monarchy and authoritarian colonial rule.

Unfortunately, Prince Yuthevong did not long survive the ratification. Sickly from childhood, he retired for a holiday at the resort town of Kep on the Gulf coast, only to contract malaria and to die in July 1947. As Huy Kanthoul later lamented, his death was 'an almost irreparable loss' to the Democratic Party. One could go further. In a political climate all too often marked by corruption and unprincipled intrigue, he stood out as an honest man—and one with great moral authority among Khmers. Had he lived he might have acted as a counterweight to Sihanouk's increasingly authoritarian tendencies. Sadly, many Khmers today seem to have forgotten his name, not the least because of a concerted effort by Sihanouk to belittle him and erase his name from Cambodia's history.

The return of the lost provinces of Battambang and Siem Reap later in the year must have lightened the gloom felt by Yuthevong's fellow Democrats. The Japanese had awarded the provinces to Thailand in 1941 as part of a treaty they imposed to end the Franco–Thai War. Their return largely restored Cambodian territorial integrity, although Cambodian grievances over the loss of Khmer lands and people in the lower delta to Vietnam remained. The following years, however, were ones of tumult and change for Cambodia. Fighting between French soldiers and Issarak guerrillas intensified and the Viet Minh controlled much of the eastern part of the countryside. Parliamentary politics, too, was proving to be much more problematic than first expected, with horse-trading, bribery and corruption widespread.

The elections of December 1947 once again returned an absolute majority for the Democrats, who could look forward in theory to a four-year term in office. However, history has shown that huge and repeated government majorities often carry the seeds of corruption within them. Minority voices can be quelled and debate cut short by the parliamentary guillotine. Many MPs from across the party spectrum used their office to line their pockets at public expense. One of the most ambitious schemers was a Democrat called Yem Sambaur, who destroyed vital evidence in a scandal involving the illegal sale of rationed commodities. Other MPs and members of the royal family ran illegal casinos and enjoyed immunity from arrest due to the protection of the corrupt police chief Lon Nol, who was to cast a long shadow over Cambodian political and military affairs.

Parliamentary horse-trading and intrigue

The Democrats lost their parliamentary majority in 1949 when Yem Sambaur left the party and set up his own group. Sambaur afterwards led an unstable coalition government until the majority of MPs backed a censure motion against him. Sihanouk dissolved parliament, but to the disgust of the Democratic opposition he refused to call fresh elections and re-installed Sambaur in office. Sihanouk's behaviour was an ominous portent of his willingness to bend and break the constitution to put his toadies in office and enhance his own power. Anger over his manoeuvres was perhaps forgotten, however, by the passage of a new

Franco–Khmer treaty, signed in November 1949, which established Cambodia as an 'independent state' within the French Union, with more powers passing over to the Cambodian government. The French, however, remained the real masters of the country and many countries refused to recognise Cambodia as a fully sovereign state.

Meanwhile, political intrigues escalated into violence on the streets of Phnom Penh. In January 1950, someone lobbed a hand grenade into the Phnom Penh headquarters of the Democratic Party, killing a party leader called Ieu Koeus. The circumstances surrounding the murder were murky and many of the huge crowd that followed Koeus' funeral cortège believed that Yem Sambaur government ministers were implicated. Others blamed the French, who for their part blamed the Issaraks. Meanwhile, the economy deteriorated and public services sank into disrepair. Further scandals followed and in May 1950, Yem Sambaur was so hated that he resigned his post. Even then, Sihanouk declined to call an election. He directed Prince Sisowath Monipong, one of the deceased King Monivong's sons, to form a new cabinet. Monipong was competent but aware that he lacked a popular mandate. Sihanouk finally agreed to call fresh elections, but only after a bizarre charade in which he publicly and histrionically declared he was about to abdicate; a crude but effective Bonapartist ploy in which he invited the people, over the heads of constitutional authority, to 'dissuade' him.

The Huy Kanthoul government

The Democrats won a convincing victory in the elections of September 1951, despite Sihanouk's public support for the rightist candidates. The French, too, had backed the Liberals with money and materials, but the people again rejected them. The Democrats won 54 of the 78 seats in the National Assembly. The Liberals limped in with 18 seats and smaller rightist parties made up the rest. The verdict on Yem Sambaur was crushing: his party won not a single seat.

The Democrat leader Huy Kanthoul formed a new government in October 1951. Had Sihanouk and the opposition parties respected the constitution, Huy Kanthoul could have expected to remain in power until October 1955. As it turned out, Huy Kanthoul's government was to be the last freely elected Cambodian government for many decades. From its inception, intriguers such as Lon Nol and Yem Sambaur worked to undermine it. The policeman-cum-politician Lon Nol was an unsavoury individual—according to French police files, he had murdered a political opponent at the Pich Nil concentration camp back in 1945—and he had little respect for the democratic process. Even without the schemers, the new government faced a difficult time; the economy was stagnant and the war against the Issaraks in the countryside raged unabated. Huy Kanthoul's problems were compounded by Son Ngoc Thanh's return from his French exile in October 1951. Again, huge crowds flocked to meet Thanh at Pochentong and his reception must have bolstered his radical mood. He founded a nationalist newspaper and gave vitriolic anti-French diatribes that embarrassed the Kanthoul government. He did not stay long in Phnom Penh, however, and soon slipped away to join the Issarak guerrillas in the countryside.

Thereafter, the government's critics stepped up their accusations that Huy Kanthoul was in league with the Issaraks. Lon Nol was one of the more vociferous of these critics and his behaviour crossed the line between dissent and subversion. In one instance he drove round the capital with a loudspeaker, openly calling for the overthrow of the government. For his pains, he spent a night in the police cells with a number of his allies. It was scarcely draconian punishment and his feigned outrage was ironic, given his penchant for robust policing. Sihanouk added his squeaky voice to the chorus, denouncing what he called the Democrats' disloyalty and alluding to a secret republican agenda. The French joined in too, alleging that the government was unwilling to take the necessary stern measures against the Issaraks. The political right were clearly in the mood for a coup.

The coup came in June 1952. Although Sihanouk denied it, it is most likely that he plotted with the French high commissioner to remove Huy Kanthoul's government. It is not credible that heavily armed French troops equipped with tanks just happened to be in Phnom Penh on the day of the coup, all the more so since they surrounded the National Assembly building while its sacking took place. This time, Sihanouk did not govern via an intermediary such as Yem Sambaur. He assumed power directly and dissolved parliament. Huy Kanthoul, the leader of the democratically elected government, went into exile in France and his political career was effectively over. Sihanouk's unelected cabinet largely consisted of the old cronies, placemen and rightist intriguers who had destabilised the elected government in the first place. A wave of strikes and protests erupted, but Sihanouk was intransigent. Many of the protest 'ringleaders' were detained without trial and others arraigned on trumped up charges, a great irony given the claim that Huy Kanthoul was a dictator for locking up Lon Nol and his cronies overnight.

The brave democratic experiment was over. Sihanouk would govern either directly or through proxies for the next 18 years, until he was himself removed in a pro-US coup led by the perennial schemer Lon Nol. It was not surprising that the French were involved in the removal of Huy Kanthoul, given the oppressive nature of their rule. Sihanouk had learned too well the anti-democratic tunes of Cambodia's colonial masters. However, it is to his credit that he soon afterwards embarked on a 'royal crusade' that would lead the country to independence.

The Royal Crusade for Independence

Sihanouk launched his 'crusade' in quixotic style in March 1953. Irritated by French refusals to grant the concessions of a new protocol on self-government agreed to in early May 1952, the king flew to Paris to argue his case with the French President, Vincent Auriol. The lack of progress was undermining Sihanouk's nationalist credentials and giving ammunition to the Issarak and Viet Minh guerrillas, who denounced

Among the crowd waiting to welcome Sihanouk on his return from Paris was this group of Buddhist monks. (Courtesy National Archives of Australia)

him as a colonialist stooge. Time was running out for the French in Indochina. French public opinion had swung against the war with the Viet Minh and although France's catastrophic military defeat at Dien Bien Phu was yet to come, the Viet Minh were increasingly confident of victory. Such a victory would render Sihanouk's position untenable and he could well look forward to a life in exile should the Issaraks come to power in Cambodia.

Shortly after his visit to Paris, Sihanouk spoke frankly to the press in New York. He called for immediate independence, warning astutely that if it were not granted his country could turn communist. He repeated his claims in Montreal and arrived back in mid-May to a tumultuous welcome in Phnom Penh. Three weeks later, the portly king was off again, travelling to Siem Reap under the protection of an ex-Issarak ruffian called Puth Chhay. It was as if a US president had suddenly sworn in Al Capone's mobsters as bodyguards and gone on tour in Nebraska or Oregon. From Siem Reap, he crossed over the border to Bangkok, causing French officials to speculate that he had gone mad. He later crossed back to Cambodia and announced that he would stay in Battambang until the French agreed to grant full independence. In the meantime, his supporters staged huge demonstrations and Sihanouk spoke frequently on radio, his high-pitched voice full of indignation, exhorting his people to keep up the pressure. On 17 August, the French agreed to grant Cambodia full sovereignty and Sihanouk returned to a rapturous welcome in Phnom Penh. Finally, on 9 November 1953, the last French troops left Cambodia, marking the end of 90 years of colonial rule. Sihanouk, in a brilliant display of political theatre, had achieved independence months before the French capitulation at Dien Bien Phu and almost one year before the final declaration of the Geneva Peace Conference on 21 July 1954 brought independence to the whole of French Indochina. He was now the undisputed master of Cambodia.

6
SIHANOUK, STAR OF THE CAMBODIAN STAGE, 1953–70

Ronald Reagan, the Hollywood actor-turned-politician, sometimes appeared to confuse real life with the silver screen, in one instance talking at Omaha Beach in Normandy as if he had actually taken part in the D-day landings. Norodom Sihanouk, too, was also both a political actor and a film star. He wrote, directed and starred in his own productions and conscripted Nhiek Tioulong and other members of the Cambodian political elite as actors, sometimes to play roles similar to those in their real lives. Arguably, Sihanouk 'wrote' his kingdom as a vast political screenplay in which he strutted in the starring role among supporting players and hordes of extras before the vast audience of the people. In 1970, the other major players would tire of the screenplay, remove the star and rewrite the script, but for over a decade, from the triumph of the Royal Crusade for Independence until the mid to late

1960s, when his grip on power began to falter, his courtiers performed to order.

Sihanouk was only 30 years old when he led his country to independence. Yet his quick intelligence and driving ambition compensated for his comparative youth, and he was able to shape a political system in which he held almost absolute power. This power derived in part from the respect afforded traditional Cambodian kingship and the monarchy as a whole, but Sihanouk added elements from modernity, and moulded the whole by force of his charismatic personality. Although often lampooned in the US media as a saxophone-playing dilettante and buffoon, Sihanouk was a complex and astute man, capable of extraordinary bursts of hard work. He could be cruel and unforgiving, and he was often arbitrary, but he nevertheless had some real achievements to his name: in Milton Osborne's words, he was both 'Prince of Light and Prince of Darkness'.

Sihanouk's least attractive trait was his craving for power; even before his Royal Crusade, he had acquired the taste for it. The shy and startled youngster who had reluctantly accepted the crown after Monivong's death in 1941 had metamorphosed into a confident and forceful adult. The 1951 coup against Huy Kanthoul's government had thrown his Democratic rivals into disarray, and he had neutralised the Issarak guerrilla chieftains by force or guile. He tolerated no rivals, recognised no equals and branded political opponents as traitors. Democracy and pluralism had no place in his script and although some who lived through 'Sihanoukism' look back upon it wistfully as a time of comparative prosperity and peace, others remember it as a time of dark shadows presaging future disaster. In truth, it was both. Sihanouk's greatest achievement was his commitment to neutrality, which kept his country out of the Second Indochina War until 1970. In the end, however, this achievement was undermined by his domestic policies and the country plunged into the abyss of the Second Indochina War and Pol Pot's bloody revolution.

An ant under the feet of fighting elephants

Sihanouk was confronted with two challenges after the success of his Royal Crusade for Independence. Firstly, as a would-be absolute ruler, he had to consolidate his grip on domestic power, and secondly, he had to maintain Cambodia's sovereignty in the uncertain world of the Cold War. The two challenges were interlinked and would remain so. Should he falter in the latter task, his domestic enemies would pounce; should he stumble in the former, he would give the cold warriors the opportunity to intervene internally. The best guarantee of peace and territorial integrity, he reasoned, was the adoption of strict neutrality. It would also strengthen his grip on power at home, by siphoning off support from the centre-left Democrats and the pro-communist *Pracheachon* (People's Group), both of which preached neutrality to a responsive electorate.

At the time, world politics was dominated by the two postwar superpowers, the United States and the USSR, both of whom controlled informal global 'empires' or blocs of allies and satellites. Although many of the emerging post-colonial states of Africa and Asia stood outside of these two blocs, the pressure on them to join one or the other was enormous. In a number of locations around the world, the superpowers or their proxies eyeballed one another across heavily fortified frontiers. Indochina was one of these flashpoints. What had begun as an anti-colonial war of liberation led by the Viet Minh had been transmogrified into a confrontation between communism and the 'Free World', with the French colonial army largely bankrolled by the US and the Viet Minh aided by 'Red China' and the USSR. In 1953, large tracts of the Cambodian countryside were still controlled by the Khmer People's Liberation Army (KPLA) and their Viet Minh allies. Cambodia was a small country with insignificant military forces, lying close to the ideological and military fault lines that divided the world. Sihanouk summed up the situation by likening Cambodia to an ant unfortunate enough to be under the feet of two fighting elephants.

Sihanouk's first task, as he saw it, was to persuade the elephants to do their fighting elsewhere, while trying to remain friends with both. He feared the Viet Minh, but was careful to insist that 'Although we are not communists we have no quarrel with communism as long as it does not seek to impose itself on us by force . . .'. Likewise, he was fearful of the anti-communist zeal of the United States, and with good reason: this was the time when US Vice-President Richard Nixon was openly canvassing the idea of using tactical atomic weapons to prevent a Viet Minh victory over the French in Indochina. Although the Viet Minh would soon win a stunning victory at the Battle of Dien Bien Phu and hasten French withdrawal, this was still some months off and Sihanouk had every reason to fear that his country would become embroiled in the war.

Sihanouk's foreign policy was never ideological in the Cold War sense. His imperatives were always pragmatic and he would seek friends where he found them, regardless of their ideological complexion. Initially, he had sought an alliance with the French, but their deviousness in the lead-up to Cambodia's independence and their revealed military weakness in the face of the Viet Minh made him reconsider. Lining up with a declining colonial power would put him offside with the Viet Minh and their allies, and the newly independent states in Africa and Asia. The United States was another potential ally and had been supplying Cambodia with military and some economic aid since 1951. Sihanouk, however, was mistrustful of the ideological bellicosity of Truman and Eisenhower and their determination to use small countries as pawns in the global battle against communism. These two US leaders saw Southeast Asia, and Indochina in particular, as a cockpit in this battle, and whereas President Franklin Delano Roosevelt had wanted the French out of Indochina, his successors saw them as a bulwark against the spread of the 'Red Peril'. Sihanouk was fearful, too, of the emerging anti-communist regime in Saigon, seeing it as the descendent of the Vietnamese invaders who had almost absorbed his country during the Cambodian Dark Ages. As the foreign relations expert Roger Smith has noted, Sihanouk's imperatives were to prevent any return to colonial or quasi-colonial status and to preserve the integrity of his borders. If he sided with either of the two Cold War antagonists or their proxies, he could end up losing some or all of his territory. Siding with either side would guarantee the hostility of the other bloc. Maintaining his distance from both might even lead them to compete for his favour.

It was both a bold and a cautious strategy, for in early 1954 the eventual outcome of the war in Vietnam was unclear. The French armies were demoralised and public opinion at home had swung sharply in favour of withdrawal, but it looked as if the United States might step in to replace France. President Dwight Eisenhower was determined to cobble together a 'coalition of the willing' against the Viet Minh, or even to launch unilateral military action to destroy them. In the event, Eisenhower was unable to get support for his plans from the American public (which was war-weary as a result of the gruelling conflict in Korea) or from Congress, and his close allies were reluctant to get involved, so he opted for the negotiating table at Geneva.

Geneva and Cambodian sovereignty

The Geneva Conference opened on 8 May 1954 with delegations from the United States, France, Britain, the USSR, the People's Republic of China (PRC), Cambodia, Laos, the (communist) Democratic Republic of Vietnam (DRV), and its anti-communist rival from the South, the Republic of Vietnam (RVN). The main item of business was to negotiate settlements of the Vietnamese and Korean conflicts. Cambodia was a tangential issue in a conference dominated by the superpowers and their big power allies, but the Cambodian delegates Nong Kimny, Sam Sary and Tep Phan, instructed by Sihanouk, left their modest mark on history. Very quickly, they were on their feet object-ing to a proposal from the DRV's Pham Van Dong (backed by the PRC and the USSR) to seat representatives of the communist-dominated 'resistance movements' from Laos and Cambodia (including the Khmer People's Liberation Army). When it became clear that the issue was a sticking point for Sihanouk's delegates, the PRC's Zhou Enlai and the USSR's Molotov persuaded Pham Van Dong to drop the demand—an early victory for the Khmer delegates.

By mid-July, the delegates had come to an agreement on most issues relating to Indochina.[4] However, Sihanouk was unhappy with the final proposals, for although they guaranteed his country's neutrality they fell short of ensuring the complete withdrawal of the Viet Minh and disarming the KPLA, and also forbade Cambodia from entering into military alliances with other countries. After weary late-night debates, the Russian and Chinese delegates pressured the Vietnamese communists to bow to Cambodia's terms and Cambodia signed the final agreement on 21 July 1954. It was a significant triumph for Sihanouk's delegates, who had fought stubbornly for their country's sovereign rights.

Cambodia's neutrality was reinforced shortly afterwards when Sihanouk came to an understanding with the PRC and the DRV, both of which guaranteed to respect Khmer sovereignty in return for Sihanouk's promise that no US military bases would be set up on Cambodian soil. The agreement displeased the US, which initially threatened to withhold all aid from Sihanouk's regime. Sihanouk did not back down and after 1955 Washington changed tack and promised large amounts of military assistance and also pledged its support for Cambodian neutrality and sovereignty. In the same year, Sihanouk attended the Bandung Conference of non-aligned nations, where he met with such luminaries as Jawaharlal Nehru, Ahmed Sukarno and Josip Tito, and was lionised as a leader of the anti-colonial struggle of Third World people. The communist bloc countries also began to provide Cambodia with economic aid on more favourable terms than those of the Americans and other capitalist countries (although US aid was consistently larger than that of all of the other donors combined).

Sihanouk consolidates power

Sihanouk had come to sovereign power in 1953 with a fund of political goodwill. His achievements on the international stage enhanced his prestige among his subjects and undercut the Democrats and the procommunist Pracheachon. He had steered his country to independence and tacked skilfully to ensure that it would be maintained on course in the face of gale force international winds. He was also a Khmer king and could expect fealty from his loyal subjects; for him, they were children and he was the father who knew what was best for them, and this was the script he would follow on the Cambodian stage. In the immediate postwar years, Sihanouk had initially flirted with the ideas of constitutional monarchy, but in 1951, when he used French tanks and infantry to close down the Huy Kanthoul government, he set off down an authoritarian path. He was not to deviate from this until his removal from power in the coup of March 1970.

Nevertheless, Sihanouk still faced considerable domestic opposition in the first years of the independent kingdom. The Democrats still enjoyed strong residual support and Sihanouk was fearful that his archrival Son Ngoc Thanh might attempt a comeback into the political mainstream. Son Ngoc Thanh remained a symbol of nationalism for the many Cambodians who could remember his role during World War II, and if anyone could challenge Sihanouk, it was this bespectacled ascetic from the lower Mekong delta. Whenever Son Ngoc Thanh had returned to Cambodia from exile, enormous crowds had flocked to welcome him back. Although he was now in the jungles with the remaining Issaraks, he was negotiating for an amnesty. Sihanouk had to move quickly.

Abdication and the Sangkum

Accordingly, in a typically audacious, but astute move in early March 1955, Sihanouk suddenly abdicated in favour of his father, Prince

Suramarit. Sihanouk reasoned that Suramarit would not use his regal powers to undermine his favourite son in the political arena. This would give Sihanouk a free hand in politics. The move also preserved the monarchy, which Sihanouk believed to be the social cement of the nation. Sihanouk's second (and linked) move was to create his own political movement. He did so in part because he was disgusted with the horse-trading and graft of the existing parties and was determined to create a grand alliance that would put the interests of the country, as he saw them, before self-interest and petty bickering. The Ministry of Information estimated that around a dozen parties existed in Cambodia in 1955 and noted that many of them were 'without defined programmes' and served as vehicles for the personal ambitions of their leaders. While this was largely true, Sihanouk's underlying motive was to entrench his own power. He instinctively distrusted the party system as a mechanism for diluting that power, and worried that it might elevate his rival Son Ngoc Thanh to high office.

Sihanouk also had to contend with pressure from the party politicians for fresh elections. Sihanouk, realising that elections conferred legitimacy on those who won them, was not opposed to ballots, but he wanted to make sure that his power would be enhanced, not challenged by them. He prepared the ground by bringing the motley collection of parties under his direct control. Characteristically, he did this via a referendum, in which 99.8 per cent of the voters approved the merger of parties into a grand 'movement of national union', which he dubbed the *Sangkum Reastr Niyum*, or Popular Socialist Community. This corporatist movement was to be the political umbrella for the whole nation and Cambodia became a de facto one-party state in which civil servants were expected to join the Sangkum. When the elections were held in September 1955, only two opposition parties remained outside of the Sangkum fold: the Left-leaning Democrats, whose existence dated from 1945, and the Pracheachon, the party which the communists had founded in 1951 as part of their two-track 'ballot box and bayonet' strategy. Another independent party, the Liberals, had collapsed in disarray when Sihanouk offered its leader, Prince Norindeth, a diplomatic post at UNESCO in Paris, with the proviso that he join the Sangkum.

Meanwhile, Sihanouk's diplomatic triumphs ensured him of continuing high levels of support. In late April he had returned from the non-aligned conference at Bandung, with the endorsement of the world's anti-colonial leaders. The following month, he signed an agreement providing for continuing US military aid, a move that soothed fears about his country's ability to defend itself, particularly among right-wingers who feared North Vietnam and China.

The 1955 elections

The elections for the National Assembly were held on 11 September 1955. Observers had expected a large vote for the Democrats and a smaller, but still respectable tally for the Pracheachon (with the outside possibility of these parties governing in coalition). The result, however, was a landslide for the Sangkum, which secured 82 per cent of the National Assembly seats, as opposed to the Democrats' 12 and the Pracheachon's 4 per cent. Sihanouk had loaded the dice: although the odds were that the Sangkum would have won anyway, he left nothing to chance. Voters were required to throw away the voting slips of the candidates they did not favour. This automatically favoured the Sangkum, as Sihanouk's face appeared on their ballot slips and it was a punishable offence to show disrespect by discarding anything carrying his image.

The flavour of these elections can be gauged by the fact that Sihanouk had appointed the brutally unsavoury Dap Chhuon—the governor of the north-western provinces—as 'director of national security' to oversee the process. On polling day, voters were harassed by Sangkum thugs and police. Moreover, in the weeks leading up to the elections, a number of opposition newspapers had been closed down and their editors detained without trial—a tactic that Sihanouk had earlier employed against dissidents during the 1951 coup. Opposition campaigners had to be physically brave. The Democrat leader Keng

Vannsak, a prominent left-leaning intellectual at the time, was bashed and his chauffeur killed, while a prominent Buddhist monk, the Achar Chung, died in jail after publicly reciting poems deemed disrespectful to Sihanouk.

The election was to set the country's political tone for the next decade and a half. Sihanouk was determined to run the country as he saw fit, relying only on an inner circle of courtiers, including Prince Monireth and his nephew Sirik Matak, along with elite commoners such as Penn Nouth, Son Sann, Sim Var, Yem Sambaur, Nhiek Tioulong, Sam Sary and Lon Nol. These men sprang from a narrow ruling class tightly bound together by ties of kinship and shared interests. Although Sihanouk was not averse to making demagogic verbal attacks on this elite, and claimed his Sangkum movement was socialist, these were populist ploys to disguise his support for the status quo.

In its more honest moments, the Sangkum media justified structural inequality as the workings of karma: the poor were poor because of the bad things they had done in previous lives, while the rich and powerful enjoyed the fruits of their virtue. As David Chandler has observed, independence meant that for the overwhelming majority of Khmers life went on as before with a new set of rulers and they 'continued to pay taxes to finance an indifferent government in Phnom Penh (or Udong or Angkor) . . .'. Cambodia had undergone a political revolution, but Sihanouk suppressed any chance of social change while cultivating the people with demagogic verbal assaults on the rich. This royal populist also made a great show of going to the people, sometimes stripping to the waist to make one or two desultory blows with shovel or mattock on a new public works project. It was cheap theatre, but it worked.

'Totalitarian democracy'

The new political system took some fine-tuning. The Sangkum was an unwieldy instrument because the amalgamation of the old parties did not end the old personal rivalries or intrigues of the corrupt cabals. In addition, many of its candidates were poor human material, dullards, grafters and time-servers unlikely to incline towards independent political thought or action. The 1955 election triumph was followed by a series of cabinet crises and resignations. But even this was grist to Sihanouk's mill, enabling him to pick and choose his men and play off rivals against one another. And if he chose, he could always have recourse to what became a favourite ploy: threatening to resign only to be 'persuaded' by stage-managed demonstrations to change his mind.

The 1955 election victory was followed by an even more dizzy success in 1958, when Sihanouk's personally handpicked Sangkum candidates won 99 per cent of the votes cast. The vast size of this majority casts doubt on its legitimacy and mirrored the state-orchestrated electoral charades of the Stalinist countries, with their party slates, police surveillance and licensed 'oppositions'. To adapt Henry Ford's words about the one choice of colour for his eponymous T-model car: in the 1958 elections you could vote for whomever you wanted, as long as they were part of the Sangkum. Opposition candidates were terrorised into withdrawing from the lists and a single courageous candidate from the Pracheachon scored less than 500 votes. It should be pointed out, however, that over 55 per cent of eligible voters in Phnom Penh failed to vote, whether from fear, disgust, apathy or a combination of motives. The deposed former prime minister, Huy Kanthoul, greatly overstates his case when he claims that by 1955 Sihanouk was 'thoroughly hated, particularly by young people', but there is no doubt that Sihanouk was slowly squandering his fund of goodwill, especially among town-dwellers and those with some education. Meanwhile, Cambodia had drifted close to what Jacob Talmon has elsewhere described as 'totalitarian democracy'—that is, dictatorship under the façade of mass participation in the political system.

Pressure from the United States and its proxies

The main potential for destabilisation of this system came from without. The 1954 Geneva Conference had resulted in a truce between the combatants in Vietnam and had guaranteed Cambodia's sovereignty, at least in the short term. But it was not to prove the lasting settlement that its more optimistic participants had hoped for. The five years after Geneva illustrate Thomas Hobbes' melancholy dictum that peace is only 'recuperation from one war and preparation for the next', with both sides arming for a resumption of the fray. In 1955–56, after France's ignominious exit from Indochina, over 60 per cent of all US foreign aid flowed to Southeast Asia, the overwhelming bulk of it military. Sihanouk had persuaded the 'elephants' not to fight near his nest and had, more-over, succeeded in extracting considerable amounts of help from them, playing one off against the other to extract the most favourable terms.

But the US was unhappy with Cambodian neutrality, which it believed was a weak point in a *cordon sanitaire* against the communist 'virus'. For the next 15 years US policy was to cajole, bluff, bribe or bully Cambodia into the Free World as a front-line state in the war against communism. Generally, the US brought pressure to bear indirectly on Cambodia via its Southeast Asian satellites and SEATO partners, the Philippines, the Republic of Vietnam and Thailand in particular. Thus, when Sihanouk made an official visit to the Philippines in early 1956, the Manila press speculated that Cambodia was about to drop its non-aligned status and seek rapprochement with the Free World. Apparently unfazed, Sihanouk reiterated his country's neutrality and cheekily announced that he had accepted an official invitation to visit Beijing.

Thereafter, Cambodia's relations with its anti-communist neighbours—and traditional enemies—in Bangkok and Saigon deteriorated. Cambodia complained of continual border incursions from Thailand by right-wing, pro-US *Khmer Serei* (Free Khmer) guerrillas linked to Son Ngoc Thanh and there were reports of similar harassment over the frontier from southern Vietnam. These neighbouring countries also imposed an economic blockade on Cambodia and in November 1958 Sihanouk broke off diplomatic relations with Thailand, restoring them after US mediation in February of the following year, only to break them again in 1961. Another running sore was the issue of Preah Vihar, an Angkorean temple on the border that was claimed by both Thailand and Cambodia (and eventually awarded to Cambodia by the World Court at The Hague in 1962). While the hardline anti-communist rulers in Bangkok and Saigon scarcely needed encouragement, Sihanouk suspected with good reason that the United States was egging them on and said that if Washington chose it could call them off. He stated publicly that US policy was unjust and 'dangerous for peace in Southeast Asia' and moved further towards diplomatic rapprochement with the communist countries. In July 1958, some 13 years before the UN and the United States took a similar step, Sihanouk gave *de jure* recognition to the PRC and two years later signed a treaty of friendship with Beijing. Anti-communist zealots in Washington, Saigon and Bangkok seethed with rage.

Pro-US plots against Sihanouk and neutrality

The overseas anti-communist chorus also struck chords in the hearts of some of Sihanouk's conservative courtiers. In 1958, Sam Sary, a long-time Sihanoukist minister and diplomat, suddenly informed Sihanouk that he wanted to set up an opposition political party, and published an independent right-wing newspaper, the *Democratic People*, which attacked Cambodia's ties with China. Sam Sary had recently been sacked from his position as ambassador in London following a scandal involving his mistress, and it seems likely that he had come under the influence of US intelligence. Observers noted that his political schemes had 'no visible means of support'. After Sihanouk denounced Sam's party as a plot cooked up by the Americans to undermine neutrality, the former diplomat fled to join Son Ngoc Thanh in Bangkok. The two exiles were not close and Sam Sary vanished a few years later, perhaps murdered, as David Chandler suggests, by one of his foreign backers.

The pro-US intrigues continued into 1959. In February, Sihanouk accused General Dap Chhuon, the governor of the north-west provinces of Cambodia, of plotting to overthrow him. Sihanouk alleged that the general had been bribed to support the installation in Phnom Penh of a pro-American government led by Son Ngoc Thanh. The evidence shows that the conspiracy was hatched by the Diem regime in Saigon, with support from Thailand and a CIA agent called Victor Matsui. The hapless Dap Chhuon was 'shot while attempting to escape' on the orders of Sihanouk's police chief, Colonel Lon Nol, a sinister character who had begun a career of murdering political opponents as far back as 1945. Six months later, a bomb exploded at the royal palace in Phnom Penh, killing the palace chief of protocol, Prince Vakrivan, along with King Suramarit's personal valet and injuring a number of other personnel. Sihanouk blamed Sam Sary and Son Ngoc Thanh and claimed that the bomb had been sent from a US military base in South Vietnam, wrapped as a gift.

While the Dap Chhuon and Sam Sary affairs did not present a real threat to Sihanouk's power, they heralded a much wider political disgruntlement that was to lead to his downfall in 1970 at the hands of other pro-US rightists. In the meantime, however, Sihanouk put the neutrality issue to a referendum and 99 per cent of voters endorsed his policy. While there were irregularities in the ballot, there can be little doubt that the pro-US stance of the plotters was deeply unpopular and that neutrality was accepted across the spectrum of political opinion. After the resumption of hostilities in southern Vietnam in 1959, few could doubt its wisdom.

The constitutional crisis of 1960

The system was plunged into sudden crisis, however, by the unexpected death of Sihanouk's father, King Suramarit, in early April 1960. Although grief-stricken, Sihanouk had to act decisively to keep the system together. His dilemma was to ensure that he kept all power in his own hands, while simultaneously maintaining the monarchy, which he believed to be the social glue that bound together the nation and the political regime he had constructed. His father had been a loyal supporting actor, never wishing to challenge his son's hold on power yet playing an essential role in the political script. There were any number of potential candidates for the throne, but Sihanouk was fearful of successors who might wish to wield real power. Sihanouk could not risk crowning a prince who might wish to be more than a figurehead. Nor did a republic appeal: Sihanouk was afraid that abolishing the monarchy would allow his archrival Son Ngoc Thanh to challenge him on new political terrain. Moreover, a republic would destabilise Cambodian society.

The logical choice for Suramarit's successor was Prince Raniriddh, Sihanouk's oldest son, but he was not yet of age and Sihanouk—perhaps forgetting his own frivolous youth—dismissed him as a lightweight more interested in fast cars and being rude to the police than in serious matters of state. Theoretically, there were around 100 other princes from whom to choose, but many of them were hopelessly corrupt, incompetent or debauched. Others craved power and the royal family was still driven by personal and dynastic intrigues, including the squabble between the Sisowath and Norodom wings. Although he did not say it publicly, neither did Sihanouk want his mother, the strong-minded Queen Kossamak, or his uncle, the stern disciplinarian Prince Sisowath Monireth, to ascend the throne as both might seek to meddle in affairs of state. Sihanouk's solution to the constitutional crisis was typically bold: he would become head of state (but not king) and Monireth would become chairman of a regency council (but not regent). Sihanouk would retain all power and monarchy would continue as the social and political glue of the kingdom.

Two months after the crisis had begun, Sihanouk let himself be 'persuaded' by demonstrators to become head of state, with Monireth as chairman of the ambiguous council. A day earlier, the National Assembly had voted to revise the country's constitution to allow for a regency of indefinite duration. Again, Sihanouk had written the script and he played the starring role beautifully for the opportunists and the unsophisticated who made up the bulk of his supporters. He had turned the crisis to his advantage and could now present himself as the indispensable father of the nation. The regency council simply faded from view.

Circuses in the style of Vichy

The modified regency had been Sihanouk's private decision, but significantly he had first broached it publicly at a mass assembly on Men Ground, adjacent to the royal palace in Phnom Penh. Going directly to the people over the heads of his courtiers was a staple of the Sihanoukist system. It was a technique he had honed in the year before the 1958 election (although he was originally influenced by the mass pageantry of the Vichy period when he had proudly reviewed the fascist-saluting ranks of adoring Yuvan). Such spectacles made for exciting political drama, indulged his ego and appealed to his instinctive belief that politics could be reduced to an aesthetic experience.

Now he adapted the style of Vichy to his own state. In September 1957, Sihanouk summoned five prominent leaders of the Democratic Party to a stage-managed 'debate' on Men Ground before a huge and murmurous crowd. The victims sat silent and dejected as Sihanouk harangued and insulted them in a marathon diatribe in his high-pitched voice. They recanted their 'heretical' views and as they slunk from the arena soldiers and members of the crowd physically assaulted them. It was coarse theatre, with overtones of a Maoist struggle session against 'revisionists'.

Such bullying highlighted Sihanouk's increasing narcissism, which went hand in hand with a deep streak of cruelty in his nature: for the Prince and crowd alike, it was a blood sport. Yet it served its purpose: the immediate outcome was the final dissolution of the Democrats, and Sihanouk was so delighted that from then on the assemblies on Men Ground were held twice a year and given a place in the country's constitution. With a cast of tens of thousands, these assemblies gave the 'extras' a sense of belonging and the illusion of popular power, and served as a safety valve for pent-up passions, while entrenching real authority firmly in the hands of the excitable little star. The Pracheachon suffered the same fate in the lead-up to the 1962 elections, with party leader Non Suon humiliated before an irate crowd, although he was spared a beating.

The large royal socialist youth movement, which boasted over half a million members by the early 1960s, also had its model in the Yuvan of the Vichy period. Again, it brought young people out of their families and villages, gave them a new sense of identity and bound them closely to the Sihanoukist state. Its members worked on public works projects, paraded the streets and participated in scouting activities that instilled them with a spirit of patriotism and loyalty to Sihanouk. The unashamedly paramilitary style of the organisation was antipathetic to democratic notions. Decisions were made at the top and orders were to be obeyed—a paradigm for Sihanoukist society as a whole. Yet the mass appeal of this movement and the other populist spectacles masked long term structural weaknesses within the system.

The flaws of Sihanoukism

All dictatorships eventually crumble, and Cambodia was no different. Sihanouk probably imagined that his system was the best in 'the best of all possible worlds' and could last indefinitely. Yet it was fraught with contradictions that would eventually lead to his political downfall. The Nobel Laureate Amartya Sen argues that the needs of a developing country are best served by a democratic system with a healthy civil society. If the Right to speak out and organise for alternative platforms are denied, he contends, there is little chance of the errors of the rulers being corrected. Cambodia was a case in point. Sihanouk's 'ruling style', as David Chandler has observed, was 'totalitarian and absurd' and had the effect of 'closing off any possibility of pluralism, political maturity, sound planning, or rational debate'.

Authoritarian regimes lack accountability and checks and balances, and encourage corruption, incompetence and plain wrong-headed policies. The civil service should be free to give objective advice to governments, but the Sihanoukist system encouraged obsequiousness, incompetence, corruption and opportunism. Sycophants were rewarded for telling their master what they believed he wished to hear, whereas honest officials and ministers were punished for speaking the truth. One suspects it was the honesty and independence of mind of the leftist ministers Hou Yuon, Hu Nim and Khieu Samphan as much as their ideology that caused Sihanouk to turn angrily against them in 1962. It was also farcical to suggest that Sihanouk had cleaned up corruption, for the Sihanoukist state was riddled with graft. This was exposed in the Labat Affair of 1960, which contributed to the resignation of the government of the day. M. Labat was an old French colonial civil servant who had stayed on after independence. When he died in early 1960 it was revealed that he had looted the equivalent of US$2 million from the public purse and that his peculations were not an isolated aberration.

Sihanouk's positive achievements

Sihanouk did have some real achievements to his name. He was not 'Snookie', the authoritarian buffoon that *Time* and *Life* sneered at during the 1960s, but he was a deeply flawed and fallible man, blinded to reality by his huge ego and sense of destiny. Some of his domestic programs were creditable. Compared to the cheeseparing French colonial administration, Sihanouk's Cambodia spent heavily on education and health. Education typically absorbed around 20 per cent of the budget throughout this period, compared with a mere six per cent in 1930, a fairly typical year under the French. Sihanouk expanded Cambodia's primary and secondary education system, and set up the country's tertiary system almost from scratch. He was quite correct in his belief that education was the key to modernisation. The trouble for the regime was that employment opportunities failed to keep pace with the stream of secondary and tertiary graduates, and this created disaffection among educated urban youth, which was to have important political repercussions.

Charles Meyer, the Frenchman who served as Sihanouk's aide during this period, is also rightly critical of the exaggerated claims that an educational revolution had occurred under Sihanouk. Much of it was 'smoke and mirrors' designed to boost Sihanouk's power and glory, yet it was still an improvement on what the French had managed throughout their 90 years in the country.

The French also had scarcely developed any industry in Cambodia, and although the country's main exports by the mid-1960s were still from the primary sector (including rice, fish and fish products, livestock, rubber, maize, pepper, cardamom, sugar, soy beans, tobacco, cotton and coffee) the country had built up a number of secondary industries since independence. These included a major cement plant, jute, textile and cotton mills, sawmills and paper and plywood factories and, towards the end of the Sihanouk period, an oil refinery at Kompong Som. According to the French economist Rémy Prud'homme, the number of industrial enterprises grew from just over 1100 in 1956 to just under 2700 in 1965. The government had also sought to develop the country via a series of national plans, including a two-year plan in 1957–58 and a five-year plan between 1960 and 1965, and had opened a blue-water port at Kompong Som (Sihanoukville) on the Gulf of Thailand in 1960. The new port was linked to the capital by an American-built all-weather road and later by a railway line, thus easing the country's dependence on shipping up the Mekong via the hostile Republic of Vietnam. Although still an overwhelmingly rural society, Cambodia's towns and cities expanded rapidly; Phnom Penh's population doubled in the ten years after 1956 to around 600 000. The 1968 *Shell Guide to Cambodia* described Cambodia as 'a modern, forward-looking state with fast-developing industries, excellent communications, and first-rate hotel and touring facilities' with 'up-to-date modern buildings . . . wide boulevards, and [a] modern way of life in the cities . . .'. This is exaggerated, and was co-written by Sihanouk's Ministry of Information, but it is nevertheless true that the prince had done more to modernise his country than the French protectorate had ever done.

The system begins to unravel

Beneath the propaganda, however, all was not well in the kingdom. Although Dap Chhuon was a chronic turncoat, the defection of the insider Sam Sary to the Khmer Serei in 1958 was symptomatic of a more serious malaise within the Cambodian political system. In the following years, dissatisfaction mounted on both Left and Right with the way Sihanouk ran the country. The suppression of the party system had not ended corruption; in fact, as the Labat Affair demonstrated, it had grown worse. Even the expansion of the education system had an important downside for the regime. It had produced the largest numbers of secondary and tertiary educated Khmers in the country's history, and many of them considered themselves intellectuals. Unfortunately, there were few jobs for this growing pool of comparatively well-educated youth, at least not in the type of employment to which they felt entitled. These volatile young people were to turn against the regime they felt had failed them, some siding with the extreme right and others with the extreme left. Many of those educated overseas returned with 'subversive ideas': Sihanouk claimed that 35 per cent of returning graduates from French universities were 'infected' with communist beliefs. Sihanoukism relied on the gullibility of the people, whereas education allowed them to think critically and formulate alternatives.

The first inkling of the depth of opposition to the government among young people came in February 1963, when students rioted in Siem Reap to protest against local incidents of police brutality and corruption. Significantly, the students also smashed portraits of Sihanouk and denounced the Sangkum, showing that they viewed the local problems as symptoms of a systemic malaise. Following student solidarity demonstrations in Phnom Penh and Battambang, the government of the day resigned. Sihanouk and his courtiers blamed both the extreme right and left for the disturbances: a convenient method to cover up the deeper causes of discontent.

Terror against the Left

These destabilising pressures were boosted after 1959, when the Vietnamese communists launched armed struggle against the Saigon regime. The war was soon lapping at Cambodia's borders, and in January 1962 the first US bombs fell on the east of Cambodia, the precursor to what would become one of the heaviest aerial bombardments in history. Sihanouk was suspicious of the loyalties of the Cambodian communists: were they with their insurgent Vietnamese comrades, or with Cambodia, which he identified with himself? Were they neutral or would they attempt to extend the conflict into a wider 'war of national liberation' involving Cambodia? Many of the older generation of communists from the Khmer People's Revolutionary Party (KPRP) had retreated to Hanoi after the 1954 Geneva Accords and Sihanouk feared that they would return to act as a pro-Vietnamese fifth column inside Cambodia. In addition, a new generation of leaders was rising through the party's ranks, and disaffected young people were attracted to an organisation that promised honesty and justice and which, never having enjoyed power, had clean hands. A secret conference in September 1960 at the Phnom Penh railway station signified a new militancy among Cambodian communists. The new party leaders included a comparatively young man called Saloth Sar, a former student in Paris who earned his living as a teacher in Phnom Penh. He would later become known to the world under his *nom de guerre* of Pol Pot.

In 1962, Sihanouk decided that the time had come to crush these insolent *Khmers Rouges* (Red Khmers), as he dubbed them. Party general secretary Tou Samouth, a veteran of the Issarak struggle against the French, disappeared and although the Australian historian Ben Kiernan speculated that he had been murdered on Pol Pot's orders as part of a factional struggle within the party, newer evidence suggests he was assassinated by Sihanouk's police and thrown into the Mekong. The government staged a purge against the legal, pro-communist Pracheachon, rounding up thousands of real and alleged members and sympathisers on trumped up charges of treason. Many were sentenced to death by kangaroo courts, although the sentences were all commuted to long terms of imprisonment. By this stage, the Vietnamese communists had established bases in the mountainous jungles along the border with Cambodia, and as the dragnet intensified many Cambodian communists quietly slipped away to join them, convinced that their lives were in danger. Some leftists such as Khieu Samphan, Hu Nim and Hou Yuon, who had been co-opted into the Sangkum, were stripped of their offices and titles, but stayed on in the capital, where they enjoyed a certain popularity as honest men in a den of thieves. In the 1966 elections, these three leftists won increased majorities against the 'official' candidates.

Sihanouk's left turn

Paradoxically, while he attacked the Cambodian communists, Sihanouk steered his domestic and foreign policies sharply to the Left. In January 1963, the government nationalised Cambodia's banking and foreign trade and embarked on a program of setting up state-owned industries: policies that had been originally proposed by Hou Yuon and the other leftists sacked from ministerial positions the previous year. On 1 May 1963, an auspicious date in the communist calendar, the Chinese President Liu Shaoqi arrived in Cambodia and shortly afterwards the two countries signed a treaty of friendship. Three months later, Sihanouk broke off diplomatic relations with the Saigon regime in protest at border violations and mistreatment of the Khmer Krom minority in the lower Mekong delta, and in November of the same year he abruptly cut off all US military and economic aid.

Although China increased its economic assistance package shortly afterwards, this could not compensate for the loss of US aid. Since Cambodia's independence, the United States had contributed almost US$404 million to the Cambodian state, more than double the quantity given by all other donors combined and amounting to a 15 per cent annual subsidy of the Cambodian treasury. The move away from US support might have been good for Sihanouk's pride, but the sudden drying up of funds was a major trauma for the Cambodian economy and alienated many army officers. Sihanouk's tactics in repressing the Left while adopting aspects of their economic program might have neutralised the communist 'peril' to some degree, but it also had the opposite effect of estranging the more conservative of his supporters. The Sangkum had voted unanimously to endorse the rejection of US aid, but the anticommunist technocrat Son Sann resigned in protest and subsequent events indicate that many conservatives shared his misgivings. Many of Sihanouk's courtiers would have privately half-agreed with the opinion of the *U.S. News and World Report* in April 1967, that Cambodia was 'a country that's "neutral" in favor of Communists'.

Brewing economic crisis

Nor was the government's quasi-socialist experiment as successful as Sihanouk had hoped, for incompetent and corrupt management and a shortage of expertise at other levels hamstrung the nationalised industries, and the state monopoly of foreign trade led to a flourishing black market. Whereas the profit motive provided incentives for efficiency on the part of the managers of private firms, nationalisation Sihanouk-style gave dishonest civil servants new openings to divert state revenues into their own pockets. By the mid-1960s, the country was suffering from the effects of spiralling inflation and decreasing government revenues. One cause of this was the trade in rice and other commodities with the Vietnamese communists in their bases along the Cambodia–South Vietnam border. David Chandler estimates that by 1967, one quarter of total Cambodian rice production was being sold to the Vietnamese communists. While this might have made individual Cambodian entrepreneurs rich, it led to a huge loss of state revenues from export taxes.

By the mid-1960s, Sihanouk's grasp on power was slipping. The country was suffering an economic crisis, and he had managed to alienate both the Left and Right. The conservatives detested his 'royal socialism' and believed his foreign policy was too closely aligned with the communist countries. They were also fearful and angry over Sihanouk's tolerance of the Vietnamese communist military bases in the east of the country, which they saw as an infringement of Cambodia's sovereignty and more fancifully as a threat to the Cambodian state itself. In the far north-east provinces of Mondulkiri and Rattanakiri, the communist guerrillas fostered a rebellion of hill peoples against the Phnom Penh government. Increasingly, Cambodian rightists must have wondered if Son Ngoc Thanh and the Khmer Serei were not correct in their calls for an anti-communist alliance with the United States and the Republic of Vietnam. After the United States decided to commit large-scale military forces to Vietnam in 1965, neutrality appeared an even less attractive option. Surely, Cambodian rightists might have reasoned, the Vietnamese communists could not stand up to the awesome firepower unleashed against them by President Johnson.

However, Sihanouk's foreign policy tilted still harder to the left. Relations with the United States and South Vietnam deteriorated throughout 1964, with mobs stoning the US embassy in Phnom Penh on several occasions, Cambodian border villages attacked by South Vietnamese troops, and US military aircraft shot down by Cambodian anti-aircraft fire. By the end of the year, Sihanouk appeared to have made up his mind to tilt even more strongly against the United States. He accepted MIG fighters and heavy artillery from China and the USSR, and in March 1965, almost simultaneously with the arrival of the first US marine forces in Vietnam, he hosted an Indochina People's Conference, which condemned US policy in Southeast Asia. The process reached its logical end after US aircraft bombed the Parrot's Beak salient on his eastern border, giving Sihanouk the pretext to break off diplomatic relations with Washington on 3 May 1965.

The US was unmoved, although it did make some conciliatory overtures via third parties, including the Australian embassy at Phnom Penh. As an internal US government memo to President Johnson pointed out, 'Cambodia has provided a variety of facilities for the Viet

Cong over a long period of time and is therefore in a poor position to criticize a single Air Force error, however tragic it is for those who were hit.' Six months later, Sihanouk further reinforced his ties with the communist countries with visits to China and North Korea. The United States, for its part, authorised its forces to undertake 'hot pursuit' of fleeing Vietnamese communist forces into Cambodia and there were a number of incursions by Khmer Serei guerrillas from both Vietnam and Thailand. In 1967, the US military stepped up its armed incursions into Cambodia with the clandestine Operation Daniel Boone search-and-destroy missions. However, a US intelligence report conceded that Sihanouk had little control over 'Viet Cong' operations along the 965-kilometre border with South Vietnam. In other words, by 1967 Cambodia was in precisely the situation that Sihanouk had striven so hard to avoid in 1953–54: it was an ant under the feet of fighting elephants.

Sihanouk was also facing increasing disaffection from the political right inside Cambodia itself. Although the leftists Khieu Samphan, Hu Nim and Hou Yuon kept their seats with increased majorities in the 1966 national assembly elections, the conservatives swept the board and in October, the arch rightist Lon Nol (now promoted to General) was installed as Prime Minister. Sihanouk offered cabinet positions to Khieu Samphan, Hu Nim and Hou Yuon, perhaps hoping that they would act as a counterweight to the growing power and independence of the rightist deputies, but they declined, not wishing to be associated with Lon Nol, the instrument of white terror against the Left.

The peasant uprising at Samlaut

By and large, the peasants had been quiescent during the years since independence and many had retained a deep reverence for Sihanouk. Their role in Sihanouk's screenplay was as extras to keep the country's rice bowls full and to supply local colour to government pamphlets

Palais du roi du Cambodge à Phnom Penh

Top:
The King's palace, Phnom Penh, soon after its construction in the 1870s. (Courtesy Cambodian National Archives, Phnom Penh)

Bottom:
The coronation of King Monivong, 1928. (Courtesy Cambodian National Archives, Phnom Penh)

Top:
At an altitude of over 3000 feet, the Grand Hotel in Bokor was a pleasant hill station for the French. It is now lies in ruin. (Courtesy Cambodian National Archives, Phnom Penh)

Bottom:
The design of Cambodian buffalo carts has not changed since the time of the Angkorean Empire. (Author's collection)

Top:
An aerial view of Phnom Penh in the 1930s. The cruciform building at top left is the art deco central market, the railway station is top centre at the end of a wide boulevard and Tonlé Sap is in the foreground. (Courtesy Monash University)

Bottom:
The art deco design of Phnom Penh's central market can still be glimpsed above the chaos of this bulging city. (Courtesy Ian Thackeray)

Top:
Built by Jayavarman V (968 to 1001), the architectural detail and carvings at Banteay Srei (Temple of the Women) are some of the finest in Khmer art. (Courtesy Ian Thackeray)

Bottom:
With few industries or natural resources, Cambodia has firmly placed its economic future in the hands of the tourist industry. (Courtesy Ian Thackeray)

and his own films. Their lives were hard, but their religion taught them the virtue of resignation and they seemed passive and docile. However, as King Norodom had warned back in the 19th century, they were like buffaloes—long suffering, yet terrible in their anger when their patience was exhausted. In April 1967, a peasant revolt flared when angry villagers killed police and soldiers and burned down government offices at Samlaut, in the north-west province of Battambang. The soldiers had been sent to requisition rice at low prices set by the government, depriving the peasants of the higher prices paid on the black market, which was controlled by private entrepreneurs who sold the rice to the Vietnamese communists. It is also likely that regionalist feeling was another factor in an area with a history of armed opposition to central governments in Phnom Penh. Sihanouk ordered a cruel repression that dwarfed anything carried out during the French colonial period. General Lon Nol crushed the rebels with bloody zeal, eager to prove his loyalty, as Sihanouk had recently humiliated him for allegedly allowing the Cambodian communists to get out of control. According to Sihanouk's own offhand estimate, as many as 10 000 peasants were killed and he has never apologised for the overkill. Disaffection spread, with scattered revolts elsewhere in the countryside and students staging demonstrations against the regime's brutality.

The government sought scapegoats for the Samlaut affair and the most obvious targets, given that most communists had gone to ground or had fled to the jungles of the north-east, were the trio of leftist former ministers who had remained in Phnom Penh and retained their seats in the National Assembly. Shortly after the end of the revolt, and fearing another anti-communist pogrom, Hou Yuon and Khieu Samphan quietly slipped away to join Pol Pot in the jungles, followed later in the year by Hu Nim. The rumour spread that they had been murdered on Sihanouk's orders and although this was not true, it further undermined the moral standing of the regime. Moreover, with the departure of the men who became known as the Three Ghosts, all hope of the incorporation of a section of the Left in the existing political system disappeared. The following January, the Khmers Rouges, as yet a small guerrilla force, launched an armed offensive against the government from the shelter of the eastern forests. By 1970, they either controlled or made unsafe up to 20 per cent of the countryside.

Sihanouk loses control

Sihanouk, once so self-confident and assured, was losing his grip on domestic politics and his foreign policy was increasingly becoming erratic. In 1968, both the NLF and the DRV opened embassies in Phnom Penh, but later in the year Sihanouk put out feelers via the French Embassy, assuring the United States of his heartfelt desire for reconciliation. As evidence of his newfound goodwill towards the country he had so often vilified, he released a number of US military personnel who had been captured inside Cambodian territory. Sihanouk was well known for dramatic changes of political course and quixotic gestures, but these flip-flops pointed towards his growing powerlessness. He also left an increasing share of the day-to-day running of the country to Prime Minister Lon Nol and his deputy, Prince Sisowath Sirik Matak. Matak, a strongly anti-communist career civil servant, was becoming increasingly alienated by the incompetence and aimlessness of his cousin's system. Sihanouk had wanted all power, but now he shirked the responsibilities it brought with it and spent much of his time making films.

Sometime during this period, Sirik Matak began to think seriously of deposing Sihanouk and began to stand up against him publicly. In August 1969, he persuaded Lon Nol to refuse to form a new cabinet unless he could choose his own ministers, who would be answerable to him and not Sihanouk. Sihanouk was forced to agree, something that would once have been unthinkable. The little rebellion struck a chord. Many prominent Cambodians were disgusted by Sihanouk's self-indulgence, highlighted in 1969 when he awarded himself a statuette cast from gold ingots taken from the country's treasury for winning first prize in a stage-managed film festival. Widespread dislike for Sihanouk's wife, Monique Izzi, also contributed to the growing disillusion and disrespect for the once all-powerful prince. In late 1969, Sirik Matak and Lon Nol humiliated Sihanouk at a conference of the Sangkum by forcing the closure of the state-run Phnom Penh casino in defiance of his wishes. By this stage, the possibility for compromise had disappeared.

Meanwhile, the war had escalated in the eastern border zones. In March 1969, the United States launched its secret bombing of communist positions in the east of Cambodia. B-52s pounded large areas of the countryside, with widespread loss of civilian lives and destruction of property, farmland and forests in a sustained bombing campaign. Cambodia was being sucked into the maelstrom and Sihanouk was powerless to prevent it. In January 1970, he went to his villa on the French Riviera to rest and regain his strength, and no doubt to ponder his political options. While members of the country's elite believed that he should have remained at his post to handle his country's mounting problems, it is possible that Sihanouk went overseas to plead with the leaders of the PRC and the USSR to lean on their Vietnamese allies to close or at least scale down their bases in Cambodia. He could then return home as a conquering hero, regain the initiative from his disgruntled courtiers and replace them with more pliable men.

Meanwhile, back in Phnom Penh, Sirik Matak struggled vainly to try to bring some semblance of order to the disintegrating system. He tried to negotiate with the North Vietnamese and NLF for a withdrawal of troops, but learned that Sihanouk in fact had secretly agreed to their presence. (It should be said, however, that Sihanouk was scarcely in any position to do otherwise, short of entering into a military alliance with the United States and South Vietnam, which would have meant the end of his country's cherished neutrality and would not have guaranteed military success.) Mobs in Phnom Penh sacked the DRV and NLF embassies with Lon Nol's covert support, demanding the withdrawal of troops from Cambodian territory. It is also likely that Sihanouk

149

approved the demonstrations and planned to use them as a bargaining chip in his discussions with Russian and Chinese leaders so that they would bring pressure on Hanoi to close the bases. In the event, they turned into full-scale riots, with a heavy rent-a-crowd of hardline Khmer Krom soldiers flown in from South Vietnam by Lon Nol for the occasion. Sihanouk had wanted something milder, and was forced to denounce the rioters. If he had planned to storm back into Phnom Penh and retake the initiative, with a signed agreement with the world communist leaders regarding the bases under his belt, he was sorely mistaken. Sirik Matak and Lon Nol had taken over writing the script and the following day they ordered the evacuation of the Vietnamese bases and cancelled agreements that allowed them to funnel supplies via the so-called Sihanouk Trail from Kompong Som. When the DRV and NLF ignored the demand to withdraw, Lon Nol's soldiers attacked the communist positions, with support from South Vietnamese artillery fire from over the border.

There is something precipitate, even hysterical about the Cambodian government's actions at this stage, for it was unrealistic to think that the Vietnamese communists could suddenly close down their bases and withdraw their troops in the middle of an all-out war. Moreover, although the bases did infringe on Cambodian sovereignty and provoke the United States into military incursions, Hanoi and the NLF could point to their deal with Sihanouk as a legitimising factor. On 16 March 1970, last-ditch talks between the Vietnamese communists and the Lon Nol government failed to resolve the problem. Sihanouk's delicate balancing act to maintain neutrality was over and from this point on the spread of full-scale war to Cambodia appeared inevitable. By March 1970, Matak had had enough. Sihanouk was still overseas while the country was sliding towards disaster.

There are times when the decisiveness or otherwise of a single individual decides the course of history. Although the Sihanouk loyalist Oum Mannorine attempted unsuccessfully to arrest Lon Nol on the night of 16 March, the General dithered. Fifty-six years of age, cautious and conservative, he had been Sihanouk's creature since he was a young man. Sirik Matak, however, was resolute and more than an intellectual and moral match for the equivocating Prime Minister. He had lost all respect for Sihanouk sometime earlier, and he was determined that the time had come to remove Sihanouk from power. During the night of 17 March, Sirik Matak and several supporters burst into Lon Nol's house, pulled him from his bed and demanded his support for a parliamentary coup against Sihanouk—at gunpoint, according to some reports. Reluctantly, Lon Nol agreed, signing a paper that called upon the National Assembly to depose Sihanouk as head of state. He is said to have wept when he signed the document, and later, when the country descended into chaos, to have expressed remorse at turning against his master.

The session of the National Assembly that followed was electric, as speakers stood to denounce Sihanouk for corruption and abuse of power, giving vent to howls of pent-up rage against the man who had often personally humiliated them. It was a revolt of men exasperated to the limit with a master who had forfeited their loyalty and respect. The assemblymen were not revolutionaries by conviction or nature. They were, by and large, the same conservatives who had supported Sihanouk since his overthrow of the Huy Kanthoul government in 1951, or men very much like them. They agreed with the plotters, voting by a margin of 86 to 3 to remove Sihanouk as head of state (later altered to be unanimous). It was the symbolic parricide of the father of the nation. Sihanoukism was dead, and some months later the mutineers voted to transform Cambodia into a republic. Cambodia, however, was rushing headlong towards catastrophe.

7
THE DOOMED REPUBLIC, 1970–75

To look back at the Lon Nol coup is to be in the presence of dramatic irony. Painful indeed is the stark contrast between the actors' euphoria and the inescapable doom that we know was their fate. If some theatre were to stage a play based on the coup, surely the audience would call out warnings to the actors! But the shades on their dusty stage are deaf to the voices of the living and shuffle inexorably towards their destiny. A carnival mood prevailed in Phnom Penh and the American journalist T.D. Allman compared the atmosphere at the time to a 'psychedelic trip'. Free of the prince who had long unmanned them, the National Assembly celebrated Sihanouk's political demise. Students paraded joyfully in the streets, the chief bonze of the Buddhist Mohanikay order praised the actions of the National Assembly, and the government granted an amnesty to a few hundred political prisoners and paid their bus fares home. The government denounced Sihanouk as a madman and vowed to put him on trial for corruption and abuse of power.

Given the dangers facing the country, it should have been a time for sobriety, but reason was washed away in the flood of jubilation. Bolstered by the empty promises of the Saigon regime, by faith in the United States, and steeped in an ineffable belief in the racial superiority of the Khmers, the Republican government prepared for all-out war. (The Khmer Republic was not declared until 9 October 1970, but for the sake of convenience the term is applied here to the entire post-coup regime from March 1970.)

Yet even Lon Nol and his ministers realised that the 35 000-strong Cambodian army was, as its former commander Nhiek Tioulong had put it, 'less effective than the Paris police'. The government called up its 3600 reservists and announced that it would immediately recruit a further 10 000 men. Thousands of young men rallied to the colours, many of them giggling self-consciously as they drilled in the city streets, yet eager to engage the enemy for all their shy smiles. They were the first instalment of human flesh for a military machine that would grow insatiable in its demands, a generation of doomed youth who, like that of Wilfred Owen, would know 'only the monstrous anger of the guns' and 'the stuttering rifles' rapid rattle'. In the end, their sacrifices only paved the way for an even more immense tragedy.

Although the new head of state, Cheng Heng, announced that his country would remain neutral, the new regime developed a de facto alliance with the United States and South Vietnam and embarked on a bloody anti-communist war that would end five years later with the fall of Phnom Penh to the black-clad Khmers Rouges guerrillas. Full of surreal optimism, Cheng Heng rejected any suggestion of a negotiated solution with the Vietnamese communists and promised to throw them out of the country. Officials scoffed at the threat posed by up to 40 000 battle-hardened Vietnamese communist regulars and NLF guerrillas and their tiny 400-strong Khmers Rouges allies. 'They amuse us,' one bureaucrat yawned. 'We are strong. In the end we will be victorious.'

The extent of US involvement in the coup

Sihanouk, China and the DRV were quick to blame the United States for the coup and to cast Lon Nol as a CIA puppet, although the coup was essentially home grown. The United States has engineered many coups and counter-revolutions around the world, and they had long schemed to undermine Cambodia's neutrality, but their involvement seems to have been indirect. As was the case with the Dap Chhuon and Sam Sary affairs over a decade earlier, the United States seemed happy to leave the actual dirty work to its Saigon proxy. Despite this, there is clear evidence that the CIA knew in advance of the impending coup and that, as British writer William Shawcross observed, if the US government did not know what was about to happen, then they were not reading their own intelligence reports. Justin Corfield, an historian of the Khmer republic, has revealed that Nguyen Cao Ky, the South Vietnamese Vice-President, 'paid . . . at least two secret visits to Phnom Penh' during the week before the coup and there were persistent reports of large numbers of anti-communist Khmer Krom 'Mike Force' soldiers flying into Pochentong airport. These crack troops were US trained and it stretches credulity to imagine that they could have been deployed without the knowledge of the American commanders.

On balance of probabilities, it appears that the United States gave tacit support to the coup, believing that Sirik Matak and his fellow plotters could oust Sihanouk with assistance from the Saigon regime, but without large-scale American intervention. Given that President Nixon had already decided on the staged withdrawal of US troops from Vietnam, it is likely that he wished to avoid a new ground war in Cambodia but welcomed an anti-communist Cambodian regime that could partially secure his rear. Lon Nol's position was made more tenuous by America's secret diplomacy, which culminated in Nixon's February 1972 visit to Beijing and rapprochement with Mao's China. Lon Nol's enemies would become Nixon's new friends. The tragedy for Cambodia is that

Lon Nol and many other supporters of the Khmer Republic believed that Nixon would not abandon them, when in fact Cambodia was a pawn on the international political chessboard. Having said that, it must be stressed that the coup resulted from pressures that had been building within Cambodia for some time. Sirik Matak probably would have moved against Sihanouk regardless of the views of Saigon and Washington.

Sihanouk determines to fight

Most Cambodians knew nothing of the secret plotting that had led to the coup, whether they were parading students, stoic peasants or ecstatic government officials. Nor did they understand the ramifications. Even Lon Nol believed that President Nixon was his personal friend and would not desert him. However, not all Khmers supported the coup and the lines were soon drawn for a savage civil war. While the coup was popular with urban Khmers, the *New York Times* correspondent Henry Kamm warned that the peasants, who made up the overwhelming bulk of the population, 'would follow the other side with equal facility'. There was a large-scale pro-Sihanouk riot in the regional centre of Kompong Cham ten days after the coup, during which a mob butchered the Prime Minister's brother, Lon Nil, and another parliamentary deputy and ate their livers. It would be wrong to reduce the conflict to a city–country divide (many people fled the war in the countryside for the comparative safety of the cities), but Sihanouk and his newfound Khmers Rouges allies did find their greatest support in the peasantry. Eventually, they would defeat the city-based republican armies.

Sihanouk first heard of the coup from Soviet Premier Alexei Kosygin, en route from Moscow airport to the Kremlin after a flight from Paris. The Prince initially contemplated retirement to his villa in the south of France, but the thought of exile among the ageing pretenders of Europe would scarcely have appealed to a man of his passion and energy. Outrage and the desire for vengeance soon replaced despair and rekindled his fighting spirit. Days after the coup, he issued a ringing appeal to the Cambodian people, calling for a united political and military struggle to remove Lon Nol from power. He met with his old friend Zhou Enlai in Beijing and the Premier pledged that 'China is determined to support Your Highness until Your Highness returns to his own country in victory'. The Soviet Union also endorsed Sihanouk and the DRV leaders announced their support for his 'just struggle'. On 23 March 1970, Sihanouk announced the formation of the National United Front of Kampuchea (FUNK after its French acronym), in which his royalist supporters would join hands with his old Khmers Rouges enemies in a war to remove the 'usurpers' at Phnom Penh. It was a declaration of war by a man who had staked his career on avoiding war.

Years later, Sihanouk claimed to have suffered misgivings over the Chinese leaders' motives. He was suspicious, he asserts, that they saw the alliance as a way of using him to install the Khmers Rouges in power. Even if this occurred to him at the time, he was boiling with rage and his lust for revenge soon overrode any doubts. Pol Pot claimed later that the alliance was his idea, but it is likely that he was encouraged by the Chinese to accept a pact of convenience with his old enemy. As it turned out, Sihanouk was supping with the devil with a very short spoon, although he could not foresee the tragic consequences of the alliance at that time.

After Sihanouk's declaration, events moved quickly. By the end of March, Hanoi and the NLF had severed diplomatic ties with Phnom Penh and savage battles raged along the eastern frontiers, with Lon Nol's troops fighting joint operations with ARVN (Army of the Republic of Vietnam) soldiers against the communists. Although the CIA speculated at this time that relations between the Prince and his former courtiers might be patched up, there was to be no going back.

The anti-Vietnamese pogroms

The initial reaction to the coup in Phnom Penh had been festive and naïve, almost innocent, but the mood darkened after Lon Nol claimed that 'Vietcong agitators' and Vietnamese plantation workers had been responsible for the pro-Sihanouk riots at Kompong Cham and else-where. While some members of the 400 000-strong Vietnamese minority might well have been involved in the disturbances, there was no excuse for the officially sponsored pogroms that broke out afterwards. Less than a fortnight after the coup, the *New York Times* reported that thousands of Vietnamese refugees were streaming across the border into the lower Mekong delta. Cambodian government leaflets whipped up race hatred and the police rounded up tens of thousands of Vietnamese civilians as suspected communists. Lon Nol labelled the entire Vietnamese com-munity as communist as a pretext for the mass detention, 'ethnic cleansing' and slaughter of civilians. *Newsweek* reporter François Sully described the horror at the Neak Luong ferry crossing on the Mekong below Phnom Penh:

> As far as the eye could see, odd-shaped bundles were slowly drifting towards us. At first I thought they were clumps of water-lilies. But the Cambodian passengers . . . identi-fied the bundles immediately as the bloated bodies of Vietnamese men and women still clad in their black pantaloons . . .

The final death toll was probably in the tens of thousands and although the government blamed the massacres on angry civilians, most were the handiwork of the Cambodian military and police. Lon Nol never apologised for the slaughter and, given his mystical racism, probably justified it as a crusade against the ancient enemy. However, even he realised that the pogroms had outraged world opinion and might well lead to a loss of overseas military aid. The murders threatened to under-mine his new-found alliance with the Saigon regime, and the *New York Times* editorialised that they 'should provoke second thoughts in Washington about the stability as well as the morality of the [Lon Nol] regime . . .'. The pogroms were called off and arms and ammunition began to flow in from the United States and Indonesia. In the end, the

Republic was kept alive only by transfusions of US economic and military aid.

The weakness of the Lon Nol regime

However, all that this military and economic aid achieved was to delay the inevitable collapse of the regime. Cambodia was drawn into the Indochina War at the time when the United States was beginning to withdraw and not even the Paris Peace Accords, which were signed in February 1973, could save the Khmer Republic. The accords resulted in the withdrawal of Vietnamese communist forces from Cambodia, but the horrors of war, coupled with the alliance with Sihanouk, were to give the Khmers Rouges a strength and legitimacy that they had lacked prior to the 1970 coup. In addition, a major problem for the Khmer Republic was that many of its political elite were men of distressingly low calibre, who preferred intrigue and financial dishonesty at the expense of the Republic.

The parliament, elected in 1966, had shown a greater degree of independence than its predecessors and had voted Sihanouk out of office, but the culture was still one of timeserving, corruption and subservience to authority. The President, Cheng Heng, was a colourless personality and Prime Minister Lon Nol was crooked and second-rate, with a mediocre intelligence, a brutal streak and a penchant for superstitious obscurantism that impeded the Republic's military operations. He consulted soothsayers before embarking on military operations and came under the malign influence of a monk named Mam Pram, who has been described as a kind of Cambodian Rasputin. The US embassy official William Harben reported that the monk convinced Lon Nol to order his soldiers to wear magical scarves to protect them from the enemy, and to enlist wizards to cast spells on the communists 'to make them believe they were confronted by vast government armies . . .'. Worse still, Lon Nol believed it was possible to cast spells to transform grass into troops. Harben's reports earned him a rebuke from the Nixon administration, which grumbled that it 'wanted no more negative reports of this sort'. Lon Nol also set up a bizarre institution called the Khmer Mon Institute, which popularised a mystical brand of racism extolling the Khmers as a kind of Asian master race. Ironically, the Khmers Rouges leader Pol Pot shared many of these beliefs.

Lon Nol was clearly unfit to govern or command armies, yet he was to linger on as the Republic's pre-eminent political figure—serving at various times as prime minister and president—until its dying days. He suffered a serious stroke as he stepped out of his shower one day in February 1971, but there was no obvious replacement for the sick man. Prince Sisowath Sirik Matak was more capable than Lon Nol and it was he who had impelled the Marshal into deposing Sihanouk, but he was deeply unpopular in ruling circles and thus unacceptable as a replacement.

Those ruling circles were riddled with intrigue. The leading plotter was Lon Nol's brother, Lon Non, 'whose efforts', as David Chandler puts it, 'were concentrated on keeping Sisowath Sirik Matak—or anyone else—from gaining power from Lon Nol'. Whether motivated by greed and the lust for power, or by loyalty to his ailing brother, the result of Lon Non's machinations was that mediocrity and corruption prevailed. The upshot was that when Lon Nol recovered, he was put back into power despite his obvious limitations. US doctors estimated that he had suffered a 20 per cent diminution of his intellectual capacity as a result of the stroke. William Harben confided this diagnosis to his diary: 'Mild schizophrenia, paranoid type; symptoms—neologisms, word salad, delusions of grandeur and persecution; IQ about 105'. No matter, Lon Nol was to remain as the ineffectual leader of the Republic until he fled before the advancing communist guerrillas in April 1975.

Republican military ineptitude

The political ineptitude of the regime was matched by its military incompetence. After his return from hospital treatment in Hawaii in April 1971, Lon Nol was promoted to Field Marshal, despite the fact that he had spent his career as a policeman, not a soldier. Although individual

Cambodian government soldiers fought bravely enough, they suffered as a result of indifferent and often criminally corrupt commanders. The Cambodian government forces (FANK after their French acronym) were out-fought almost from the beginning of the war, and the Republic quickly lost control of vast swathes of the countryside. The situation had been greatly worsened by the US–ARVN invasion of eastern Cambodia in April 1970, which had the predictable effect of driving the communists deep into Cambodian territory. Although the CIA's Douglas Pike claimed that the Vietnamese communists controlled up to ten per cent of Cambodia before the coup, a map prepared by the Lon Nol government's General Sak Sutsakhan suggests that they occupied only scattered salients of territory in the extreme north-east of Rattanakiri province, the Parrot's Beak, and elsewhere along the 965-kilometre frontier. This was to change dramatically within months of the coup, as Cambodia became the scene of what the US President himself called 'the Nixon Doctrine in its purest form'.

When Nixon was sworn in as the 36th president of the United States in 1969, it was apparent that America could not win the increasingly unpopular war in Vietnam, despite the deployment of over half a million troops. The President formulated what became known as the Guam or Nixon Doctrine: the United States would disengage its ground forces, while providing its Southeast Asian allies with air cover and large amounts of military and economic aid to hold the line against communism. Implementation of the policy began on 20 April 1970, when Nixon announced he would remove 150 000 US ground troops from Vietnam, the first in a series of staged withdrawals. Nixon's field commanders felt vulnerable. There was a danger that the Vietnamese communists would take advantage of the withdrawals to step up attacks down the Ho Chi Minh Trail, so Nixon decided to attack the enemy bases inside Cambodia. Operation Menu—full-scale carpet-bombing—had begun the previous year but this had not eliminated the threat; the communists never had a static 'Pentagon East' and their command posts were always on the move. Nixon decided to launch a full-scale ground assault to root out COSVN, the communists' supreme command headquarters, which he believed was situated in the 'Fishhook' area of Cambodia.

Operation Shoemaker

The invasion, code-named Operation Shoemaker, began on 30 April 1970. Tens of thousands of infantrymen, supported by tanks, aircraft and artillery, stormed over the border. It was not an occupation, Nixon said on US television. US troops would not stay longer than six to eight weeks and their aim was to destroy the enemy's bases and supplies in order '[T]o protect our men who are in Vietnam, and to guarantee the success of our withdrawal and Vietnamization program . . .'. The Saigon regime let it be known that they did not consider themselves bound by the timeline (and in fact stayed for some months longer than the US troops). Nixon did not bother to inform Lon Nol of the attack until after he had announced it on American television. The invasion had nothing to do with the security of Cambodia, although Lon Nol presented it as a response to his appeal for military assistance and wrote Nixon a pathetic letter of thanks. US diplomatic staff in Phnom Penh were under no illusions about the likely effects of the invasion. *Chargé d'affaires* Mike Rives warned Washington in telegraphese:

> US and ARVN presence in Eastern Cambodia seems bound to worsen situation in Cambodia by forcing . . . [Vietnamese communists] westward. No one here credits Cambodian army with capability defending against these . . . forces. Appears to us that in absence of any immediate chance of negotiation, Cambodia faced with prospect of de facto partition and of becoming battlefield fought over and occupied by foreign troops.

Publicly, the US military commanders presented Shoemaker as a resounding success. Nixon boasted that over 11 000 enemy soldiers had

161

been killed and vast amounts of war matériel captured, although his field commanders gave more sober estimates in their internal reports. What Nixon didn't talk about publicly was the invasion's effect on Cambodia, including Mike Rives' analysis quoted above. Nor did he discuss the effects on Cambodian civilians and property, although these were reported in internal State Department correspondence. Samuel Berger, the US deputy ambassador in Saigon, informed his superiors in Washington that there had been many civilian deaths as a result of US tactical air operations, which included the use of napalm. Berger also reported that there was a 'problem of distinguishing [communist soldiers killed in action] . . . from civilians killed' and that this was 'obviously difficult where [helicopter] gunships [were] involved'. There were also reports of widespread looting and atrocities against civilians, particularly, although not exclusively, by ARVN troops.

The other immediate effect of the invasion was that many thousands of peasants had flocked to the FUNK guerrilla forces. Berger reported that US commanders were 'surprised' by this, but that it was true. Significantly, many who joined or sympathised with the guerrillas wanted Sihanouk to return, and Berger expected the trend to continue as the death and destruction continued. A slogan daubed on the walls of a gutted hospital in Saang asked, 'If the Lon Nol government says it wants to protect the Khmer people, why did it destroy the town?' The invasion was a cynical piece of *Realpolitik*, and bore out Lord Palmerston's famous aphorism, repeated by John Foster Dulles, that the United States has interests, not friends (a fact sadly lost on Lon Nol, who continued to bombard his 'friend' in the White House with adoring letters). Cambodia had been dragged into the war just as the US was leaving it.

By August 1970, Lon Nol's writ had been restricted to bands of territory around Phnom Penh, the Great Lake, Battambang, Pursat and Siem Reap, along with corridors linking Kompong Som, Takeo, Kampot and Svay Rieng with the capital. In January 1971, communist gunners almost completely destroyed the government's air force in a barrage on

Pochentong airport. Some of the Cambodian army's operations were little short of farcical. An early example was the 'siege' of Saang, 32 kilometres south of Phnom Penh, which was found to be empty of communists (dead or alive) following a sustained artillery bombardment by Lon Nol soldiers. In the early years of the war, the government launched a number of grandiosely named campaigns, including Chenla I and Chenla II, but these rapidly bogged down and never captured more than a few narrow ribbons of territory before being abandoned.

Observers such as Mike Rives believed that if they wished, the Vietnamese communists could have occupied the entire country. This was also the opinion of the DRV's Pham Van Dong, who told Sihanouk's wife, Princess Monique, that they could have captured control of the country within 24 hours. Their main aim, however, was to drive out the United States and its Saigon 'puppet regime' from Vietnam. Occupying and administering Cambodia was not a realistic or desirable option. Mike Rives believed it '[M]ore likely that the communists intend to protect their interests in the border area while applying a range of pressures—short of all-out military attack—against the current [Phnom Penh] regime in the hope of bringing it down'. In the early stages of the war, the FUNK forces (Khmers Rouges and Sihanoukists) were not strong enough to achieve this by themselves and had to rely on the Vietnamese communist 'umbrella'. They were, however, to grow rapidly in strength and numbers in the coming years. Indeed, as early as March 1972 there were reports of Khmers Rouges troops fighting their way to within 16 kilometres of the capital, and by the next month the *New York Times* claimed that all of Cambodia east of the Mekong, with the exception of some regional capitals, was in the hands of the communists.

The crisis of the Republic

The war quickly sapped the foundations of the Cambodian economy, which were shaky even before the coup due to decades of corruption and mismanagement. The five years of the Khmer Republic were marked by chronic economic crisis: galloping inflation, the collapse of exports, a mounting budget deficit and growing dependence on US subventions. Cambodia's major exports had been rice and rubber, but the communists rapidly overran many of the rubber plantations on the left bank of the Mekong, and others were damaged or destroyed. Secondary industries were hamstrung by a shortage of spare parts and skilled labour: many of the most skilled workers had been Vietnamese and had fled during the pogroms. Tourism was dead, with heavy fighting near the Angkor ruins from early in the war. For much of the life of the Republic, the lower Mekong was impassable or dangerous for shipping due to floating mines and other guerrilla activity, and the road and rail link to the blue water port of Kompong Som (Sihanoukville) was intermittently cut and, in the end, permanently closed to government traffic.

A continuing feature of the Republic was the drip feed of US food aid, with flights beginning in November 1970. There were shortages of petrol, food and many other commodities, and prices were pushed up by the burgeoning black market, which sent inflation levels soaring. During September 1972 food riots broke out in Phnom Penh, a symptom of the grim lives of the city poor. Unemployment leapt as hundreds of thousands of refugees flocked to the cities to escape the war: within six months the population of Phnom Penh swelled from around 700 000 to over one and a half million.

Earlier, in late October 1971, the government had declared a State of Emergency, with Lon Nol insisting that he would no longer 'play the game of democracy and freedom'. All political meetings and opposition demonstrations were banned, and civil rights indefinitely abolished. The crisis was exacerbated by the incessant budgetary demands of the armed forces, which bloated out from around 35 000 men at the time of the coup to over 210 000 within twelve months, and with Lon Nol eventually demanding the Republic place 600 000 men under arms. The drain on a country of seven and a half million people (less if those in the communist zones are excluded) was colossal. The situation was not helped by the Cooper–Church amendment to US Senate appropriations in December 1970, which restricted military and economic aid to a small country that the Nixon administration ominously insisted was a neutral country, not an ally.

City of Bonjour, Republic of Corruption

Corruption has been a depressingly regular facet of developing societies such as Cambodia. It thrives where civil society is weak, the media is muzzled and the separation of powers is blurred. Sihanouk's Cambodia was corrupt. People's primary loyalty was often to patrons rather than the state or community, and responsible office was seen as a ticket to self-enrichment, as when civil servants helped themselves to the profits of state-owned enterprises and government ministers pilfered from the public till. Princess Monique's peculations shocked all but the most hardened cynics and Sihanouk himself fudged the distinction between public and private assets. Many of his courtiers, including Yem Sambaur, Sirik Matak and Lon Nol, had murky records, so it should not be surprising that the 1970 coup did not usher in a new era of financial probity. Yet the extent of corruption before the coup pales by comparison with the astonishing levels of sleaze and dishonesty under the Khmer Republic. The veteran politician Sim Var's concern that the declaration of martial law in mid-1970 would serve to cover up corruption proved all too true. Indeed, corruption was the only growth industry in Cambodia at the time. One Khmer writer later described Phnom Penh as 'The City of Bonjour'. ('Bonjour' here means corruption, from bribes passed with a handshake and the French greeting.)

The most profitable pickings were to be found in the US economic and military aid program and those best placed to benefit from it were high-ranking army officers. Sim Var's newspaper, *Sethkech Khmer*, exposed many examples of corruption in the armed forces, but all too often those sent to root out corruption were themselves dishonest and Lon Nol was indifferent to it. Officers stole their men's rations and sold them in the city markets, soldiers 'shook down' travellers at army

165

checkpoints and Cambodian soldiers copied the widespread ARVN practice of selling weapons and ammunition to enemy agents. Some officers even sold artillery pieces to the Khmers Rouges. However, the most egregious racket in the armed forces was the 'phantom soldiers' scam, in which army commanders padded the numbers on the payroll and pocketed the difference. Other officers failed to report soldiers killed or missing in action, with the result that many detachments were seriously under strength yet intact on paper. R.P.W. Norton, writing in the *Far Eastern Economic Review*, estimated that a year after the coup there were 30 000 such phantom soldiers. These treacherous rorts were costing the treasury almost US$11 million per annum, and cost the lives of countless Khmer soldiers and civilians. While ordinary Khmers fought and died, cavorting fops lived the high life at glittering balls and parties, even as rockets and shells landed in the capital's outer suburbs. William Harben recorded the disgust of the Korean wife of a retired US general, who asked, 'When they have war, why they have party rike [like] this?'

Nixon, Kissinger and the aerial bombardment

In spite of its bungling and corrupt leaders, the Khmer Republic hung on for five years, for the last two in deadly combat with the Khmers Rouges alone. The war was fought with a ferocity that defies description, but in the welter of bloody superlatives the US carpet-bombing stands out. Although few literate people can be unaware of the horrors that befell Cambodia under Pol Pot, the US bombing is largely forgotten and nobody will ever face court for it. In the words of the American ecologist Arthur Westing, the air war over Indochina aimed at the 'massive, intentional disruption of both the natural and the human ecologies of the region'. The technology of death from the skies involved colossal amounts of high explosive, incendiaries such as phosphorus and napalm, and the chemical destruction of forests and farmlands by defoliants such as the dioxin-rich Agent Orange. A single B-52 squadron was capable of dropping as many bombs in one year as the US air force dropped in the entire Pacific theatre during World War II. From 1970, when the bombing was stepped up following the Lon Nol coup, the US dropped almost 540 000 tons of bombs on Cambodia.

After the Paris Peace Accords came into force in February 1973, and ended the bombing of Vietnam, the US commanders turned their entire aerial firepower on Cambodia, with B-52s flying thousands of sorties from carriers in the Gulf and bases in Thailand and Guam. The bombing reached a crescendo in the first half of 1973, when 260 000 tons of bombs fell on Cambodia. By way of comparison, the Allies dropped a total of 160 000 tons of bombs on Japan in all of World War II. Admittedly, Japan was a more urbanised society, but the extent of the destruction inflicted on Cambodia should not be downplayed. Estimates of the total death toll from bombing vary from 150 000 to the US historian Chalmers Johnson's perhaps inflated estimate of 750 000. A Finnish Commission of Inquiry estimated 600 000 directly war-related deaths between 1970 and April 1975, although in truth the exact numbers will probably never be known. To this day, hundreds of Khmer peasants are killed and mutilated every year by the cluster bombs and other unexploded ordnance littering the countryside, although some of this is caused by landmines sown by Cambodian troops of one ideological complexion or another.

US Congressmen had on a number of occasions tried to stop or limit the bombing, but Nixon and his chief advisor, Secretary of State Henry Kissinger, ignored their directions. The bombing only ceased after Donald Dawson, a B-52 co-pilot on leave in the United States, saw television footage of the carnage inflicted on a Cambodian wedding party at Neak Luong by a US raid. B-52s fly at a tremendous altitude, so high that their engines cannot be heard on the ground and the first inkling of their presence is when the bombs begin to punch huge craters in the ground. The air crews are shielded from the horror below and think only in terms of dropping their bombs according to pre-arranged map coordinates in long, narrow areas known as 'boxes'. When he realised the horror of what he had done, Dawson refused to fly any more sorties. He was threatened with a court martial, the public outrage halted legal proceedings and the US Congress ordered the complete cessation of bombing.

The British writer William Shawcross, who documented the bombing in his book *Sideshow: Nixon, Kissinger and the Destruction of Cambodia*, believes that there is a *prima facie* case that the United States breached international law. Professor Mark Selden, historian and trenchant critic of US policy, insists that area bombing is a war crime and in clear breach of the 1949 Geneva Convention. When one ponders how a great and civilised nation could inflict such atrocities, the contempt in the words of General William Westmoreland, the supreme commander in Vietnam, should not be forgotten: 'The Oriental doesn't put the same high price on life as does a Westerner. Life is plentiful, life is cheap in the Orient.'

The death agony of the Republic

After the Paris Peace Accords came into force in January 1973, the Vietnamese communists effectively disengaged themselves from the fighting in Cambodia. Indeed, a rift opened up with their erstwhile allies, with US intelligence reports of fighting between Vietnamese communist soldiers and the Khmers Rouges. The conflict in Cambodia was now a straight civil war, with neither side strong enough to win an immediate breakthrough. Even when the US bombing was finally ended in mid-August 1973, the Khmers Rouges could not overpower the Republican forces. A grim war was played out in the countryside, with neither side giving quarter, and horrible atrocities occurred on both sides. Phnom Penh came frequently under attack from communist rockets and howitzer fire and when the United States terminated the supply of war matériel to the FANK air force after June 1974, they edged ever closer to the capital.

The Khmer Rouge's half-starved soldiers rolled unopposed into Phnom Penh on 17 April 1975. (Courtesy Newspix)

After 1 January 1975, when the Khmers Rouges launched their final offensive, Phnom Penh was effectively cut off from the rest of the world except for US supply flights which ferried food, ammunition and medical supplies into the city. Inside the city, now swollen to a population of perhaps three million, there was great suffering as people died from malnutrition and sickness, or huddled beneath makeshift shelters, or fell victim to Khmers Rouges artillery fire. The Mekong was sealed off to the Republic's shipping and the US airlift was called off in late March, after a ferocious rocket barrage on the airport.

Despite some diplomatic overtures by the Republic, the Khmers Rouges were confident of victory and spurned all talk of a negotiated solution. With the capital squeezed by communist troops, the United States bowed before inevitable defeat and on 4 April began the evacuation of its embassy staff. Lon Nol and some hundreds of top Republican cadres also flew to safety, many of them weighed down by the proceeds of their scams. As Haing Ngor, a doctor and officer in Lon Nol's army put it, 'Our society had lost its moral direction. And that's why we lost the war.' Some Republican leaders, most notably Sirik Matak, had the decency and courage to share the fate of the common people, but such cases could not make up for the regime's moral bankruptcy. On 17 April 1975 the final collapse came, with government soldiers throwing down their weapons and burning their uniforms as the guerrillas filed into the city. Peace had come, but it was the beginning of Cambodia's greatest agony. For many, it was to be the peace of the grave.

8
POL POT'S SAVAGE UTOPIA, 1975–79

It is a sad irony of history that it took Pol Pot's savage 'utopia'—or rather dystopia—to put Cambodia on the current world map. Prior to the establishment of Democratic Kampuchea (DK), Cambodia was for most westerners (if they knew of it at all) an exotic backwater that was home to the fabulous ruins of Angkor. It was 'the gentle land' of smiling peasants and lissom dancers ruled by an eccentric prince, a stereotype that was shattered by Lon Nol's hopeless war and the brutal fanaticism of Democratic Kampuchea.

A byword for horror

Today, Cambodia is a byword for horror, and the ubiquitous motorbike taxi drivers in Phnom Penh often assume that tourists come to visit the killing fields outside the city. Behind the conflicting stereotypes, Cambodia is a country inhabited by ordinary human beings who do the things people everywhere do, albeit in particularly Khmer ways.

One is entitled to ask why western visitors to Bali or Java rarely wonder at the massive slaughter that befell those islands in 1965–66, yet define Cambodia by the killing fields. Yet, unfair as the stereotypical image is, we cannot avoid the horror of the Pol Pot years. According to the CIA, the population of Cambodia stood at around 7.3 million in 1975, with other estimates of up to 8 million. Around 1.7 million of these people were to die during the brief period of DK, up to quarter of a million of them murdered as real or imagined enemies of the paranoid regime. The rest perished due to malnutrition and overwork, lack of medical care and sometimes despair and heartbreak.

When Phnom Penh fell to the Khmers Rouges, Cambodian society and economy had been traumatised by five years of war. Any regime, no matter what its ideological complexion, would have faced enormous challenges of reconstruction but the victorious Khmers Rouges only worsened the suffering of the people through a murderous combination of dogmatic quackery, ignorance, ineptitude and deliberate cruelty. In the end, their revolution failed miserably and almost destroyed the country in the process. There were no democratic mechanisms to allow for the correction of the policies of the rulers, despite their arrogation of the word 'Democratic' in the country's new name. That the suffering of the Cambodian people only ended in 1979 with their liberation by their traditional enemies from Vietnam is another irony of history, albeit a happier one.

Prince Sihanouk was the first head of state of the new regime, but the Khmers Rouges made clear to him that he was to be a mere figurehead. His alliance with them had been very much a marriage of convenience between old adversaries. Perhaps he believed that his old friend Zhou Enlai would ensure he would at least share power with the Khmers Rouges, but if so he was mistaken. After his return to Phnom Penh in September 1975 following a goodwill mission to twenty countries, Sihanouk was effectively a prisoner in the royal palace, and in April 1976 the Khmers Rouges forced him to retire and appointed Khieu Samphan as the new head of state. Many of Sihanouk's family died during the DK years and what perhaps saved him from the same fate was his high international profile and his friendship with the Chinese leaders, plus the possibility that he might be useful for the regime in future. He spent much of his time under house arrest, reading and growing vegetables in his palace, terrified of the irrational violence of his Khmers Rouges 'friends'. He had supped with the devil and now he had the time and the solitude to ponder the wisdom of what he had done. Whether he did so at the time is a matter for debate, for his continuing alliance with Pol Pot after the downfall of DK points to a character ruled by egotism and visceral emotion.

The forced evacuation of the cities

Eyewitness accounts agree that the people of Phnom Penh were awash with conflicting emotions when their city fell to the Khmers Rouges on 17 April. As the Cambodian memoirist Haing Ngor points out, most city-dwellers had a friend or relative on the other side. Many believed that Prince Sihanouk was the supreme commander of the guerrillas and that he would save them from harm, but stories of infernal atrocities had also made them apprehensive. Some residents welcomed the guerrillas with food and drink, but most stood in doorways and by windows to see what would happen. No one seems to have been prepared for the sudden mass evacuation of the city's population.

The heavily armed guerrillas, filing through the streets in black peasant garb or rudimentary khakis, were serious and disciplined in contrast to the lackadaisical and demoralised Lon Nol soldiers. Some accepted the food offered them but most padded past in grim silence on their rubber sandals. Most of them were dark-skinned back-country Khmers and many were young adolescents and children, some as young as ten years old toting AK47s almost as big as themselves. Some spontaneously broke into shy country smiles when pressed with kind words to accept food or drink, but most smouldered with rage against the city and its denizens. The French author François Bizot (himself a former prisoner of the robotic Khmers Rouges executioner Ta Duch) wrote that beyond the French Embassy gate there raged 'a violence so terrible and explosive that I felt totally disheartened'. Haing Ngor felt there was 'something excessive in their anger' and mused darkly that 'something had happened to these people in their years in the forests'. Indeed it had. Although it is not easy to see these young guerrillas as victims, given the horrors of the regime they served, they had been moulded by what the French writer Serge Thion has called 'the most savage onslaught ever launched against a peasantry'. Part of the price of the civil war and the American bombing was the brutalisation of the young and the destruction of family ties. These young people were part of an immense tragedy that began when the 1970 coup dragged their country over the edge of an abyss.

For many guerrillas, this was their first sight of a big city and they must have been as apprehensive of the city-dwellers as the latter were of them. For these farm boys (and girls), Phnom Penh was a strange foreign place, where they might witness marvels beyond their wildest imaginings: white-skinned westerners, running water, electricity, women with high heels and make-up, whitegoods and televisions, brick buildings, iced drinks and sweet pastries, people wearing glasses, children wearing shoes, the royal palace. Haing Ngor recalls a young guerrilla marvelling at the 'fresh' water in a toilet. Phnom Penh was also a kind of Sodom on the Mekong, a place of ill repute that the Khmers Rouges cadres had long warned them against. These child and adolescent soldiers, uprooted from their families, impressionable and unschooled, were the praetorian guard of the new regime, harsh and fanatical, yet pliable in the hands of the leadership they knew only as *angkar*, 'the organisation'. A book written from their point of view would make fascinating reading, but is unlikely to appear for most of them were illiterate.

Haing Ngor was about to operate on a badly wounded Lon Nol soldier when a guerrilla burst through the hospital door. 'He was, at most, twelve years old,' the doctor recalls, and like most of the other guerrillas he encountered the boy's face bore a fierce and angry expression. In a voice that had not yet broken, he screamed at the hospital staff to leave at once, emphasising the words with jabs of his rifle. The staff complied, leaving the soldier to die on the operating table. Outside in the streets all was chaos, with Khmers Rouges soldiers yelling at the people to get out of the city, occasionally punctuating their words with bursts of AK47 fire into the sky. Some said that the evacuation would be only for a few hours, because the Americans were going to bomb the city, yet it took hours to move even a few city blocks in the crush. Finally, the orders came that everyone must make their way to their home village, that there would be no exceptions. Some guerrillas chanted slogans against the 'US imperialists' and the Lon Nol government, or hailed their own victory, their words full of exaggerated hatred or praise. A *mit neary*—woman comrade—endlessly harangued the crowd: 'The wheel of history is turning . . . If you use your hands to try to stop the wheel, they will be caught in the spokes.' She had evidently learned the speech by rote, and the expelled population would hear it from many other mouths in the coming days and weeks.

The entire city population, up to three million strong, was on the move: children, pregnant women, the well fed and half-starved, the old and infirm, rich and poor, long-time city-dwellers and refugees alike. Most walked, some shoved motor scooters or even cars through the throng, while others pushed handcarts piled high with ill-assorted possessions: television sets, boxes bulging with personal effects, pots and pans, and the proverbial trash and treasure. Some carried bags crammed with Lon Nol currency, only to discard it when they learned there would be no money in the new society. Dr Haing Ngor's 'exodus of the sick and crippled' flowed from the hospitals: wounded soldiers on crutches, wobbly old women and even a man with both legs amputated, whose relatives pushed his hospital bed with the intravenous drip bag still attached. The French priest François Ponchaud estimates the hospital population of the city at 'liberation' at up to 20 000. Many patients, along with the very young and very old, would perish in the exodus. Some civilians tried to turn back when they reached the suburbs but the Khmers Rouges shot recalcitrants on the spot as a warning. The engineer Pin Yathay recorded the fate of one young man who went back to get something from his house: a guerrilla stood 14 metres from the boy's corpse, 'smoke still wafting lazily from his AK47'. The evacuation was relentless, and when Haing Ngor returned a few days later with a guerrilla escort to pick up some medicines, Phnom Penh was already a ghost city. Official DK sources admit that between 2000 and 3000 people died during the evacuation, but the total was certainly much higher.

The mass expulsion was an atrocious act, but the deportation of populations has a long history across many civilisations. The Romans scattered the Jews from Palestine in the Diaspora of 70 AD. Ferdinand and Isabella deported the Sephardic Jews from Spain in 1492 and the last of the Muslim *Moriscos* followed them in 1614. Stalin expelled the Crimean Tartars, the Volga Germans and the Chechens to Siberia during World War II, and after 1945 some 14 million Germans were driven westwards from their homes in Central and Eastern Europe. The mass transfer of Muslim and Hindu populations marked the end of the British *Raj* in India in 1947 and more recently Bosnia was 'ethnically cleansed' by murder and expulsion. All of these cases depended on the mobilisation of hatred which targeted a clearly identifiable ethnic or at least religious 'other'. What is singular about the Cambodian experience is that Khmers expelled Khmers. In the mental universe of the guerrillas, medieval prejudices jostled with half-baked corruptions of Marxism and the city-dwellers had become, as a group, the 'class enemy'. The urban-dwellers, so the Khmers Rouges leaders told them, were in league with the US imperialists and thus collectively responsible for the sufferings of the peasantry. For the guerrillas, Phnom Penh was more malignant than the 'Great Wen' (boil or carbuncle) of 19th century London was to any English peasant or bucolic reactionary, and was to be drained of its 'tainted' people. The north-west town of Battambang, its population swollen to over quarter of a million by refugees, suffered the same fate as the capital.

Although apologists for DK defend the expulsion as a necessary precaution against possible US bombing and mass starvation, it is clear that the decision was made on ideological grounds some months beforehand and in secret. Even bearing hindsight in mind, it was extremely unlikely at the time that the United States would bomb the city. The US Congress had put an end to the American bombing almost two years earlier and the war-weary American people had no stomach for a fresh war in Asia. Feeding the bloated urban populations did present a real problem, but the Vietnamese communists managed to feed the people of Saigon without recourse to draconian measures when that city fell a fortnight later. Undoubtedly, there was a compelling case for the orderly, humane and voluntary repatriation of the refugees to their home villages, but none of these caveats apply to what happened after 17 August 1975.

Building 'utopia' from day one of the revolution

There were two interrelated immediate reasons for the expulsions. The first was the relative weakness of the Khmers Rouges forces, which had been only just strong enough to defeat Lon Nol's army. The second was the fear that the cities would act as reservoirs of counterrevolution. It did not matter that over half the urban population were civilian refugees from the countryside, or that most city-dwellers welcomed the end of hostilities and favoured national reconciliation. For the high command of the secretive *angkar*, it was a case of 'if you're not with us, you're against us'—logic that they shared with both Sihanouk and Lon Nol, for whom dissent meant treason. Underlying the immediate practical necessity of evacuation (as the Khmers Rouges saw it) was an ideological imperative. The Khmers Rouges leadership was determined to begin the total transformation of Cambodian society on the day that Phnom Penh and Battambang fell and this was predicated on the dispersal of the old urban populations. Even before the end of the war, the Khmers Rouges had begun its radical experiments in the so-called liberated zones under its control. The ideological basis for the expulsions is clear from Pol Pot's orders, summed up by a Khmers Rouges regimental political commissar quoted by the historian Ben Kiernan:

Immediately upon liberation on 17 April 1975, there was a Special Centre Assembly for Cabinet Ministers and all Zone and Region Secretaries. Eight points were made at the Assembly, by Pol Pot:

1. Evacuate people from all towns.
2. Abolish all markets.
3. Abolish Lon Nol regime currency, and withhold the revolutionary currency that had been printed.
4. Defrock all Buddhist monks, and put them to work growing rice.
5. Execute all leaders of the Lon Nol regime beginning with the top leaders.
6. Establish high-level cooperatives throughout the country with communal eating.
7. Expel the entire Vietnamese minority population.
8. Dispatch troops to the borders, particularly the Vietnamese border.

Here, we have the nub of Pol Pot's plan for the sweeping transformation of Cambodian society. The construction of 'utopia' would begin from the first day of the revolution on the ruins of the old society. The towns were seen as parasitic growths and hotbeds of spies, foreign ideologies and capitalism. The urban populations, henceforth known as 'new people', would join the 'old people' in productive labour on collective farms in the countryside and their labour would provide the wealth to build the future paradise. There would be no freedom of movement and no freedom to choose one's occupation. Families would be split up. There would be no singing or dancing save to glorify the regime, and even the music of the new regime sounded discordant to Khmer ears.

The people would be denied spiritual sustenance. The Khmers are an intensely religious people and their religion has often served as a consolation for the hardships of life, but Pol Pot would have none of it. Monks were defrocked and put to work and their orders closed. The regime would not tolerate any other source of authority that might undermine its own. The January 1976 Constitution of DK granted freedom of worship, but cancelled it with the qualification 'except for reactionary religion'. The entire country would be sealed off from the 'contaminating' influences of the outside world. There was to be no respite after the rigours of war, no chance for the people to heal their wounds and mourn their dead. There would be no time for love, no reconciliation after a fratricidal war that had pitted brother against brother and sister against sister. The new people would submit or perish. There would only be a life of unremitting toil in the paddy fields and, in what was really the socialisation of poverty, the entire population would be levelled to the position of the poorest and least educated member of society. The country, as David Chandler has put it, would become one huge 'prison farm'.

Partly this was an act of revenge, but the regime saw it as necessary for the rebuilding of Cambodian society according to a utopian blueprint dreamed up in the remote jungles, based on a romanticisation of the primitive communism of the hill peoples among whom Pol Pot and his comrades had lived. The dream formed the basis for the regime's Four-Year Plan of 1976, which foresaw the rapid development of light industry, followed by heavy industry, regardless of the lack of skilled labour, raw materials, infrastructure and professional expertise. Cambodia would catch up and overtake the capitalist West by an act of will, and Cambodians would regain their true stature as the people who had built Angkor, dreamed Pol Pot. The foreign exchange needed for this plan would be earned by increasing Cambodia's agrarian exports. Cambodia would, in a gigantic act of Maoist-style 'voluntarism', acquire the wealth with which to industrialise the country and build a glorious future. That future justified whatever hardships the people might suffer.

Although Pol Pot claimed that his revolution had no foreign models, and he kept the existence of the Communist Party a secret until a marathon radio speech in September 1977, one of his models was Stalin's Russia, where 'primitive socialist accumulation' was based on the violent expropriation of the peasantry and slave labour. The extreme voluntarism—the belief that human beings can overcome all obstacles by sheer willpower alone—mirrored the ideology of Maoist China, which had produced the absurd Great Leap Forward of the late 1950s that ended in the catastrophic famine of the early 1960s. To this, we might add Stalin's idea of socialism in one country, Mao's doctrine of self-reliance, and Kim Il Sung's *Juche* dogma, all of which preached autarchy, or the virtue of countries going it alone economically and socially.

Yet, on another level, DK *was* unique. As Philip Short has pointed out in his magisterial study of Pol Pot, some semblance of 'normal life' was possible in Stalin's USSR or in Nazi Germany, whereas in DK it was impossible. There was no private life nor any respite from the incessant demands of the state and its black clad minions.

Pol Pot believed Cambodia's transformation would be so swift that there would be no need for 'transitional' mechanisms such as money and markets. Private property was abolished overnight. Eating was socialised, both on moral grounds and to ensure collection of the maximum surpluses of agricultural commodities for sale overseas. As a result, towards the end of the regime there was often almost nothing on the communal tables to eat, but it was a crime for individuals to supplement their meagre rations with 'wild food' from the forests as Khmers had always done in times of privation. A Khmer woman told the Australian communist journalist Darryl Bullen soon after the liberation from Pol Pot that members of her commune were forbidden to eat from the wild sugar palms, coconut trees and wild bananas, even though they were starving. Although food was comparatively plentiful during the first year of the new regime, supplies rapidly dwindled afterwards. Chronic malnutrition coupled with overwork and medical neglect carried off hundreds of thousands to the grave. In some places, the people resembled the walking skeletons, the so-called Musselmen of Hitler's concentration camps, or the *Zeks* of Stalin's Gulag.

How many people perished during DK?

The Khmers Rouges soldiers and cadres would sing, apparently without irony, their national anthem, which began: 'Bright red blood which covers the fields and plains/Of Kampuchea, our motherland!' Given that many of their victims were dispatched in the fields with a blow to the back of the head or neck with an ox cart axle, the words take on a grim meaning unintended by their writer.

The degree of hardship and terror differed from region to region and from time to time in the same regions. The Khmers Rouges had replaced the old provinces with seven large zones and these were further broken down into 32 smaller administrative regions. Some of these, such as the North Eastern and Eastern zones, were comparatively well run (sometimes local administrations were almost 'benign' comments the Australian author Margaret Slocomb, a long-time resident of Phnom Penh and author of a book on the post Pol Pot People's Republic of Kampuchea). Local administrators differed: some were cruel thugs, such as Ta Mok (known as The Butcher) and the other commanders of the North Western and Western zones, who were notorious for their brutal incompetence. Others were merely ignorant and incompetent, whereas survivors remember others for their kindness. Members of the Muslim Cham minority suffered terribly, with their numbers dropping by 36 per cent during DK, 'a proportion sharply higher than the losses sustained by the rest of the population' Milton Osborne tells us. On the other hand, the 2.5 to 3 million 'old people' who had lived in Khmer Rouges-controlled zones before 1975 were generally treated better than the 4 to 5 million 'new people' who fell into Pol Pot's hands after the fall of Phnom Penh. Overall, however, life was hard and became worse as the years wore on.

The exact death toll during DK will probably never be known, although 1.7 million is a reasonable estimate. One problem is that after 1979, the incoming People's Republic of Kampuchea (PRK) government sought to legitimate itself by exaggerating the number of dead, which they routinely put at 3 million. The Vietnamese also blurred the political nature of the Pol Pot regime and spoke of an 'Asian Auschwitz' when in fact the closest parallel with DK is not Nazi Germany but Stalinist Russia or Maoist China. Another problem is that there was no way of keeping accurate population statistics during the five years of war that preceded Pol Pot, so calculating the exact number of people in Cambodia as of 17 April 1975 is difficult. Millions of people were displaced from the countryside between 1970 and 1975 and although there is no precise record of the number of war-related deaths these were colossal, probably in the high hundreds of thousands, many of them a result of the maniacal US bombing. (A Finnish Commission of Inquiry estimated that the war cost 600 000 lives, while the writer Eva Myslwiec considers one million to be likely.)

The population at the time of the Khmers Rouges takeover in 1975 was 7.3 million according to the CIA, 7.1 million according to the UN, although the last complete census was taken in 1962. In fact, it may have been as high as 8 million as all the statistics are a bit rubbery. Perhaps as many as 200 000 people fled or were expelled immediately after the DK victory. (The overwhelming bulk of the Vietnamese minority was deported across the eastern border, and perhaps 50 000 people fled to Thailand.) Six years later, after the fall of DK, the total population had decreased by around one million: PRK census figures put the population at 6.7 million in 1981, although the CIA believes that it was around 6.3 million to 6.4 million. This is a decrease of around 20 to 25 per cent, despite the steep increase in the birth rate after the liberation from Pol Pot and the return of around 400 000 refugees after 1980.

It is clear that we are looking at a demographic catastrophe. Given that the birth rate between 1965 and 1970 was 2.8 per cent, Cambodia's population should have risen to around 9 million by 1980 had there been no war and no DK. The Finnish Commission concluded that Cambodia's population fell by 30 per cent in the decade after 1970 and estimates of a net loss of around 1.7 million people during the DK years ring true. How many were executed is a moot point: the Finnish Commission calculated up to 150 000 murdered, Chandler suggests 200 000 and PRK figures were much higher. If Chandler is correct, the Khmers Rouges executed just under three per cent of the country's population. By way of comparison, the equivalent figures for hypothetical holocausts in Australia, the United States and the United Kingdom at the beginning of the 21st century would be 600 000, 8 850 000 and 1 800 000 executed respectively. Similar death rates from all causes as in DK would be astronomical.

Enemies of the people

The new regime showed its brutal colours from the first days of the revolution. Pol Pot had stipulated in his 17 April speech to the Khmers Rouges assembly that there would be no mercy for the cadres of the defeated regime. Foreign embassies were not respected as places of sanctuary: even the gates of the Soviet legation were blown in with a bazooka. Prince Sirik Matak was taken from the French Embassy and executed. Displaying exemplary courage, 'nothing in his life became him like the leaving of it'. One of the most harrowing passages of François Bizot's autobiographical book, *The Gate*, concerns the fate of Madame Long Boret (wife of the Republic's penultimate prime minister) and her infant son, whom Bizot and a gendarme were forced to turn away from the embassy gates. Thirty years on, Bizot's anguish still burns as he recalls her desperate pleas to them to save her child.

The arm of revenge reached right down the hierarchy of the defeated regime. On the day of the evacuation, Haing Ngor narrowly escaped induction into a 'recruitment centre' set up by the Khmers Rouges on the outskirts of the city to lure unwary Lon Nol soldiers. The centre was full of former soldiers and officers, some of whom waved to their fellows if they saw them on the road, inviting them in to share what they saw as their good luck. They were loaded onto trucks, driven into the country, and shot. Afterwards, it would be the turn of the intellectuals and professional employees, even of skilled manual workers supposedly 'tainted' by the city. Later, the Khmers Rouges leader Thiounn Mumm lured overseas Khmers back home by promising them a role in the reconstruction of their country, only to have them executed when they stepped back on Cambodian soil.

Intellectuals and 'book learning' were treated with particular contempt in Pol Pot's Cambodia, although one also senses the fear that the new regime had of them. The wearing of spectacles was sufficient to brand one as an intellectual and therefore an enemy of the people, and the consequences were often lethal. The relentless animosity towards intellectuals and experts was fundamentally self-defeating, but a hallmark of a regime in which ignorance was a virtue. Haing Ngor records one of many interminable harangues delivered by Khmers Rouges cadres to the 'new people' when they reached the countryside:

> 'We don't need the technology of the capitalists,' he [the cadre] went on. 'Under our new system, we don't need to send our young people to school. Our school is the farm. The land is our paper. The plow [sic] is our pen. We will "write" by plowing [sic]. We don't need to give exams or award certificates. Knowing how to farm and knowing how to dig canals—those are our certificates . . . We don't need doctors anymore. They are not necessary. If someone needs to have their intestines removed, I will do it'. He made a cutting motion with an imaginary knife across his stomach. 'It is easy. There is no need to learn how to do it by going to school.'

Shortly afterwards, the anguished doctor was forced to watch as two young Khmers Rouges 'doctors' incompetently administered a lethal injection of thiamine to a sick baby. 'The country was ruled by the ignorant,' Haing Ngor laments. Three examples could serve as symbols of the officially sponsored ignorance of the DK years: the conversion of the National Library at Phnom Penh into a pigsty, the transformation of the state archives building into a dwelling place for the top cadres' servants, and the closure of the state agricultural college and its conversion into a Khmers Rouges ammunition dump. In the end, this contempt for academic learning and technical expertise was to cause the regime to commit monumental blunders and contribute to its downfall. The engineer and memoirist Pin Yathay records trucks being cut up and turned into ploughs, canals dug in which the water would have to flow uphill, dams built without spillways and farming practices that would make an agronomist wince. Contempt for medical knowledge was to cause the deaths of hundreds of thousands of people struck down by overwork and illness in an infernal calculus that saw them as expendable.

Again, there are parallels here with the Stalin and Mao regimes. Stalin's GPU massacred 14 000 Polish officers, professionals and intellectuals at Katyn Wood in 1941 and earlier tried and executed countless Soviet experts as 'saboteurs'. Mao launched the Hundred Flowers campaign that 'lured the snakes from their holes', as he puts it, in 1950s China and followed this up with the massive persecution of intellectuals during the so-called Cultural Revolution. Contempt for experts was also a cornerstone of the Maoist ideology of self-reliance.

The Khmers Rouges leadership

Paradoxically, those who presided over DK were a close-knit band of well-educated men and women, related by ties of blood and marriage. Hu Nim, Hou Yuon and Khieu Samphan, the 'Three Ghosts' who had fled Sihanouk's White Terror back in 1967, had Paris PhDs and Brother Number One, as Pol Pot was known, had studied in Paris and worked as a teacher in the Cambodian capital before he slipped away to the jungles. Brother Number Three, Ieng Sary, a scholar with an aptitude for mathematics, had also studied in Paris, as had another Khmers Rouges leader, Son Sen, who became director of studies of the National

Teaching Institute at Phnom Penh after his return from France in the 1950s. Pol Pot's first wife, Khieu Ponnary (whose sister was married to Ieng Sary), was the first Cambodian woman to earn her *baccalaureate* and she had attended literary *soirées* with Sihanouk and the top French officials in Phnom Penh. Many of the Khmers Rouges leaders were from comfortable backgrounds and had never done manual labour, although Pol Pot claimed to have been a rubber worker when 'elected' to the DK National Assembly in March 1976 and other leaders claimed to have been peasants. Thiounn Mumm and his brother Prasith were grandchildren of Thiounn, an immensely rich and powerful civil servant under the French. Pol Pot, whose real name was Saloth Sar, came from a well-off farming family with palace connections—indeed his sister, Sarouen, was King Monivong's favourite concubine, and the king had died in her arms at his Bokor estate back in 1941. Pol Pot had studied radio mechanics in Paris in the 1950s, and while there he had mixed in anti-colonialist circles and joined the Communist Party of France (CPF).

When Pol Pot and Ieng Sary were in Paris, the CPF was the largest single party in France and although it was one of the largest communist parties outside of the Soviet bloc, it had a reputation for slavishly following the Moscow line. As a result, the young men absorbed a solid dose of the Stalinist ideology that was to form the bedrock of their ideas. The features of this were always apparent: dogmatism; narrow-mindedness; contempt for democracy; a belief in the infallibility of the party line and the party leader; and a deterministic view of history that saw the final triumph of communism as inevitable, and that justified the most brutal means as necessary in achieving the utopian end. To this were later added specifically Maoist elements, the idea of self-reliance in particular, which held that Third World revolutionaries should scorn western technology and expertise, rely on their own strength and learn from the people. While there is much to be said for respecting the people, the downside is the worship of ignorance. Pol Pot also turned to the idea of the peasants as the revolutionary class as a result of Maoist dogma. The working class, such as it was in Cambodia, was to get short shrift at his hands and whereas Marx had sneered at 'the idiocy of rural life' Pol Pot took the Maoist idea of surrounding the cities from the countryside a stage further and emptied them of their people. In his mental universe, the poor peasantry were to be the locomotive of Cambodian history and all the urban classes were considered reactionary. The evacuation was an integral part of a great levelling that he saw as necessary before Cambodia could become great.

While in Paris, the young revolutionary must also have become aware of the Stalinist purges and show trials of Old Bolsheviks during the 1930s. He must also have learned shortly after his return to Cambodia of Khrushchev's 1956 'secret speech' that retrospectively denounced these crimes. However, given his own later methods, Pol Pot must have agreed with Mao's rejection of the speech as revisionist. For hardline Stalinists like Pol Pot, the victims of the trials were forever condemned as spies and wreckers, and the lesson was that one must remain forever vigilant against such elements in one's own party. On the evidence, Pol Pot did not murder party secretary Tou Samouth, as Ben Kiernan claimed, but he most certainly did turn on 'Khmer-Viet Minh' who had returned from Hanoi from at least 1973. Moreover, in August 1975, in the worst traditions of Stalinism, the veteran leftist Hou Yuon was murdered, most likely on Pol Pot's orders. Hou Yuon had opposed the evacuation of the cities even at the 17 April assembly where Pol Pot roughed out his immediate program, and four months later he made a public speech denouncing the expulsions, calling on the party to show mercy to the people. It was a brave, humane and alas futile gesture for which he was executed and his body thrown into the Mekong. If this was the fate of a high-ranking party leader who dared voice dissent, there could be no freedom of speech for any other subject of DK.

Hou Yuon's fate presaged a later, much larger hunt for spies within the party that resembled the witch-burning frenzies and the hunt for heretics by the Inquisition in Europe. In 1977, following torture, Hu Nim 'confessed' to having been an agent of the CIA, although like the

Old Bolshevik Nikolai Bukharin before him during the Moscow trials, he left clues to posterity attesting to his innocence. He confessed to serving the CIA by 'presenting my activities as those of a "progressive", whereas my true essence was reactionary'. The admission was worthless, obtained as it was by repeated whippings and 'stuffings' with water, but we should not see everything he wrote in Tuol Sleng prison as the invention of DK's inquisitors. Reading between the lines, we can see Hu Nim as a revolutionary who had grown disillusioned with the trajectory of the movement to which he had dedicated his life. Most likely there were many other loyal party members who despaired at a dream gone sour, their doubts regarded as treachery by a party leadership ever more deeply steeped in blood.

Hu Nim hinted that he had grown tired of the ongoing terror, that he wanted the people to live normal lives in a stable and prosperous country at peace with its socialist neighbour Vietnam. He recorded the opinions of the other dissident party leaders that the state ought not rely on sheer muscle power, but should mechanise and accept foreign aid. Furthermore, he reported that other socialist countries, even North Korea, had currency, so why not Cambodia? Pol Pot, he hinted, did not want a 'system of plenty', but one in which the people were worked long hours for the benefit of the state.

Taken together, these beliefs were heresy in the Cambodian dystopia. The confession reveals that Hu Nim and others like him supported an alternative platform: a gentler and more gradual road to socialism. He was tortured and murdered for his pains. However, as the Australian scholar Ben Kiernan has pointed out, Hu Nim was a talkative person who was used to winning arguments. Although on the surface he appears to have submitted to the arguments of Brother Number 1, in the court of history he had the final word.

In the final years of the DK regime, fear and paranoia burned out of control within the party, with tens of thousands of members arrested and executed, many after torture in the notorious S21 establishment set up at Tuol Sleng in the Phnom Penh suburbs under a former teacher called Duch (François Bizot's former captor). Duch's meticulous records show that around 20 000 unfortunates were tortured and executed at Tuol Sleng and that the interrogations did not stop until the Vietnamese soldiers were almost in the city's suburbs. There were only eight survivors, three adults and five children.

Hatred of Vietnam, glorification of Cambodia

As the purges unfolded, they revealed Pol Pot's extraordinary hatred of his communist neighbour, the Socialist Republic of Vietnam, which he had come to see as his country's greatest enemy. Although the charge of being in league with the CIA was still routine, suspected enemies were increasingly described as having 'Vietnamese minds inside Cambodian bodies'. Among the first of these were the old Pracheachon leaders, Non Suon and Keo Meas, who were arrested, tortured and executed in late 1976. The pair's downfall came as a result of their dating the foundation of the Communist Party to 1951, the year of the formation of the Khmer People's Revolutionary Party, rather than 1960, when Pol Pot rose through the ranks at the Communist Party conference held at the Phnom Penh railway workshops.

The obsession with the Vietnamese 'threat' is linked to another central element of Pol Pot's ideology: an extreme Khmer nationalism that he shared with Lon Nol and which was close to the racist mystical mumbo-jumbo of Keng Vannsak's 'Khmer–Mon Institute' during the Khmer Republic. He once boasted that the people who had built Angkor could do anything, and bragged of his superb leadership, which allegedly resulted from Khmer nationality. This racist chauvinism was to lead Pol Pot down an increasingly irrational and blood-soaked path and to DK's destruction at the hands of the Vietnamese.

Marxism is an internationalist doctrine, even in its deformed Marxist-Leninist variant, but Pol Pot's ideology was as nationalist as it was Marxist-Leninist. One can see traces of this even in his formative political years in Paris when he signed an article in a revolutionary magazine under the pseudonym of 'The Original Khmer'. Although Pol

Pot sheltered under the wing of the Vietnamese communists in the jungles of Cambodia's north-east for many years he resented his subservient position and what he saw as the patronising attitudes of his communist 'elder brothers', who insisted that Cambodia had to wait its turn for 'liberation' until the United States and its Saigon client had been defeated.

In 1964–65, Pol Pot had travelled to China and Vietnam, and the Vietnamese communist leader Le Duan had ticked him off for his impatient nationalism, telling him to subordinate his own struggle to that of Vietnam. From Pol Pot's point of view, this advice made little sense: given that Sihanouk's police were hunting down Cambodian communists in the towns and cities, they had little choice but to flee to the jungles and wage armed struggle. Cambodian nationalism had always had a reactive quality to it, and from the 1930s on it was often at least as much anti-Vietnamese as anti-French, sometimes more so.

Lon Nol had ordered hideous pogroms against the Vietnamese in 1970 and Pol Pot shared the same irrational and mystical Khmer nationalism that led to such racist atrocities. According to the CIA, open fighting broke out between Vietnamese and Cambodian communist units as early as 1973, following the Paris Peace Accords, and there are reports of clashes as early as 1971. Significantly, the last two planks of Pol Pot's 'action program' announced at the 17 April Assembly were to 'expel the entire Vietnamese population' (something of which Lon Nol would have heartily approved), and to 'dispatch troops to the borders, particularly the Vietnamese border', where fighting broke out shortly afterwards over disputed islands in the Gulf of Siam. Cambodians had had reason for dissatisfaction with the border since the French had drawn up the arbitrary Brevié Line to demarcate it in 1939, but Pol Pot's actions dramatically weakened the possibility of compromise. More than that, the gesture hints at the paranoia and delusions of grandeur that were to be his undoing. In later years, as famine broke out, this overarching 'ideological' antipathy for Vietnam meshed with Pol Pot's need to divert attention from the results of his regime's failed ultra-left policies. This bore out Dr Johnson's celebrated observation that 'patriotism is the last refuge of a scoundrel'.

International dimensions of the Kampuchea–Vietnam conflict

Pol Pot's antipathy towards Vietnam also impelled him into an alliance with China, which for its part was delighted to gain an ally against Hanoi, which it saw as an upstart agent of 'Soviet social imperialism' on its southern border. The communist world, it should be recalled, had been riven in two by the Sino-Soviet split of 1960, when Mao denounced the leaders of the USSR as revisionists seeking to impose their domination over the rest of the bloc. Pol Pot suspected that the Vietnamese wanted to revive the old federation of Indochina under their hegemony and his suspicions deepened when they signed a treaty of friendship and cooperation with the Lao communist regime in 1977, a move he interpreted as encirclement. After delivering the September 1977 speech in which he announced the existence of the Communist Party of Kampuchea, Pol Pot flew to Beijing for discussions with Hua Guofeng, the successor to Mao and the 'Gang of Four'. The hostile alignment of the Indochinese states within the communist world was completed in 1978, when Vietnam, suspicious of China's ambitions in Southeast Asia, signed a 25-year treaty with the USSR.

The move accelerated the deterioration of relations between DK and Vietnam. DK broke off diplomatic relations with Hanoi in early 1978. There had been sporadic fighting along the border and in December 1977, the Vietnamese decided to teach Pol Pot a lesson by dispatching an invasion force that penetrated deep into eastern Cambodia and routed Khmers Rouges forces. They soon withdrew but took a number of Cambodian villagers with them and, more importantly, there was an increasing stream of Khmers Rouges over the border as

Pol Pot's purges began to spiral out of control and local Khmers Rouges commanders attempted to defend themselves or escape. Pol Pot was suspicious of Eastern Zone cadres such as Sao Phim (a former militant of the old Indochinese Communist Party) and some hundreds of them were tortured and killed at Tuol Sleng prison during this period. Sao Phim himself committed suicide after receiving a sinister summons to travel to the capital for 'discussions'. Among those who fled to Vietnam in 1977 and 1978 were two men called Heng Samrin and Hun Sen. The latter, a young Khmers Rouges regimental commander, had lost an eye during the war against Lon Nol, and is Cambodia's premier and 'strongman' today. Heng Samrin headed the Vietnamese sponsored National Salvation Front, in effect a government-in-exile formed largely of disaffected former Khmers Rouges. Heng Samrin's forces participated in the invasion of Cambodia on Christmas Day 1978 and he was president of the PRK between 1979 and Sihanouk's return in 1991. Today he is honorary president of the ruling Cambodian People's Party.

The downfall of Democratic Kampuchea

Vietnam and Cambodia were on a collision course, with Pol Pot acting as a proxy in a broader global conflict, much as Lon Nol had acted as a surrogate in a wider war until 1975. Increasingly belligerent and buoyed by an unrealistic sense of power, Pol Pot rejected a Vietnamese offer to submit the border dispute to international arbitration and both sides massed troops at the frontier. Khmers Rouges guerrillas increasingly slipped over the border and raided villages on the Vietnamese side, committing horrible atrocities that were recorded by the journalist Nayan Chanda for *Far Eastern Economic Review* at the time. It was necessary, claimed the Khmers Rouges, to 'annihilate' the Vietnamese on their own territory. What this meant was that 'In house after house bloated, rotting bodies of men, women and children lay strewn about. Some were beheaded, some had their bellies ripped open, some were missing limbs, others eyes.' General Tran Van Tra, the commander of the Vietnamese army in the Mekong delta, seethed with rage and another officer who witnessed the massacres was 'overcome with nausea' when he recalled them 12 months later, Chanda has written. The raids displaced almost half a million people on the Vietnamese side of the border, and caused around 100 000 hectares of farmland to be temporarily abandoned. While the local Vietnamese army commanders chafed, the Hanoi government continued its fruitless efforts at a negotiated solution. In one memorable speech, Pol Pot boasted that the disparity in size and population between Cambodia and Vietnam was of no consequence, for if every Khmers Rouges soldier killed 30 Vietnamese, they would win the war. He was also banking on Chinese support, but the Chinese were no more inclined to dispatch troops to help him than the Americans had been to protect Lon Nol.

The end came swiftly for the Pol Pot regime. On Christmas Day 1978, an invasion force over 100 000 strong, backed by tanks, artillery and aviation, poured over the border from Vietnam, driving the Khmers Rouges forces before them. Although Pol Pot had always boasted that his army had defeated the Americans, this was false: he had won a civil war against the ramshackle and corrupt Khmer Republic, not its powerful backer. Now the Khmers Rouges guerrillas faced one of the most formidable, battle-hardened armies the world has seen. The Vietnamese had competent generals and superior firepower, and they were not blinded to reality by mystical rhetoric. They also had the advantage of fighting a regime that had long ago forfeited what little support it ever had among the Cambodian people, most of whom welcomed its demise.

Phnom Penh fell to the advancing Vietnamese soldiers on 7 January 1979 and Pol Pot fled before them in a helicopter, with Ieng Sary, Nuon Chea and the other top leaders scurrying away by train towards Battambang. The Khmers Rouges guerrillas were thrown back in disorder to the remote borders with Thailand. They had been smashed and the country liberated, albeit by the Khmers' traditional enemies from the east. It should have been the end of the Khmers Rouges but,

Pol Pot in 1981. (Courtesy Newspix)

as has been so often the case, Cambodia's fate was to be decided by forces outside of the country, and the suffering of the people was not yet over. Pol Pot, however, was never to regain power, despite fighting a guerrilla war along the borders for many years.

The old despot died while under house arrest in a Cambodian frontier village in April 1998, a sad, sick old man of 70 years, despised even by the rump of the Khmers Rouges, who cremated his corpse in a makeshift pyre of old rubber sandals and other rubbish. He never expressed remorse for his disastrous policies. The American journalist Nate Thayer, who interviewed Pol Pot shortly before his death, said, 'The one regret I had in my several encounters with Pol Pot was that he didn't feel sorry. He felt what he did was justified.' To the end, this old schoolmaster-turned-guerrilla epitomised what a wiser revolutionary, Leon Trotsky, had meant when he wrote that the ultra-left sectarian saw life as a great school and himself as the teacher. The Cambodian people had failed him, not the other way round. Pol Pot liked to think he was in tune with the ineluctable laws of history, but in the end he failed and turned his country into a bloody shambles. We cannot forecast how much weight future historians will give to the three and a half years of his regime but if the aftermaths of other outbreaks of mass butchery provide any guide, the vivid memories will fade. The Young Turks killed one and a half million Armenians in 1915–16, but Adolf Hitler recognised the human potential for forgetting when he sold his coming Holocaust to wavering generals by asking them 'who today remembers the extermination of the Armenians?' Sadly, he was right. Perhaps in the future some other budding mass murderer will ask the same question of Cambodia.

9
PAINFUL TRANSITION: THE PEOPLE'S REPUBLIC OF KAMPUCHEA

It is now over a quarter of a century since the demise of Pol Pot's Democratic Kampuchea, during which time the country has undergone a number of painful transitions. Cambodia today is still desperately poor and underdeveloped and although it has clawed its way back from barbarism, dark shadows still linger and huge problems beset the Khmer people. Some of these are new. Others seem timeless and have a sense of *déjà vu*, not the least of which is official corruption and authoritarian government. Cambodia is also a divided society and one of the greatest sources of discord concerns attitudes towards the Vietnamese invasion/liberation that began on Christmas Day 1978. To many Khmers, the 7 January holiday commemorates the anniversary of their country's liberation from Pol Pot's tyranny and the rebirth of the nation. To others, it is a day of infamy marking the beginning of over a decade of foreign occupation.

Cambodia has lived through two regimes since Pol Pot. Immediately after the Vietnamese invasion, the leaders of the Hanoi-backed National Salvation Front declared the People's Republic of Kampuchea

(PRK) on a broad platform put forward at Snoul on the eastern border in December 1978. This regime (renamed the State of Cambodia in 1989) lasted until the Paris Peace Agreement of 1991, when the warring factions in Cambodian politics, helped by international diplomatic initiatives and the end of the Cold War, decided on a course of national reconciliation and democratisation that resulted two years later in the reconstitution of the Kingdom of Cambodia.

The PRK failed in its avowed socialist objectives and its non-communist successor has yet to live up to the democratic hopes of its domestic and international sponsors. Although the Kingdom of Cambodia holds regular elections, like the old Sihanouk and Lon Nol regimes it is an authoritarian state ruled by a strongman—the ex-Khmer Rouge guerrilla Hun Sen, who first rose to prominence under the PRK, abandoning its socialist principles along the way. Given the catastrophes of the recent past, and the country's longer history of authoritarian rule, it was unlikely that Cambodia could make a pain-less transition to democracy, with respect for human rights, the rule of law and social justice. It was also unlikely that the PRK could introduce successful socialist measures in a country traumatised by Pol Pot's bloody version of socialism and in the face of the patent indifference and even hostility of the people.

Whether Cambodia will be able to overcome its entrenched prob-lems of underdevelopment and authoritarianism remains to be seen. Today, around 50 per cent of Cambodia's budget comes from overseas aid, corruption is rife even at the highest levels of government and the civil service, poverty and landlessness are increasing, serious social evils fester, there is an HIV/AIDS pandemic, and the country is facing a burgeoning ecological crisis. For all their faults, however, the post-DK regimes have done much to rebuild a shattered society, and the Pol Pot years are a receding nightmare for older Cambodians and a bogeyman story for their children.

The PRK's manifesto

Cambodia's deliverance from its modern Dark Age began on 2 December 1978, when a 44-year-old former Khmers Rouges Eastern Zone commander stood up to read a manifesto to his Khmer People's Revolutionary Party (KPRP) comrades at a captured rubber plantation near Snoul on the Vietnamese border. The speaker, Heng Samrin, had fled over the border earlier that year and had become the leader of the Solidarity Front for National Salvation, created under the auspices of the Vietnamese communists. He promised to liberate Cambodia from those he described as tyrants who had reduced the people to neo-slavery. He swore to rebuild Cambodia as 'a truly peaceful, independent, democratic, neutral, and non-aligned country . . .'. Once the Khmers Rouges had been defeated there would be national elections and a new constitution. The people would have the Right to vote and to live, work and travel where they wished within the country.

The new regime would be avowedly socialist but there would be a mixed economy, with rural cooperatives established only with the full consent of the peasants, and there would be an eight-hour working day. Banks, currency and trade would be re-established. Family life and religion would be respected and the state would provide its citizens with proper health care, and education at all levels. There would be support for war victims, the elderly and the numerous orphans. Finally, Heng Samrin held out the hope of national reconciliation, promising that the new state would be lenient with former Pol Pot supporters who had genuinely reformed.

Given the state of the country at the time, it was as ambitious and lofty a declaration as any in human history and it was sincerely meant. It would also prove far more difficult to implement than its authors imagined. The PRK did try to keep its promises but, as American writer Evan Gottesman has said, the hints of pluralism in Heng Samrin's speech were subsumed within 'the sort of inclusion espoused throughout the communist world'. Although the French priest François Ponchaud had coined the term 'Year Zero' to describe Cambodia at the inception of DK in April 1975, in another sense it is more fitting to apply it to the country in early 1979, when normal society had collapsed and the country was on the verge of extinction. The new leaders proclaimed a new revolution, but as Gottesman eloquently puts it: 'there was nothing to overturn, just an emptiness to fill'.

Beyond the imagination of mankind

The Australian communist Darryl Bullen, who flew up to Phnom Penh from Ho Chi Minh City shortly after the liberation from Pol Pot, described 'a pock-marked landscape' with 'gaping craters, the size of buses' scattered to the horizon, 'the . . . legacy of saturation bombing by B-52s'. The journalist John Pilger landed on the 'beaconless runway' at Pochentong airport some months later, and described 'a pyramid of rusting cars' on the edge of a forest, 'like objects in a mirage'. The cities were still virtually deserted, he wrote, and the hustle and bustle of Asia stopped at the PRK's borders. Although Pilger is often (sometimes very unfairly) criticised for exaggeration, he was right when, struggling to find words to describe what he saw, he quoted the correspondent of *The Times* at the liberation of Belsen, who had written, 'It is my duty to describe something beyond the imagination of mankind' and added, 'That is how I and others felt in the summer of 1979' in Cambodia.

The enormity of what Cambodia had suffered is beyond the imagination of most of us. A staggering 30 per cent of the population had died since Lon Nol's coup in March 1970 sent the country down the road to disaster. A country already devastated by war had been reduced to the extremes of destitution, its citizens pauperised and almost all the infrastructure of civilised society destroyed. There was no currency or banks, no markets or public transport, and the country's roads and railways were badly damaged. There was no postal system, no telephones or telegraphs, no clean water supplies or sanitation services, hardly any electricity and no schools or hospitals. There were virtually no consumer goods. The people were in rags. There were virtually no professionals or skilled workers; as one historian of the period records, 'Only 15 per cent of the nation's intellectuals, doctors, engineers, educators, *et cetera*, remained in Cambodia by 7 January 1979'. The others were either dead or had fled. Of the 450 doctors in Cambodia before 1975, only one tenth remained. There had been around 1600 agricultural experts in the early 1970s, but this number had dwindled to only 200, including ten graduates, of whom one was a veterinary surgeon. The latter had his work cut out, for of an estimated two and a half million draught animals before the war and revolution, less than 800 000 had survived, most of them weakened or sick.

All was chaos, a kind of debilitated anarchy. The Vietnamese general Bui Tin observed 'hundreds of thousands of gaunt and diseased people, dazed as if they were returning from hell, [who] wandered shoeless along dusty roads . . . reduced to a state where they did not speak or smile any more'. Earlier, a Yugoslav television crew who had been granted access to Democratic Kampuchea observed that only Pol Pot smiled in that land of sorrow. Several hundred thousand people fled the country, but 400 000 people returned to chance their luck, joining the throngs who trekked from their places of exile to their old homes. Fear was their constant companion after living so long with death at their heels. Even at the end of Pol Pot's Democratic Kampuchea, there had been a final round of slaughter in some districts, with the Khmers Rouges forcing families to volunteer their strongest members, ostensibly for labour but in reality for execution. As historian Margaret Slocomb explains, 'Like roads and bridges, and a ripe harvest, human assets had to be destroyed to spite the conquerors.' One suspects it was also to prevent them from joining the invaders, arms in hand, to wreak vengeance on their tormentors.

Normal social life had also collapsed. Often, the old familial relationships had broken down, leaving people without safety networks in a society devoid of social welfare of any kind. There were many more females than males in the general population but significantly, the imbalance was not present in the under-16 age group. The children, however, had suffered greatly. Helen Ester, who went to Cambodia on behalf of the Australian Council for Overseas Aid in 1980, reported that 70 per cent of the children in a new Phnom Penh orphanage she visited were illiterate because education had ceased under Pol Pot. Of the 20 000 teachers before Pol Pot, less than 7000 remained and they had not practised their profession since the inception of DK. Ester wrote, 'I feel almost more shock at the past neglect of Kampuchean children than at the outright atrocities. The children suffered forced separation from nurturing and the love of their parents and relatives and the criminal neglect of their learning development.' Perhaps Cambodia's tragedy is summed up in Ester's report of an orphan who sang of 'how her mother and father died, of how her father's throat was cut and he died in a pool of blood'. It was, said the orphanage staff, the child's way of coping with the horror.

Cambodia was on the brink of famine when Vietnam invaded. The retreating Khmers Rouges soldiers took a quarter of the rice crop with them and burned down granaries and even destroyed the crops in the fields. Still more rice rotted on the ground as people deserted the DK's prison-villages, some for the nearest frontier, others for their old homes. In the midst of the chaos, much of the next rice crop was not planted. There was also a shortage of basic agricultural implements, seed, draught animals and means of transportation. Fish teemed in the rivers and in the Great Lake, but there were virtually no nets or boats to catch them. Although some food aid came from Vietnam and Eastern bloc countries, augmented by smaller amounts from some Western charities, it was not enough to stave off disaster. After living to see the end of DK, between 325 000 and 625 000 people died within the first year of liberation, many from starvation. By way of comparison, this alone is a disaster almost on the scale of the Irish famine of the mid-19th century.

Pragmatic policies of the new government

The new government, the Kampuchean People's Revolutionary Council, was established in Phnom Penh on 8 January 1979, under the presidency of Heng Samrin. It was basically a coalition, with Heng Samrin and Hun Sen representing the former Khmers Rouges who had broken with Pol Pot, and another group of former 'Khmer Viet Minh', such as Pen Sovann and Keo Chendra. The latter group had spent most of the time since 1954 in exile in Hanoi, although some had returned to fight Lon Nol during the early 1970s, only to flee Cambodia again to escape Pol Pot's assassins. There were also a number of non-socialist technocrats who wished to help rebuild their country.

Although avowedly socialist and revolutionary, the new government took a pragmatic approach to the country's economic affairs. Priority was given to getting basic services operating and encouraging food production, and to defence and foreign affairs. (As we shall see, the Khmers Rouges remained an irritant militarily and the new regime was isolated internationally.) All taxes on crops were waived for the first few years of the new regime. Vietnamese engineers and technicians re-started electricity and water supply plants, and as factory workers returned to their old workplaces there was a modest revival of industrial production, though this was hampered by a lack of spare parts, skilled labour and general infrastructure. The retreating Khmers Rouges had also sabotaged the few plants they had kept in production. In the first months, trade was carried on by barter, with cans of rice acting as units of exchange. As markets slowly revived, Vietnamese *dong* and Thai *baht* were used as currency until Cambodian *riels* could be printed.

In the countryside, the government allowed private farming but made some tentative steps towards collectivisation by organising peasants into *krom samakki*, or production solidarity groups, and by setting up a number of model villages in which work was done on a cooperative basis. However, as Belgian writer Viviane Frings has recorded, 'What emerged in fact after the anarchy of the first few months of 1979, was a reappearance of private ownership of the means of production, in accordance with the preferences of the peasants.' The PRK, despite its avowedly socialist principles, was never more than half-hearted about collectivisation. There were a number of practical factors involved here, including a lack of dedicated cadres and a dearth of state assistance to collective farms or cooperatives. The underlying reason, however, was that the government was afraid to push its program because, although non-coercive in the main, it smacked of the DK years, when the population was forced into collective forms of life and work. 'The Pol Pot experiment had alienated the people of all social strata from both socialist theory and practice', writes Margaret Slocomb, so 'If the revolution was to survive, the state had to secure the consent and full cooperation of the masses.' This would have been difficult even if DK had never existed, for as the anthropologist May Ebihara wrote in her classic 1968 study of traditional Cambodian rural society, 'A striking feature of Khmer village life is the lack of indigenous, traditional, organized associations, clubs, factions, or other groups that are formed on non-kin principles'. In the end, as Slocomb argues, the lukewarm socialism of the PRK failed, and where the regime was successful it was 'at the expense of its ideological principles'.

The PRK: an international outcast

The PRK years were marked by gruelling poverty, with the new regime and its Vietnamese sponsor attempting to rebuild a society almost from scratch. What was a daunting task was made much harder by the enforced international isolation of the PRK at the hands of ASEAN, China and the United States. Once again, Cambodians were suffering as a result of international political decisions beyond their control. The very countries that had conspired to drag Cambodia to its ruin were now set on blocking its recovery. Once again, Khmers were the victims of the Cold War and of age-old patterns of East Asian *Realpolitik* that preceded it. It was a case, as Oxfam's Eva Myslwiec argued, of 'punishing the poor' for offences they had never committed, regardless of disputes about the legitimacy of the Heng Samrin government. However, it must be acknowledged that the PRK regime contributed to Cambodia's isolation by its secretive and closed nature.

The rising big power in the East Asian region at this time was the People's Republic of China, itself an international pariah until it was brought in from the cold by the American President Richard Nixon in 1972. Although ostensibly Marxist internationalists, the Chinese leaders operated within a paradigm of international relations inherited from China's imperial past, when the Southeast Asian states were tributaries of the 'Middle Kingdom'. China had befriended Pol Pot partly out of ideological affinity; China was itself in the last throes of Mao Zedong's ultra-left Cultural Revolution when Pol Pot came to power. However, Chinese support continued after the death of Mao in 1976 and the subsequent downfall of the 'Gang of Four' ultra-leftists and their replacement with Deng Xiaoping's pragmatists, which suggests that China's Cambodia policy was driven primarily by perceived national self-interest rather than ideology. Central to this was China's growing animosity towards Vietnam, which it feared as a pro-Soviet expansionist usurper of its own 'rightful' sphere of influence in Southeast Asia. Relations between the Chinese and Vietnamese communists, once proverbially 'as close as lips and teeth', had rapidly deteriorated after 1975 and, as Australian specialist in international law Gary Klintworth puts it, had 'reverted to the kind of hostile dynamic the two countries had often shared over the previous two millennia'.

For these reasons, China had encouraged Pol Pot's belligerence towards Vietnam. DK would act as a counterweight to Vietnamese power in Indochina and serve as a buffer against its possible expansion into the rest of the region. It is unclear whether the Chinese wanted Pol Pot to goad the Vietnamese into a full-scale invasion, but they took full advantage of the opportunities the invasion provided to turn Cambodia into a military quagmire, to isolate Vietnam internationally and weaken it economically. The Chinese never had any intention of committing 'volunteers' as Pol Pot had hoped; they were content to cause Vietnam the maximum aggravation with the least damage to themselves. In the process, they helped create what looked like an intractable problem until Vietnamese troop withdrawals (completed in 1989) and the end of the Cold War created the opportunity for a negotiated solution.

The Chinese were perhaps surprised by the ease with which General Bui Tin's army overran Cambodia, however. In February 1979, both in order to teach Vietnam a lesson and to lessen Bui Tin's pressure on Pol Pot's guerrillas, China launched a massive invasion of Vietnam's northern provinces, capturing control of the border town of Lang Son before withdrawing a month later. Many of the world's governments welcomed the Chinese action. The People's Republic of Kampuchea was widely regarded around the world as a Vietnamese puppet and many international jurists believed that the Vietnamese invasion of Cambodia was an infringement of international law and the principle of national sovereignty. Be that as it may, an immediate consequence of the Chinese military operation was that Pol Pot's troops stormed out of their jungle hideouts and massacred undefended Cambodian villagers in revenge. The many governments that shared China's obsession with punishing Vietnam overlooked such bloody 'facts on the ground'. For Cambodian villagers in this period, the Vietnamese army was the only bulwark against the return of Pol Pot's murderous zealots, but for many of the world's leaders, the Khmers were pawns on the international chessboard. While the principle of national sovereignty should not be dismissed lightly, there were unusually compelling reasons for the Vietnamese invasion. In any case, behind the lofty talk of principles on all sides, there lurked more narrowly pragmatic and self-serving agendas.

China's Indochina policy won support in the United States and the non-communist countries of Southeast Asia. These countries had enjoyed warmer relations with China since Nixon's 1972 visit and these thawed further with the cessation of Chinese support for communist guerrilla insurgency in Thailand. The United States was still smarting from its crushing defeat in Vietnam and was determined to isolate and punish the Vietnamese communists: Washington did not recognise the Vietnamese government until 1995, after 20 years of diplomatic and economic embargo. The non-communist countries making up the Association of South-East Asian Nations (ASEAN)—Thailand, Singapore and Indonesia in particular—were also frightened of what they saw as Vietnam's hegemonic intentions in the region; this was still the era of the domino theory. As a result, Thailand gave sanctuary to Pol Pot's guerrillas, allowing them to operate with impunity from bases in refugee camps inside its border. This was done with the full support of China and the United States.

In June 1982, the Khmers Rouges were joined by Sihanouk's royalist FUNCINPEC party (after its French initials) and Son Sann's republican Khmer People's National Liberation Front (KPNLF) in an unlikely Coalition Government of Democratic Kampuchea (CGDK), which was immediately recognised by China, the United States and the ASEAN countries (with Lee Kwan Yew's Singapore particularly zealous in its support). Militarily, Pol Pot's forces, estimated to number 200 000 in 1979 and stabilising thereafter at around 35 000, dominated this coalition. FUNCINPEC and the KPNLF never managed to muster effective fighting forces. According to the United Nations, the total number of people under CGDK control in the refugee camps was slightly more than 260 000 in 1987. There is evidence that many people under Khmers Rouges control in particular would have left if they could. Because the PRK was widely regarded as Vietnam's puppet, the CGDK gained widespread diplomatic recognition, with the Khmer Rouge Khieu Samphan occupying Cambodia's ambassadorial seat at the United Nations General Assembly. In contrast, only 11 countries recognised the Heng Samrin government, and only one of them, India, was outside of the Soviet bloc.

Early attempts to end or at least scale down the conflict proved fruitless. In 1980, Thailand flatly rejected a Vietnamese proposal for a demilitarised zone along the Cambodian border and the following year the Soviet bloc boycotted a UN-sponsored international conference on Kampuchea, along with an ASEAN proposal for the UN to disarm all of the Cambodian factions, in combination with withdrawal of all Vietnamese troops and free elections. In 1983, China blocked a proposal by the Non-Aligned Summit for a round-table conference of all the parties to the dispute. Three years later, Austria offered to chair direct talks between the parties, but the proposal failed due to Chinese opposition. International events, however, allowed in the end for the relatively speedy resolution of the conflict, but for the best part of a decade it was intractable.

For the vast majority of Cambodians, who lived under PRK control, the results of these international intrigues were painful in the extreme. During the 1979 famine, for instance, the country was denied the economic and humanitarian aid it so desperately needed and although conditions improved in subsequent years with better harvests, Cambodia remained one of the world's poorest countries. Oxfam's Eva Myslwiec was forthright in her criticism: 'Seven million Kampucheans are being denied the Right to development and many are suffering directly because of the decisions taken by China, ASEAN and Western nations.' The PRK was ineligible for any of the assistance normally available for other Third World countries, many of which were ruled by governments much more corrupt and brutal than the PRK or Vietnam. The PRK was cut off from assistance from the UN Development Programme, the Asian Development Bank, the IMF and the World Bank, with only a trickle of humanitarian aid from UNICEF and the International Red Cross, whose rules did not preclude them from operating in disputed territories. 'Kampuchea,' pointed out the Oxfam patron Sir Robert Jackson, 'remains in the unique position of being the only developing country in the world—and it is almost certainly the country most in need—that is prevented from receiving any of the normal development and other assistance provided by the UN system.'

A Stalinist regime

These facts should not blind us to PRK's Stalinist nature, whatever the democratic and pluralistic reforms Heng Samrin had pledged at Snoul. An Amnesty International (AI) report published in 1987 criticised the regime for unfair trials, the detention without trial of political prisoners, torture during interrogation, and holding prisoners in cramped and unsanitary conditions. The report stressed that people were liable to be labelled 'traitors to the revolution' for 'crimes' such as holding private meetings, distributing leaflets, refusing to accept government posts and criticising the administration. The report attacked the regime for its treatment of political prisoners in the T3 detention centre at Phnom Penh and at a 'reform centre' at Trapeang Phlong in Kompong Cham province. Prime Minister Hun Sen did not respond to a letter from Amnesty International raising these concerns. During the first three years of the regime, security was almost entirely in the hands of Vietnamese secret police, because former members of Pol Pot's hated *nokorbal* (security service) were not allowed to serve the new government. The Vietnamese left a distinctly Stalinist stamp on those they trained. AI was also critical of the CGDK for abuse of human rights in the camps under its control.

Perhaps the PRK's greatest abuse of human rights began in 1982–83, when the regime launched the ambitious K5 Plan in the preparation for the huge 1984–85 dry season offensive against the Khmers Rouges. Under the K5 blueprint, the regime moved to seal off the border with Thailand with a great line of forts, ditches and dikes, walls, fences and minefields. Although Khmer People's Revolutionary Armed Forces (KPRAF) personnel and Vietnamese soldiers worked on the fortifications, the regime also conscripted some 50 000 civilian labourers. Indifferent food and poor sanitation, combined with heavy manual work, cost the lives of thousands of these civilians. By way of comparison, the loss of life was much greater than on the construction of the French pleasure centre at Bokor during the 1920s, which had been deservedly condemned for its inhumanity. K5 and the following offensive could be rated a military success, but it was deeply unpopular and cost the PRK a great deal of support among those it claimed to serve. However, we should not forget that it was the continuing support for Pol Pot by China, the West and ASEAN (and in particular Thailand) that necessitated the fortifications in the first place.

Nor was there anything new about the PRK's methods. As Michael Vickery has pointed out, 'For the rural 80–90 per cent of the Cambodian people, arbitrary justice, sudden violent death, [and] political oppression . . . were common facts of life long before the war and revolution of the 1970s.' The French had subjected the peasants to onerous taxation and brutally repressed them when they protested in 1916, and Sihanouk and Lon Nol had drowned the Samlaut rebellion in blood. Oppression is still part of the lives of the Khmer peasantry.

The eclipse of the 'Khmer Viet Minh' veterans

In general, however, the PRK was nowhere near as repressive as its DK predecessor, and nor was it guilty of deliberate mass murder. Nor was the Khmer People's Revolutionary Party swept by the bloody purges that had bled DK. For all that, however, it was a rigid Marxist-Leninist party modelled on the Vietnamese party and, more distantly, on the Communist Party of the USSR. Two curious incidents underline the party's Stalinist organisational methods and the domination of Hanoi over it during this period: the sacking of Prime Minister Pen Sovann in late 1981, and the death of his successor, Chan Si, in Moscow in 1984. Both men were former 'Khmer Viet Minh' and while more committed to socialist policies than the Hun Sen-Heng Samrin wing of the KPRP, they were also more nationalist-minded and inclined to be critical of the Vietnamese. This was ironic, given the fact that they had trained in Vietnam during their long exile after 1954.

Pen Sovann from all accounts was a sincere and competent albeit prickly man, an idealist who had devoted his life to the communist cause. One day, he simply disappeared from public view. This Khmer prime minister was incarcerated in a Vietnamese prison for a number of years and thereafter placed under house arrest in Hanoi. In total, he was deprived of his liberty and exiled to a foreign land for ten years without charge or trial. When Khmer civil servants asked why his portrait had disappeared from office walls, they were told not to ask, with dark hints of the consequences of persisting. The Vietnamese initially told Kong Korm, the PRK ambassador to Hanoi, that the prime minister was ill. Pen Sovann had become a 'non-person' in a nightmare that might have been dreamed up by Franz Kafka. When he pushed for explanations for his arrest, none were forthcoming; privately he was only told that he was well aware of why he was being punished. There would be interrogation, but no trial. The words of the historian David Burman about the fate of European heretics under the Inquisition also fit Pen Sovann's case perfectly:

> The prisoner . . . was kept in ignorance of the reasons behind his arrest and imprisonment . . . There was no precise charge, and therefore little possibility of making a plausible defence . . . He was required to confess to a crime that he attempted desperately to imagine . . .

The difference is that finally the Catholic Inquisitors would inform their victims of the charges against them—Pen Sovann was never told. His 'crime' would appear to have been that he was too independent-minded, a communist 'heretic' whose views were coming into conflict with the party line decided by the Politburo in Hanoi. The Vietnamese would no longer tolerate what Gottesman has called the 'steely autonomy' of Pen Sovann to advocate policies of economic nationalism and resistance to Vietnamese immigration. The fact that Pen was arrested by the Vietnamese and imprisoned in Vietnam cuts across any theory that he might have fallen victim to an anti-Vietnamese push within the KPRP. On the other hand, perhaps the Vietnamese had already concluded (as they had done in the days of the old Indochinese Communist Party back in the 1930s) that Cambodia was not ripe for socialism, and that idealistic communists such as Pen Sovann had to be removed from office. The truth of the matter awaits the opening of the state archives by some future Vietnamese Gorbachev, although the prospect is a distant one.

Chan Si, who succeeded Pen Sovann as prime minister, was also a competent and well-educated man, albeit considerably more 'mild mannered and accommodating' than his predecessor. However, he too demonstrated a capacity for independence of thought, most notably by his refusal to cooperate in the K5 Plan described above. Although he appears to have been in good health, Chan Si was suddenly struck down by a mysterious illness during a trip to Moscow. He was cremated after a full state funeral in Phnom Penh and publicly the regime mourned his loss. Years later, following his release from prison in Vietnam, Pen Sovann told the *Cambodia Daily* that Chan Si had been murdered on Hun Sen's orders. The opposition politician Sam Rainsy repeated the charge and Pen Sovann subsequently published a book (in Khmer) detailing his claims. It is difficult to imagine how Pen Sovann could have known the details of Chan Si's death as he was in prison at Hanoi at the time, and unless fresh evidence emerges the official explanation of his death will have to stand.

Chan Si's death was certainly fortuitous for the party pragmatists and former Khmers Rouges, however. By 1985, power had fallen largely into the hands of the Hun Sen wing of the KPRP, and their pragmatic policies prevailed over the Khmer Viet Minh's socialism. The remaining Khmer Viet Minh cadres were eased from their positions and replaced with former Khmers Rouges who Pen Sovann in particular had previously excluded. As Margaret Slocomb has observed, Chan Si's death 'dramatically marked a major turning point in the history of the PRK and in the revolution itself'. The regime introduced a kind of *perestroika* from 1988 (mirroring the Vietnamese party's *doi moi* free market reforms) and the collectivisation project in the countryside was abandoned. In September 1989, just prior to the fall of the Berlin

Wall and coincident with the final withdrawal of Vietnamese troops, the PRK changed its name to the more neutral-sounding State of Cambodia (SOC). The KPRP renamed itself as the Cambodian People's Party (CPP) and dropped its socialist aims and ideology. It had simply given up on the socialist project in the face of overwhelming domestic and international pressures and the seductions of power. However, by this stage the regime had also demonstrated that it was no longer the mere Vietnamese puppet that its detractors had claimed.

Momentous changes in international relations

These internal ideological shifts mirrored momentous international changes, which in turn impacted on Cambodian politics. The 1979 Vietnamese invasion had coincided with an intensification of the Cold War, which saw US President Ronald Reagan wage an implacable—and successful—struggle against what he saw as the 'evil empire' of the USSR. The Soviet Union became bogged down in a hopeless war against US-backed Islamist insurgents in Afghanistan, while at the same time its economy and society stagnated under an increasingly sclerotic bureaucracy and the debilitating strain of the arms race. By the end of the decade the pressures were so great that the Soviet Union began to crack, despite the best efforts of President Mikhail Gorbachev to preserve it by his reformist policies of *perestroika* and *glasnost*. The year 1989 saw the fall of the Berlin Wall and the 'velvet revolution' in Czechoslovakia, with the Soviet President refusing to intervene to save the Eastern European communist regimes. Two years later, the Soviet Union itself collapsed and the Cold War was over.

The same period had also seen a gradual thaw in relations between China and the USSR and an increasing willingness by a more pragmatic, post-Maoist Chinese leadership to embrace the capitalist world. The fall of communism in Eastern Europe also jolted them into the realisation that regardless of Stalinist dogma, they could not assume that their own regime was permanent. Finally, with the Cold War over, US (and ASEAN) intransigence towards Vietnam and the PRK/SOC made little sense. This general thaw in international politics provided the opportunity for a negotiated solution to the hitherto intractable problem of Cambodia.

The process was also assisted by the staged withdrawal of Vietnamese troops from Cambodia, begun in 1982 and completed in 1989. Although the CGDK and its backers initially claimed these were little more than troop rotations, the assertion wore thin in the face of the evidence. It was also increasingly apparent to the outside world that the PRK was no longer a Vietnamese puppet and had established itself as an effective government. This was underlined when, despite widespread fears that the PRK/SOC might not be able to prevent the return of the Khmers Rouges after the Vietnamese withdrawal, the Cambodian army was able to keep them at bay for the best part of four years before the arrival of UN peacekeeping forces. The regime had also boosted food production and re-established the basic infrastructure destroyed during the years of war and revolution.

Increasingly, too, it was difficult to justify support for the embarrassing Pol Pot. British Prime Minister Margaret Thatcher had once tried to sidestep awkward questions about DK's murderous history by claiming that there were both good Khmers Rouges and bad, and the United States maintained the fiction that its support for the CGDK did not mean support for Pol Pot. But such claims were untenable and increasingly unacceptable to world opinion. In 1986 the Australian Foreign Minister Bill Hayden said what many others were thinking when he called publicly for the trial of the Khmers Rouges leaders by an international tribunal. Any close ideological affinity the Chinese had once shared with Pol Pot was finished, with Beijing's new leadership turning their backs on the violent ultra-leftism of Mao's time in favour of market reforms and integration into the world economy.

By the late 1980s the ASEAN countries and Thailand in particular had begun to warm towards both Vietnam and the PRK as it became apparent that they had no plans (or capacity) to export revolution to the rest of the region. In short, after the Vietnamese withdrawal and the end of the Cold War, China, the West and ASEAN had little to gain from their continued support of the Pol Pot dominated CGDK, and much more to gain from embracing Hun Sen. On the other side, Gorbachev had everything to gain by moderation and the Vietnamese were preoccupied with rebuilding their own weakened economy and seeking rapprochement with their neighbours.

Prince Sihanouk, whose political antennae were always finely tuned, was also aware of the implications of these changes and began to distance himself from his unsavoury coalition partner, Pol Pot. In fact, Sihanouk had proposed direct talks with the PRK in Paris as early as August 1984, but the plan had failed because of vehement Chinese opposition. The following year the PRK announced its willingness to talk with the coalition, providing that the Khmers Rouges were excluded. Some years later, Sihanouk admitted that DK's aggression had triggered the Vietnamese invasion and said that Hun Sen was 80 per cent good and 20 per cent bad: 'he is my son, a bad boy but not so bad!' Perhaps it had finally dawned on Sihanouk that his alliance with the Khmers Rouges had been a major strategic error, even if he never seems to have considered the ethical problem of consorting with mass murderers over a period of two decades. With the lessening of Cold War tensions and improved relationships between China, the USSR and Vietnam, Sihanouk saw Pol Pot as expendable. In July 1987, Sihanouk proposed talks between all the parties, with no pre-conditions, although the proposal failed because all parties did set conditions.

Two years later, as Gary Klintworth observes, the final withdrawal of Vietnamese troops presented the UN, ASEAN, China and the United States with a *fait accompli*. At a stroke, it also removed any credibility from Sihanouk's claims that the PRK/SOC was illegitimate. Now, it served no one's interests save the Khmers Rouges to continue the conflict and on 23 October 1991, following some skilful diplomacy, all four of the Cambodian factions signed an agreement in Paris that allowed for free elections to be supervised by the United Nations. Pol Pot was unhappy with the arrangement, but his Chinese mentors had effectively abandoned him and he had no option but to go through the motions. From now on, he would be a dangerous nuisance but not a contender for power. From March 1992, the United Nations Transitional Authority in Cambodia (UNTAC) would oversee the country's affairs, and the factions would cooperate in the Supreme National Council under Sihanouk's presidency to ensure the continuation of Cambodian sovereignty.

The loathing and contempt felt by most Cambodians for the Khmers Rouges was underlined by the humiliation of Khieu Samphan when he flew in from Thailand in November 1992 to organise the Khmers Rouges' election campaign. Although there appears to have been some orchestration of events by Hun Sen, the spontaneous outrage of the people cannot be denied. Khieu Samphan was almost hanged from a ceiling fan in front of French journalists before scurrying ignominiously to the airport under CPP military guard, his bleeding head hastily bandaged in a pair of Y-fronts, jeered at by all who saw him.

A balance sheet of the PRK

Margaret Slocomb has argued that although the PRK failed as a revolutionary socialist regime, it did largely keep faith with the promises made by Heng Samrin at Snoul back in December 1978. The first point is indisputable, but the latter is true only up to a point, for the democracy Heng Samrin promised never eventuated. However, the PRK had rebuilt the country under conditions of great difficulty. There were, once again, schools and hospitals, functioning public transport, banks and currency, some industry and a revitalised agricultural sector. Moreover, even after the final withdrawal of Vietnamese troops in September 1989, the KPRAF soldiers were able to keep the Khmers Rouges at bay for the best part of four years until the arrival of UNTAC troops. In the end, the PRK/SOC leaders had cooperated with other factions and the United Nations to bring peace and security back to the country. While not highly popular, neither was the PRK unpopular, Slocomb argues. As long as it allowed people to piece together their shattered lives without too much interference, they would bow before it. This, after all, has been the pattern of life in Cambodia throughout the centuries, whether the rulers were kings or colonial administrators.

Most Khmers had accepted the PRK and the Vietnamese as the only way to keep Pol Pot out, but this does not mean that they supported the original Marxist-Leninist aims of the government. This is summed up in the words of a Khmer civil servant quoted by the University of Kentucky's Thomas Clayton, a writer on Cambodian affairs: 'At that time [January 1979], we were as if submerged under water. Someone came to us and held out a stick for us. We did not think at that time about who was holding the stick. We only knew that we needed to grasp the stick or we would die.' It is a fair comment.

Although the most pressing reason for the Vietnamese invasion was to eliminate the Pol Pot regime as a menace to Vietnam's own security, it nevertheless did liberate the Cambodian people from an atrocious regime. Although it is possible that the regime might have collapsed under the weight of its own incompetence and the debilitating effects of the purges, it is more likely that the country would have reverted to anarchic barbarism under petty regional despots. One is entitled to be sceptical of the claim of an anti-Vietnamese student, cited by Evan Gottesman, that 'Really, they [the Vietnamese] came here to kill people and take our property'.

For all their manipulation of Cambodian affairs, the Vietnamese government did its best to provide economic and humanitarian aid that it could scarcely afford. The war in Cambodia cost Hanoi dearly and was deeply unpopular with the Vietnamese people. Up to 50 per cent of Vietnam's budget was spent on the military during the occupation and this colossal drain turned their own war-damaged country into an economic basket case. Vietnam and the PRK were shunned as international pariahs while Pol Pot's sinister entourage basked in the sun of international recognition. The tragedy is that it took 13 weary years before the 'international community' could agree on a solution to a problem they were largely responsible for creating in the first place.

A final spasm of violence

Despite the diplomatic breakthrough in Paris that ushered in the UNTAC mission, Cambodia's problems were far from over. The last days of the PRK/SOC regime saw an explosion of political violence against students and other critics of widespread corruption and the lack of human rights in the country. Between 17 and 21 December 1991, Phnom Penh students staged a number of demonstrations against official corruption, during which at least ten people were killed and dozens wounded when security forces opened fire with live ammunition. Armed police also stormed into the Phnom Penh university medical faculty to disperse students who had not been involved in the street demonstrations. One student told the Australian observer Helen Jarvis that, 'This was a police manifestation [demonstration] not a student manifestation.' An undisclosed number of students were held without charge or trial or contact with friends or relatives.

Foreign Minister Nor Namhong announced on television that the demonstrations amounted to 'an armed insurrection with a political aim' and hinted at Khmers Rouges involvement. There was a plot by 'armed elements' to 'create instability for the government' and to 'prevent the implementation of the Paris peace accord', he fumed. Human rights agencies denied his claims and a special United Nations rapporteur agreed, noting that 'Reportedly, none of the demonstrators . . . had been equipped with firearms, nor had any of those killed used Molotov cocktails.' Amnesty International reported that 'eyewitnesses reported no firing on the police' and asked the government to release prisoners who were held 'solely for the peaceful expression of their opinions'. Although Hun Sen vowed to prevent Cambodia from becoming an 'anarchic' and 'lawless country', his government failed to

217

fully investigate the incidents and took no legal action against members of the security forces for their murderous rampage.

Shortly afterwards, Tea Bun Long, a leading civil servant and scathing critic of corruption, was kidnapped in broad daylight outside his house and murdered on the outskirts of the city. Tea had been especially critical of the role of National Assembly president, the ex-Khmer Rouge Chea Sim. One week later another government critic, a former government minister called Ung Phan, was shot outside his home, but recovered from his wounds after seeking refuge at Hun Sen's house. Both Tea Bun Long and Ung Phan had been involved in discussions to set up a new political party and indeed Ung Phan had only recently been released from prison for the 'crime' of trying to set up such a party. The journalist Nate Thayer, a long-time observer of Cambodian affairs, wrote in *Far Eastern Economic Review* that 'Long's killing was ordered by a powerful faction inside the government which is afraid of losing power in the liberalised political situation brought about by UN intervention . . .'. In March 1992, according to Human Rights Watch, another former political prisoner named Yang Horn was savagely assaulted 'shortly after being summoned with Ung Phang to an encounter with his former jailers who warned both not to engage in political activity'.

The PRK/SOC, which had done much to rebuild the country after the death and destruction of the Pol Pot years, thus departed from the historical stage with a final shameful blot on its record. Ruthless and astute, Hun Sen was determined to hang on to power despite the changed political circumstances that the UNTAC operation would bring. This final spasm of officially condoned violence presaged episodes of much greater violence that were to come and was in depressing counterpoint to the solemn declarations of the Cambodian political factions to respect democracy and human rights.

In many former Soviet bloc countries, the old ruling communist parties were either eclipsed or reinvented themselves politically and made a genuine commitment to play by the rules of democracy and pluralism. This did not happen in Cambodia. The Khmer People's Revolutionary Party, rebadged as the Cambodian People's Party, was determined to maintain its monopoly of power. Evan Gottesman has expressed this succinctly:

> No Berlin Wall fell in Cambodia. No Vaclav Havel or Lech Walesa came to power. The regime did not collapse; it negotiated the terms of its survival. Impoverished and isolated, the SOC understood that it needed legitimacy and assistance from the United Nations and the West. This meant complying with the expectations of the international community, when necessary, and protecting power in undemocratic and frequently violent ways, when possible.

Part of the price was the abandonment of the party's socialist ideology, and therefore its apparent *raison d'être*. Nor did the party reinvent itself as a social democratic party, with a residual commitment to social justice. From now on its imperatives would be those of power and wealth, devoid of egalitarian concerns, and backed up by its control of the country's 'prisons and bodies of armed men' inherited from the PRK.

10
TOWARDS AN UNCERTAIN FUTURE

The arrival of UNTAC in 1992 marked another painful transition for Cambodia. Unlike previous UN missions in other countries, which had concentrated on policing ceasefires and disarming the combatants, UNTAC's task was multi-dimensional. The UN Security Council charged UNTAC with peacekeeping, but added new duties which included the arrangement and supervision of national elections and the 'civic, economic, humanitarian and political reconstruction of the country'. It was a difficult order and although UNTAC did manage to run what was perhaps the freest election in Cambodian history, in other respects the intervention was less successful. As Amalia Branczik of the University of Colorado has observed:

> Of two billion dollars spent on the UNTAC mission in Cambodia, most was spent on UN staff salaries (an estimated 118.5 million dollars) and travel costs (62 million dollars). Almost 9000 new vehicles were purchased at a cost of approximately 81 million dollars, and all senior

UN bureaucrats were given a daily hardship allowance of 145 dollars to supplement their salaries. At the time, the average annual income in Cambodia was 130 dollars.

The 1993 elections

The UNTAC-sponsored elections were held in May 1993 and boycotted by Pol Pot's faction, which also launched military attacks on SOC forces and threatened to kill people who voted. They also refused to allow UNTAC personnel into their zones. These difficulties were compounded by widespread political violence and intimidation by the parties that participated, especially Hun Sen's Cambodian People's Party (CPP), which made full use of its 'coercive state power' against its opponents. Twenty parties contested the polls, the four most important being Son Sann's KPNLF; a CGDK partner reinvented as the Buddhist Liberal Democratic Party (BLDP) under the direction of an old Lon Nol general, Sak Sutsakhan; Hun Sen's CPP; and the royalist FUNCINPEC, headed by Sihanouk's son Prince Ranariddh.

Just over four million valid votes were cast, in spite of the Khmers Rouges' threats. The UN and most independent observers agreed that the election had been free and fair in spite of attempts at intimidation, although the CPP immediately disputed this. No party gained an absolute majority, but FUNCINPEC secured the largest vote, of 45.47 per cent. The CPP gathered 38.23 per cent and the other parties managed 12.59 per cent between them. This translated into 58 seats for FUNCINPEC, 51 for the CPP, 10 for the BLDP and 1 for the small Moulinaka party. As the largest party, it was possible for FUNCINPEC to form a minority government, but this would hardly have made for stable government in the face of the mutual hostility of the other parties.

Clearly, it was necessary to form a coalition but this was difficult, given that the BLDP were the political descendents of Sihanouk's old enemies Son Ngoc Thanh and Lon Nol. They were also the enemies of the CPP. They had coexisted out of necessity with FUNCINPEC and the Khmers Rouges inside the border coalition, but now had no reason to act with forbearance. With the Khmers Rouges rampaging in the countryside and the CPP disputing the election count, there was a clear danger that the country might revert to civil war.

For his part, Norodom Sihanouk saw the opportunity to regain the position he had held prior to the Lon Nol coup as unelected head of government as well as chief of state. He had behaved very erratically during the UNTAC period. He was often out of the country and he blew hot and cold in his attitude to UNTAC itself. After the elections he announced that he would head up a coalition government, acting as president of council of ministers and commander-in-chief of the armed forces despite the fact that he hadn't been elected to anything. Surprisingly, Prince Ranariddh, the FUNCINPEC leader, rejected the plan, leaving Sihanouk sputtering about 'disobedience', which was somewhat rich as he had behaved with all his old deviousness in playing Hun Sen and his son off against one another. As it turned out, it was the last chance that Sihanouk would have to regain his old supremacy and impose a Sangkum-type solution on the country. Henceforth, back on the throne as King Sihanouk, he would play a largely ceremonial role in a regime dominated by Hun Sen until his retirement in favour of another son, Sihamoni, in October 2004. 'Sihanoukism' was dead, although the king remained popular.

A bizarre compromise

The crisis was resolved when the CPP and FUNCINPEC agreed to share power in a new provisional government that became the Royal National Government of Cambodia on 29 October 1993, leaving the BLDP out in the cold. There was a curious twist to this coalition. In what was perhaps a world-first achievement, Ranariddh became First Prime Minister and Hun Sen Second Prime Minister. Despite the ranking, it was clear who really held the power in this arrangement. As Mao Zedong had once observed, 'power grows out of the barrel of a gun' and in

Cambodia in 1993, the CPP dominated the country's police and armed forces. The veteran *New York Times* journalist Henry Kamm noted crisply in his book *Cambodia: Report from a Stricken Land* that 'UNTAC, pleased with its successful elections, offered no objections to the perversion of their result.' Other observers mused that the peacekeepers had lost more soldiers to AIDS than to hostile fire. To be fair, one wonders what they could have done about Hun Sen's manoeuvres, short of waging war and plunging the country into a new abyss of chaos and destruction.

Plus ça change, plus c'est la même chose

The Khmer political scientist Sorpong Peou believes that the post-UNTAC period marked the beginning of the 'slow death' of the democratisation process that UNTAC was supposed to have begun. Henry Kamm was more forthright, declaring that a 'clique of thugs' ran the country, caring nothing for the Cambodian people, most of whom lived in misery as they had always done. Immediately after the elections, the new finance minister Sam Rainsy went on an international tour, seeking to boost donations of foreign aid to his country. Yet, as Daniel Ten Kate noted in the *Cambodia Daily* at the time, 'While appealing for money abroad, the new government voted to increase their salaries tenfold. Policemen earned an average of [US] $9 to $12 a month. Soldiers netted a maximum of $13. Now legislators would take home $650 every month.' The country was also sliding into the same kinds of official corruption that had marked the Sihanouk and Lon Nol regimes, a case of what the French call *plus ça change, plus c'est la même chose* (the more things change, the more they stay the same). Sam Rainsy, who has a reputation as Cambodia's 'Mr Clean', denounced the rampant corruption and was expelled from FUNCINPEC and from the National Assembly for his temerity, with the full support of Hun Sen's CPP, without even a vote.

The coalition government also slid easily into the same old patterns of authoritarianism that had characterised previous regimes. Although the new period had seen a blossoming of independent media (from around 14 newspapers before 1993 to 51 after 1994), the government often clamped down heavily on its critics. It should be noted that Prince Ranariddh, well schooled by his dictatorial father, was no more enamoured of press freedom and freedom of speech in general than his CPP 'Second Prime Minister' Hun Sen. For Ranariddh, like many authoritarian Asian leaders with their rhetoric of 'Asian values', democracy equated with economic development, and he had no understanding of the essential links between successful development and full political and civil rights in a flourishing civil society (a theme developed by the Nobel Laureate Amartya Sen in his book *Development and Freedom*).

In November 1994, the anti-government *Khmer Ideal* was suspended from publication for caricaturing Hun Sen and Ranariddh as 'dogs'; intemperate language to be sure, but something that would be accepted as part of the political cut and thrust in a free society. The following year, the paper was closed down on the orders of the Phnom Penh municipal court and the publisher fined US$4000 for describing Hun Sen and Ranariddh as 'greedy dictators'. Human rights organisations slammed the presence of heavily armed riot police in the courtroom. In April of the same year Michael Hayes, the American editor of the English-language *Phnom Penh Post*, was charged with 'misinformation' following publication of a number of articles critical of the government. Although King Sihanouk assured Hayes of a pardon, Khmer journalists were not so lucky. Many were imprisoned or fined for speaking out against government policies, and four journalists paid with their lives for their outspoken criticism during the first few years of the new regime. The most notorious case was that of Thun Bun Ly, the 39-year-old editor of the *Khmer Ideal*, who was gunned down by unidentified assassins as he travelled to work one morning in 1996. Armed police blocked the route of his funeral cortège at Phnom Penh's Independence Monument, yet in previous years they had done nothing to prevent mobs from sacking the offices of opposition newspapers.

Although Hun Sen had previously warned against allowing the country to fall back into anarchy, the security forces were often the worst abusers of the rule of law. There were persistent reports of police routinely abusing their power, especially in Battambang province where the Special Intelligence Battalion carried out rape and torture. The country's problems were compounded at that time by the Khmers Rouges insurgency, which made large sections of the countryside unsafe for travel, although there was little likelihood of them ever returning to power.

Hun Sen emerges as the undisputed 'strongman'

Meanwhile, relations between FUNCINPEC and its CPP coalition partner deteriorated, with both parties correctly suspecting the other of trying to stitch up deals with factions of the Khmers Rouges. From 1996 onwards, there were massive defections from the guerrillas. Ieng Sary, Nuon Chea and Khieu Samphan made their peace with the government, and the Khmers Rouges were reduced to a small rump under Son Sen and Pol Pot in the Dangrek Mountains near Anlong Venh on the Thai border. David Roberts, in his book about 1990s Cambodia, quotes Hun Sen's candid comments on Ranariddh: we do not 'hug and kiss each other, we do not love each other. In fact, we barely speak. We do not have regular scheduled meetings because we have little to discuss.' The writer William Shawcross described Hun Sen in an article which appeared in the 14 November 1996 *New York Review* as 'an increasingly dangerous psychotic' who had shown that he would not stop at violence to get his way.

A showdown was looming, and it was clear which side would prevail. Hun Sen had the military muscle, in contrast to Ranariddh's ineffectual forces. In July 1997, the calm of a Phnom Penh morning was rent by the clanking of tanks and heavy gunfire. Hun Sen had launched a bloody coup against his coalition partner. Fighting raged for the next two days, although the conclusion was never in doubt as the FUN-CINPEC forces were outnumbered and outgunned. Dozens of people were killed and many hundreds more wounded in the gun battles in the capital's streets. Ranariddh fled and a number of his leading associates

Hun Sen in 2002. (Courtesy Newspix)

were executed, some after torture, and others were 'shot while trying to escape'. The CPP troops engaged in an orgy of looting, stripping the airport buildings at Pochentong, raiding factories and even hospitals, and making off with their booty tied atop tanks.

Disputes still continue as to whether Hun Sen's actions constituted a coup d'état. From the CPP point of view, they had staged a pre-emptive strike to prevent a looming merger between FUNCINPEC and the main body of Khmers Rouges who had been their CGDK partners for over a decade on the Thai borders. There is some evidence to support this claim. Whatever interpretation one favours, Hun Sen had emerged triumphant as the country's most powerful figure. King Sihanouk was a figurehead, the royalist party was weakened, and the following year Pol Pot died peacefully in a remote village after being tried by the remnant of the Khmers Rouges for ordering the execution of his lieutenant, Son Sen. Cambodia was now ruled effectively by a dictator, a 'strongman' whom the US scholar Stephen Heder had once described as 'both a competent political administrator and a ruthless political criminal'.

The astute Hun Sen was aware that force alone does not legitimise a regime. Despite its corruption and abuse of human rights (the latter documented in Amnesty International's annual reports and the publications of Human Rights Watch and Citizens for Public Justice etc.), the regime maintained a populist façade, claiming to care for the poor who made up the overwhelming bulk of the population. In fact, a study by the UN Development Programme published in March 2003 indicates that poverty has become much worse under Hun Sen, and the rate of infant mortality rose from 79 deaths per 1000 in 1987 (under the PRK) to 95 per 1000 in 2000. Trade unionists—including women textile workers who attempt to organise to improve their standards of living and conditions of work—have been brutally repressed and/or subjected to officially condoned private violence.

In 1998, however, Hun Sen surprised his critics by announcing that the country would hold fresh elections for the National Assembly. The elections, which were held on 26 July, were supervised by a team of international observers from the European Union, ASEAN and NGOs, all of whom, to FUNCINPEC's chagrin, proclaimed them to have been free and fair in the main. The result was a clear victory for the CPP, although it fell short of the two-thirds majority necessary under the constitution for it to govern in its own right. As a result, the CPP formed a new coalition with FUNCINPEC, which accepted some junior portfolios.

The following year saw Hun Sen win another important political victory when his country was accepted as a member of ASEAN. The CPP's pre-eminence was reconfirmed in July 2003, when the party again won a majority of votes, and is unlikely to be challenged in the near future. As summed up in *The Economist* at that time, the CPP has more powerful electoral assets than brute force: more money than the opposition, a more effective party machine, the administration's power of patronage and control of the media. The opposition parties' many flaws are also an asset to Mr Hun Sen. Prince Ranariddh . . . offers little effective leadership [and] his party's popularity has slipped.

The magazine also pointed out that while Sam Rainsy is a courageous voice against corruption in what he calls a mafia state, 'his autocratic style as leader of the party that bears his name alienates allies almost as fast as he recruits them'.

Nor has the government displayed much interest in coming to terms with the horrors of the DK years, either through trials or via a 'truth and reconciliation' process as in post-apartheid South Africa. The PRK, it is true, made the S21 torture centre at Tuol Sleng into a 'museum of the genocide', but there has been little progress in bringing the top Khmers Rouges leaders to trial. Indeed, at the time of writing, only two of the worst leaders have been indicted: Ta Mok, the one-legged former commander of the DK's South-west Zone, and Duch, the schoolmaster-turned-torturer who ran Tuol Sleng. Pol Pot and Son Sen are dead and although the Cambodian government came to an agreement with the United Nations in May 2005 to set up a tribunal to try the other former leaders, it remains to be seen whether this will happen.

Hun Sen does have a valid point when he complains of Western hypocrisy. It is true that many of the countries that now call for indictment were happy to recognise the legitimacy of the Khmers Rouges when it suited their own purposes. However, this does not justify Hun Sen's refusal to proceed against the remaining DK leadership, of whom Ieng Sary, Khieu Samphan and Nuon Chea live in comfortable retirement in Cambodia, protected by the government. Nor can there be any justification for Hun Sen's refusal to accept a United Nations proposal for an international trial, rather than a trial overseen by the notoriously corrupt pro-CPP Cambodian judiciary.

Deeply entrenched social problems

Today, Cambodia remains one of the poorest nations on earth. Between one third and one half of its 13 million people live in abject poverty on less than US$1 per day, and the numbers rise every year. Fifty per cent of the country's children under five are underweight. Corruption scares off foreign investment and the country's rate of economic growth has slumped, with the World Bank predicting that it could fall to less than 2.5 per cent in 2005. The estimated per capita GNP was US$280 in 2002. The country relies heavily on foreign aid donations, which make up some 50 per cent of its budget, yet the US Agency for International Development estimates that corrupt officials siphon off up to US$500 million per year. Michael Hayes of the *Phnom Penh Post* says that 'Corruption is there up and down the chain of command, from the top to the bottom', adding that 'Hun Sen has to start with his own party members for a start.' Indeed, he has to start tackling corruption even closer to home, as many observers believe that his own family members and cronies are involved in illegal logging scams that cost the country dearly both financially and ecologically. Certainly, as the environmental NGO Global Witness has shown, the government has permitted widespread illegal logging and has threatened whistleblowers with imprisonment. Chea Vanath, of the Centre for Social Development in Phnom Penh, says, 'Corruption is across the board and the more poor you are, the more you are affected by corruption. The poor who depend on the health sector, the education sector and rural administration are among those [worst] hit.' Cambodia, as much as post-communist Russia, fully deserves to be known as a kleptocracy, a country ruled by thieves.

In the past, landlessness was never a problem of the same magnitude as it was in neighbouring countries. The old crown land system allowed those who farmed the land to live on it indefinitely and the French cadastral laws granted land titles to those who could prove continued use of it. The upheavals of the 1970s and collectivist experiments meant that many peasants and even city-dwellers cannot now produce proof of ownership and they are liable to be expelled from their land and homes by ruthless officials and developers. Any tourist who walks the Phnom Penh streets at dawn cannot but notice the country people who have drifted to the city in the hope of finding work, waiting for contractors to hire them. For most, this consists of dangerous and underpaid casual work on construction sites, or as *cyclo* (bicycle taxi or rickshaw) drivers. Women often have little choice but to turn to prostitution, or are shanghaied into sex slavery by criminal gangs.

Prostitution—including child prostitution—is a major social problem in Cambodia. There are an estimated 60 000 to 80 000 prostitutes in the country, one third of them below the age of 17. In one survey, 70 per cent of children interviewed in the vicinity of Angkor said that Westerners had approached them for sex. Given the poverty of the country, it is not surprising that many accept. In the capital, parents can sell their 12-year-old girls to a brothel for between US$300 and $1000, a vast sum in a country where much of the population lives on less than a dollar a day. Although Western sex tourism is a problem in Cambodia (much of it involving children), most brothel customers are Khmer men. Some young men in Phnom Penh have made a sport of gang rape (*bauk*, or 'plus' in Khmer) and they clearly regard their victims as less than human. Such attitudes are perhaps inevitable in a society traumatised by decades of war and suffering. As the writer Raoul Jenner has lamented, Cambodia has become 'a society governed entirely by the strongest', in which 'the price placed on a human life is less than that placed on a motorbike'.

The psychological damage and emotional trauma of the past casts a long shadow and manifests itself in anomie or social breakdown, a loss of values, greed, selfishness, violence and crime. Prostitution in turn is the main cause of the country's HIV/AIDS pandemic, with the main route of transmission from male clients to their regular partners. AIDS accounted for over 17 000 deaths in Cambodia in 2002 and the prevalence rate is around 2.6 per cent for adults, though perhaps considerably higher. Between 170 000 and 280 000 people in the 0 to 49 age range are infected. However, cooperation between Cambodian health authorities and NGOs in condom awareness programs has at least led to a decline in HIV infection rates from 42.6 per cent in 1998 to 28.8 per cent in 2002 among female brothel-based prostitutes. This modest success is one bright spot in a country fraught with enormous problems.

Widespread ecological damage

In Chapter 3, the idea was discussed that ecological devastation might have contributed to the decline of Angkor, a theory closely associated with Bernard-Philippe Groslier and Roland Fletcher. Those we might term 'social archaeologists' believe that logging on the watersheds north of Angkor led to erosion, silting and other environmental problems that disturbed the delicate ecology of the complicated anthropogenic wetland that was Angkor. Today, Cambodia is once again facing a major ecological crisis as illegal logging and pollution threaten the country's primary natural system, the Mekong River and the Great Lake. The annual floods of the Mekong, which back up into the lake, allow the world's fourth largest catch of freshwater fish and provide work for over a million people. The fish form the largest single source of protein for the Cambodian population. It is also estimated that up to 80 per cent of the rice production in the lower Mekong basin depends on the river's annual floods.

Much of the wildlife has abandoned the Great Lake or died. Birds are relatively scarce, reminding us of the legend of the kingfishers, and the once ubiquitous crocodiles have almost vanished. Not all of this is Cambodia's fault, but stems in part from a series of dams and irrigation schemes built far upstream in China's Yunnan province and on some of the Mekong's tributaries in Vietnam. These projects have led to at least a 12 per cent decrease in river levels since the works began and erratic flows that disrupt fishing and agriculture along the banks.

What of the future?

Unfortunately, the world has largely forgotten about Cambodia since the UNTAC period. There have been other crises and other conflicts to absorb the world's attentions: wars in the Middle East, the Asian tsunami, genocides in Africa and the Balkans, terrorist attacks in the heartlands of the Western world, and the threat of global warming to name just a few since UNTAC pulled out and left the Cambodians to their own devices. Cambodia, too, is a small country without appreciable supplies of vital raw materials such as oil that might bring it to the centre of world attention. One trusts that the Cambodian proverb *srok khmer moun de soun* (the country of the Khmers will never die) will prove true.

Looking back over the past quarter of a century (let alone the earlier Dark Age that beset Cambodia in the first half of the 19th century) it is difficult to imagine that anything worse could befall the Khmers. Cambodia has staggered from crisis to crisis since 1970 and in the absence of a developed civil society there is little check on the arrogance of government and the corruption of the administration. With entrenched rulers primarily interested in their own power and wealth, there seems little prospect of change in the near future.

On the other hand, as Gottesman points out, 'There are many indications of a budding civil society', including a number of human rights organisations, ecological organisations and other NGOs that maintain offices in Phnom Penh and regional centres. In a way, for Cambodia to have survived is itself a triumph, but there is no guarantee that it will not become a failed state, as was a real possibility before the establishment of the French protectorate in the 19th century. However, those readers who hope for remedies to social problems and forecasts of what might be will be disappointed. We might do worse than remember the social historian Roy Porter's wise words at the conclusion of his book on London, where he warns against Cassandras and oracles:

The temptation at the conclusion of a volume like this is to offer either a blueprint for . . . regeneration or a funeral oration . . . Historians, however, make rotten physicians, worse planners and appalling prophets. I shall therefore resist the temptation to offer diagnoses and prescriptions.

Glossary and abbreviations

AK47   Assault rifle designed by the Red Army's Mikhail Kalasnikov

ARVN   The armed forces of the pro-US Saigon regime in Vietnam before its collapse in 1975.

ASEAN   Association of South-east Asian Nations

Baray   A large pool or reservoir.

Belle époque   Literally, beautiful or fine period.

BLDP   Buddhist Liberal Democratic Party

Bodhisattva   Incarnation of Buddha.

Cambodia/Kampuchea   Both attempts to render the Khmer name for their country in English. Earlier variants include Camboja, Camboia and Camboxa. The French know the country as Cambodge, the Germans as Kambodscha.

CGDK   Coalition Government of Democratic Kampuchea

Cham   A Muslim minority people with their own language in Cambodia and Vietnam (some are Hindu in the latter). Descendents of the people of Champa.

Champa   Indianised kingdom of the Chams east of Cambodia before its sack by the Vietnamese in 1471. In its heyday, the kingdom of Champa stretched across what is now central modern Vietnam.

CIA   Central Intelligence Agency

Corvée   Compulsory labour on roads etc.

CPF   Communist Party of France

CPP   Cambodian People's Party

Dangreks   Range of sandstone mountains along Cambodia's northern border with Thailand.

Darul Islam   'House of Islam', roughly equivalent to Christendom.

Devaraja   God-kings of Angkor.

DK   Democratic Kampuchea

DRV   Democratic Republic of Vietnam declared by Ho Chi Minh in December 1945. After the partition of Vietnam in 1954 and until re-unification in 1975, the name applied to communist North Vietnam.

ENSO   El Niño/Southern Oscillation Index

FANK   French acronym for Khmer National Armed Forces

FUNCINPEC   French acronym for National United Front for an Independent, Neutral, Peaceful and Cooperative Cambodia

FUNK   French acronym for National United Front of Kampuchea

Geneva Conference   Peace conference held in Geneva in 1954 to resolve the wars in Indochina and Korea. The conference recognised Cambodia's independence and granted independence to Laos. It also resulted in the de facto partition of Vietnam into a communist North and a non-communist South.

Glasnost   Literally 'open-ness', political reforms launched by Soviet President Mikhail Gorbachev in the 1980s.

IMF   International Monetary Fund

Kampuchea Krom   The lower Mekong delta lands around Saigon, which passed from Khmer into Vietnamese hands by 1780.

Kamrateng jagat   'Lords of the universe', the god-kings of Angkor.

Karma   In the Buddhist doctrine of reincarnation, the quality of people's new lives after rebirth depends on how much merit they have accrued in the previous life. Good works will result in good karma, a bad life in bad karma.

Kempetei   The Japanese military police in World War II.

Khmer   Means both the language and the majority ethnic group of Cambodia, and more generally is used as an adjective to describe something from the country. Khmer is also generally used as a synonym for Cambodia and although this can lead to semantic problems, I have adopted this usage.

Khmerité   'Khmerness', a term used by the French administration during the Vichy period in World War II to try to harness Khmer national–cultural feeling behind their regime.

Khmer Krom The Cambodian minority in the Vietnamese lower Mekong delta.

Khmer Loeu Hill tribes in remote regions of Cambodia. More commonly known by the pejorative name of 'Phnongs'. Known as Montagnards by the French.

Khmer Serei Pro-US or pro-Thai and pro-South Vietnamese, republican political and guerrilla force linked to Son Ngoc Thanh.

Khmers Rouges Literally 'Red Khmers', a term probably first used by King Norodom Sihanouk. Came to mean more narrowly the Pol Pot faction of the Communist Party of Cambodia.

Khmer Viet Minh Pro-Vietnamese faction of the Cambodian Communist Party, many of whom spent much of the time after 1954 in exile in North Vietnam.

Kompong Small town or village, a word derived from the Malay kampong.

KPLA Khmer People's Liberation Army

KPNLF Khmer People's National Liberation Front

KPRAF Khmer People's Revolutionary Armed Forces

KPRP Khmer People's Revolutionary Party

Krama Chequered coloured scarf-cum-towel worn by many Khmers.

Mahayana 'Greater Vehicle' Buddhism, influential at Angkor until the coming of the Theravadin Buddhists in the 13th century.

Mission civilisatrice French for the alleged 'civilising mission' of colonialism. A variation of Rudyard Kipling's 'white man's burden', perhaps.

Nagaravatta Khmer for Angkor Wat and also the name of a Khmer proto-nationalist magazine in the 1930s until its suppression during World War II.

NGO Non-Government Organisation

NLF National Liberation Front

Obbareach Heir apparent to the Khmer throne.

Oxfam Oxford Committee for Famine Relief

Pecul (picul) A measurement equivalent to 60 kilograms.

Perestroika   Economic reforms launched by Soviet leader Mikhail Gorbachev in the 1980s.

Pochentong   Suburb of Phnom Penh and site of the city's airport.

Pon   Chieftain or petty king in pre-Angkorean societies of what is today Cambodia.

Pracheachon   'People's Group', legal pro-communist political party set up in Cambodia to contest elections in Sihanouk's Cambodia after independence.

Prahoc   Fermented fish paste. A staple Cambodian food and leading source of protein for most Khmers.

PRC   People's Republic of China

Prei Nokor   Cambodian name for Saigon/Ho Chi Minh City and name of the original settlement in that place when it was part of Cambodia.

PRK   People's Republic of Kampuchea

Quatre Bras   'The Four Arms' formed by the confluence of the Mekong and Tonlé Sap rivers and the bifurcation of the main stream into the Mekong and Bassac at Phnom Penh.

Quoc ngu khmer   Khmer language rendered in Latin script.

Realpolitik   German word used by political scientists to describe actual existing power politics.

Résident   Leading French official at Phnom Penh after the Treaty of 1863.

Résident Supérieur   Top French official overseeing four of the five components of French Indochina: Cambodia, Laos, Tonkin and Annam. The colony of Cochin-China was administered by a governor. The other divisions were protectorates.

RVN   Republic of Vietnam, the US-backed anti-communist regime in South Vietnam between 1954 and 1975.

Sampot   Colourful ankle-length dress worn by Khmer women.

Sangha   Any community of monks, members of the Theravada Buddhist orders in Cambodia and elsewhere in southern Asia.

Sangkum   Sangkum Reastr Niyum, political party or movement set up by Norodom Sihanouk after independence and created by amalgamation of most of the existing parties.

SEATO South-East Asia Treaty Organisation

Siva (Shiva) One of the chief gods of the Hindu pantheon, afforded higher status in Angkorean Cambodia than in India.

SOC State of Cambodia

Srok A Khmer word meaning land or country, but it would be a mistake to equate it historically with the idea of a modern nation-state. As David Chandler has observed, 'Cambodian ideas about political geography did not include the notion that "Cambodia" was defined primarily by lines on a map.' Srok meant the place where people spoke Khmer and 'more narrowly' where official titles and seals of office were given out by the Khmer king.

Sticklac(k) Shellac, substance produced by insects and used in sealing wax, glues, plastics etc.

Tagal Malay or Filipino palace guards in Cambodia.

Theravadism 'Lesser Vehicle' Buddhism brought to Cambodia from Ceylon (Sri Lanka) in the 13th century. Distinguished from Greater Vehicle by its emphasis on the need to do good works to achieve nirvana.

Tirailleur Colonial (including Cambodian) sharpshooter or light infantryman in the French army.

Tonlé Sap The Great Lake of Cambodia and the river that drains from it into the Mekong at the Quatre Bras.

UNICEF United Nations International Children's Emergency Fund

UNTAC United Nations Transitional Authority in Cambodia

Varman Suffix added to names of Cambodian kings, meaning 'protector'.

Vichy Authoritarian, pro-Axis regime set up with a seat at the spa town of Vichy after the fall of France to the Nazis in 1940. Some colonies, including Indochina, were administered by Vichy officials during this period. Others, such as New Caledonia, were run by pro-Allied officials.

Vichyite Supporter of Vichy.

Viet Minh   Communist-led anti-French guerrillas in Indochina during the 1940s and 1950s.

Wat   Buddhist temple.

Wittfogelian   Karl Wittfogel held that Asian societies such as China and India were static because the need to irrigate large areas of land for food production demanded authoritarian centralised states and large bureaucracies that were hostile to change. Wittfogel's views were summed up in his 1957 book, *Oriental Despotism*. In fact, Chinese society was technologically ahead of that of Europe until the onset of the Industrial Revolution. One 18th century Scottish visitor wrote, 'In a word, I look upon China to be the richest and best-governed empire in the world.' However, although Wittfogel overgeneralises, conflates very different societies and is doubtless guilty of what Edward Said later called 'orientalism', it has to be admitted that much of what he says does seem to fit Angkorean society. This is particularly so if the 'hydraulic city' thesis is accepted.

Notes

1. Chinese astronauts have reported that the Great Wall of China is not visible from outer space, as was previously believed. To clear up a common misconception, Angkor Wat (*wat* means temple) is only one of the many structures of the city of Angkor.
2. Javanese power had gone into decline around this period, but the Khmers had only recently thrown off their yoke.
3. From the 16th century on, European missionaries devised a system that used the Latin script and diacritic symbols to express the tones of the Vietnamese language. *Quoc ngu* is now used throughout Vietnam. Strictly speaking, it is inaccurate to apply the term to the Latinised Khmer script.
4. The conference did not resolve the Korean conflict.

Further reading

General

The best general history is David P. Chandler's *A History of Cambodia*, Second Edition (Allen & Unwin, Sydney, 1993). Prior to the Pol Pot period, there was a comparative dearth of general books on Cambodia, especially in the English language. Two general histories were written in French during the 19th and early 20th centuries by French Cambodia 'mandarins': Adhémard Léclère's *Histoire du Cambodge depuis le ler siècle de notre era* (Librairie Paul Geuthner, Paris, 1914) and Jean Moura's two-volume *Le Royaume du Cambodge* (Ernest Leroux, Librairie de la Société Asiatique de l'École des Langues Orientales Vivantes, Paris, 1883). There was also Étienne Aymonier's monumental three-volume work on Cambodian society, *Le Cambodge* (Ernest Leroux, Paris, 1901). These, however, remain untranslated and in any case have been to some degree superseded by subsequent scholarship and the passage of the years. They can be found in large academic libraries, particularly those with an emphasis on Asian studies.

Madeleine Giteau published her *Histoire du Cambodge* (Didier, Paris) in 1957 and Achille Dauphin-Meunier his book of the same name (P.U.F., Paris) in 1968, but the first attempts at English-language histories appear to have been Martin Herz's modest *A Short History of Cambodia from the Days of Angkor to the Present* (F.A. Praeger, New York, 1958) and Manomohan Ghosh's *A History of Cambodia: from the earliest time to the end of the French Protectorate* (J.K. Gupta, Saigon, 1960). Both are somewhat dated, Ghosh's work is not always reliable, and Herz has been criticised for excessive pro-US bias but his work nevertheless contains interesting information on the Sihanouk era. The most recent bibliographic guide to books and other sources on Cambodia is Helen Jarvis' useful *Cambodia* volume of the *World Bibliographical Series* (Clio Press, Oxford and Santa Barbara, California, 1997). Also worth consulting is Justin Corfield and Laura Summers' *Historical Dictionary of Cambodia* (Scarecrow Press, Lanham, Maryland, 2003).

Chapter 1: The people and their environment

For general information on Cambodia, see Ian Mabbett and David Chandler's *The Khmers* (Blackwells, Oxford, 1995) or Chandler's *The Land and People of Cambodia* (HarperCollins, New York, 1991), which is pitched to secondary students. Another book worth considering is David J. Steinberg's *Cambodia: its people, its society, its culture* (Hraf Press, New Haven, 1959). The best and most comprehensive work on Cambodian peasant society, Jean Delvert's *Le Paysan Cambodgien* (Mouton, Paris, 1961), unfortunately remains untranslated from the French. The anthropologist May Ebihara's *Svay* (University Microfilms, Ann Arbor, 1971) is a fascinating study of Khmer village life but is not available outside of specialist academic libraries. Ebihara also contributed an interesting account of the importance of Buddhism in Cambodian life: 'Interrelations between Buddhism and Social Systems in Cambodian Peasant Culture' in Manning Nash et. al, eds, *Anthropological Studies in Theravada Buddhism* (Southeast Asia Studies, Yale University, New Haven, 1966). Those seeking an accessible travel guide should consider Nick Ray's *Lonely Planet Cambodia* (Lonely Planet, Melbourne, 2002), which contains maps and general information for the visitor to Cambodia.

Chapter 2: Cambodia before Angkor

Very little of a non-specialist nature has been written about pre-Angkorean Cambodia, especially outside of scholarly journals. Mabbett and Chandler's previously mentioned *The Khmers* contains some material on the period, as does Chapter 2 of Chandler's *History*. The French epigrapher George Coedès' classic *The Indianized States of Southeast Asia* (University of Hawaii Press, Honolulu, 1968) contains valuable detail. Coedès' *Angkor: an introduction* (trans. and ed. Emily Floyd Gardiner, Oxford University Press, London and New York, 1963) contains some information and argument on this period in its opening chapter. The same is true of Christopher Pym's *The Ancient Civilization of Angkor* (Mentor, New York and Toronto, 1968) and Lawrence Palmer Briggs' *The Ancient Khmer Empire* (White Lotus, Bangkok, 1999, originally published 1951). The only book-length study dealing with Cambodia before Angkor is Michael Vickery's detailed and fascinating *Society, Economics and Politics in Pre-Angkor Cambodia: the 7th and 8th centuries* (Centre for East Asian Cultural Studies for UNESCO, The Toyo Bunko, Tokyo, 1998), which is written from a Marxist perspective. Vickery is perhaps the pre-eminent scholar of the pre-Angkorean period and readers interested in finding out more might also consider looking at his essay 'What and where was Chenla?' which appeared (in English) in *Récherches Nouvelles sur le Cambodge* (École Française d'Extrême-Orient, Paris, 1994, pp. 197–212). The University of Hawaii is also conducting research into the civilisations of the pre-Angkor period through its Lower Mekong Archaeological Project (LOMAP). Details of LOMAP can be found on the web at <http://www.anthropology. hawaii.edu/projects/cambodia/cambodia.htm> accessed 1 February 2005.

Chapter 3: The ancient Angkorean civilisation

There is only one eyewitness account of the Angkorean Empire during its heyday. This is the chronicle of the Chinese traveller Zhou Daguan (check also under the old spelling Chou Ta-Kwan when searching). Zhou has left us a vivid record of his visit to the kingdom in the 13th century in *The Customs of Cambodia* (trans. from Paul Pelliot's French version by J. Gilman D'Arcy Paul, The Siam Society, Bangkok, Second Edition, 1992). Whatever else we know about Angkor came until recently from stone inscriptions from around the kingdom and from pictorial scenes on the stone friezes of Angkor Wat and the Bayon. More recently, social archaeologists have used satellite imaging and other high-tech methods to further our understanding of Angkorean civilisation.

Among the best books on Angkorean history and society are George Coedès' *Angkor: an introduction* and Lawrence Briggs' immensely detailed *The Ancient Khmer Empire*, both previously cited for Chapter 2. Christopher Pym's detailed book, *The Ancient Angkorean Civilization* (also already cited) is perhaps the most highly readable introduction to Angkor. Less recommended is John Audric's *Angkor and the Ancient Khmer Empire* (Robert Hale, London, 1972) which, while accessible, sometimes makes claims not borne out by the available evidence. A more recent, highly readable introduction is Michael D. Coe's *Angkor and the Khmer Civilization* (Thames and Hudson, London, 2003). Good guidebooks to the ruins include Dawn Rooney's *Angkor: an introduction to the temples* (Fourth Edition, Odyssey Publications, Hong Kong, c.1999) and Jean Laur's *Angkor: an illustrated guide to the ruins* (trans. Diana Pollin, Paris, 2002).

Most people are primarily interested in the ancient monuments of Angkor, but in recent times archaeologists have shifted their focus to the civilisation that produced them. This has given rise to furious debates about whether Angkor was a hydraulic city in which a large population was sustained by irrigated agriculture. Although earlier authors assumed the existence of large-scale irrigation, the thesis was developed in a series of essays written in the late 1970s by the celebrated archaeologist Bernard-Philippe Groslier. (See, for instance, his 'La Cité hydraulique angkorienne: exploitation ou surexploitation du sol?' in the *Bulletin de l'École Française d'Extrême-Orient*, Vol. LXVI, Paris, pp. 161–202.) Two writers in particular vigorously contested the thesis: W.J. van Lière in his essay 'Was Angkor an hydraulic society?'

(*Ruam Botwan Prawasit*, Vol. 4, Silpakorn University, Bangkok, pp. 36–48) and Robert Acker in his 'New geographical tests of the hydraulic thesis of Angkor' (*South East Asia Research*, 6 (1), pp. 5–47). The debate is the subject of a fascinating special volume of the *Journal of Sophia Asian Studies* (No. 18, Institute of Asian Cultures, Sophia University, Tokyo, 2000). The volume contains argument and counter-argument by such writers and scholars as James Goodman, Yoshiaki Ishizawa, Elizabeth Moore, Hisashi Nakamura, Akiro Goto and Christophe Pottier. Some of the most interesting research into the hydraulic hypothesis has been undertaken by the Australian archaeologist Roland Fletcher. Leigh Dayton has summarised Fletcher's ideas in an article entitled 'The Lost City' (*New Scientist*, No. 2273, 13 January 2001, pp. 30–33).

Chapter 4: From Angkor's end to the French protectorate

Apart from the general histories cited above, books and articles on the period between the decline of Angkor and the coming of the French are scattered and generally found only in academic libraries and scholarly journals. Those with a knowledge of French wishing to read more about the decline of Angkor might wish to consult Bernard-Philippe Groslier (in collaboration with C.R. Boxer), *Angkor et le Cambodge au XVI Siècle d'après les sources Portugaises et Espagnoles* (Presses Universitaires de France, Paris, 1958). This book has its origins in the discovery by C.R. Boxer of a lost manuscript written by the Portuguese traveller Diogo do Couto, who visited Angkor in the 16th century. Another early European account of post-Angkorean Cambodia is *The Suma Oriental of Tomé Pires* (trans. Armando Cortesao, Hakluyt Society, London, 1944). Other early European accounts have been collected and edited by C.R. Boxer in his *South China in the Sixteenth Century*.

Being the Narratives of Galeote Pereira, Fr. Gaspar da Cruz, O.P., Fr. Martin de Rada, O.E.S.A., (1550–1575) (Hakluyt Society, London, 1953). See also Michael Vickery's 'Cambodia After Angkor: The Chronicular Evidence for the Fourteenth to Sixteenth Centuries' (University of Michigan Dissertation Service, Ann Arbor, 1977), which fleshes out a rounded picture of the period in its later sections. The attempt of Iberian conquistadors to gain an Asian mainland foothold in Cambodia is recorded in C.R. Boxer's splendid article 'The Spaniards in Cambodia' (History Today, Vol. 21, April 1971, pp. 280–87). Little has been written on Cambodia in the 18th and early 19th centuries, but those interested should take the time to seek out David Chandler's fine but unpublished PhD thesis, 'Cambodia Before the French: politics in a tributary period', which can be consulted on microfilm and hard copy in some university libraries (University of Michigan, Ann Arbor, 1973).

Chapter 5: The French protectorate, 1863–1953

Books about the French colonial period are rather more plentiful than for the previous period. The period is covered briefly in a number of general works cited above and in a number of more specialised texts. The latter include Milton Osborne's The French Presence in Cochinchina and Cambodia: rule and response (1859–1905) (Cornell University Press, Ithaca, 1969); Alain Forest's Le Cambodge et la Colonisation Française: histoire d'une colonisation sans heurts (1897–1920) (Editions l'Harmattan, Paris, 1980) and V.M. Reddi's A History of the Cambodian Independence Movement, 1863–1955 (Sri Venkateswara University Press, Tiraputi, 1970). See also my Cambodia Under the Tricolour: King Sisowath and the 'Mission Civilisatrice', 1904–1927 (Monash Asia Institute, Melbourne, 1996) and France on the Mekong: a history of the protectorate in Cambodia, 1863–1953 (University Press of America, Lanham, 2002). Virginia Thompson's well-written French

Indo-China (Octagon Books, New York, 1941) also contains valuable information on the colonial period. Milton Osborne's stirringly told *River Road to China: the Mekong River expedition, 1866–1873* (George Allen and Unwin, London, 1975) relates the story of the French attempt to find a trading route via the Mekong to Yunnan. Michel Igout's *Phnom Penh Then and Now,* with photographs by Serge Dubuisson (White Lotus, Bangkok, 1993), is a beautifully illustrated history of the Cambodian capital city. Donald Lancaster's *The Emancipation of French Indochina* (Oxford University Press, Oxford, 1961) contains valuable information on the struggle for independence. Philippe Preschez's unpublished French-language thesis on the democratic experiment in Cambodia after World War II is an important source of information for elections during that period. (The title is 'La Démocratie Cambodgienne', written as a thesis for the Diplôme de l'IEP, Paris, 1961.) King Norodom's auto-biographical works, while not always reliable, are worth reading. These include his *Souvenirs doux et amers* (*Bittersweet memories*) (Hachette, Paris, 1981). There are also a large number of what we would now call travel books written by visitors to Cambodia during the 19th and early 20th centuries, some of them particularly well written. Although to be treated with caution as source material, they nevertheless can provide vivid snapshots of Cambodian society at the time. While out of print, they can be found in some large metropolitan libraries. The best of these in the English language include Harry Franck's *East of Siam: ramblings in the five divisions of French Indo-China* (The Century, New York, 1926); Harry Hervey's *King Cobra* (Cosmopolitan Books, New York, 1927); Eleanor Mordaunt's *Purely for Pleasure* (Martin Secker, London, 1932); J. MacGregor's *Through the Buffer State* (F.V. White, London, 1896); and Frank Vincent's *The Land of the White Elephant* (Sampson, Low, Marston, Low and Searle, London, 1873). Finally, there is the English-language translation of Henri Mouhot's two-volume *Travels in the Central Parts of Indo-China* (John Murray, London, 1864).

Chapter 6: Sihanouk, star of the Cambodian stage, 1953–70

A number of writers have written good accounts of the 'Sihanoukist' period between the winning of independence in 1953 and the Lon Nol coup in 1970. David Chandler's A *History of Cambodia* (Chapter 11, 'From Independence to Civil War') provides a good brief introduction to the period. More specific works include Milton Osborne in his *Politics and Power in Cambodia: The Sihanouk Years* (Longman, Melbourne, 1973) and his biographical study *Sihanouk, Prince of Light, Prince of Darkness* (University of Hawaii Press, Honolulu, 1994). Osborne's *Before Kampuchea: preludes to tragedy* (George Allen and Unwin, London, 1979) is also worth reading, all the more so because the author was able to draw upon his own experiences in 1960s Cambodia. Roger M. Smith's *Cambodia's Foreign Policy* (Cornell University Press, Ithaca, 1965) is a detailed and perceptive study of the twists and turns of Cambodian foreign policy during this period, although it was written before Sihanouk began to lose control of the situation and his country was dragged towards war. David Chandler's magisterial *The Tragedy of Cambodian History: politics, war and revolution since 1945* (Yale University Press, New Haven, Connecticut, 1991) is the best book of all on the period, full of fascinating details and insights.

Chapter 7: The doomed republic, 1970–75

Again, Chandler's *Tragedy* is indispensable reading for this period of Cambodia's recent history. A harrowing account of the US bombing is contained in William Shawcross' *Sideshow: Kissinger, Nixon and the destruction of Cambodia* (Touchstone Books, Simon and Schuster, New York, 1981). Arnold R. Isaacs' *Without Honor: defeat in Vietnam and Cambodia* (John Hopkins University Press, Baltimore, 1983) deals mainly with Vietnam, but is well worth reading to gain an overall picture of Cambodia in this period. For a general history of the period sympathetic to the point of view of the Lon Nol regime, see Justin Corfield's *Khmers Stand Up! A history of the Cambodian government, 1970–1975* (Centre of Southeast Asian Studies, Monash University, Melbourne, 1994). For an opposing viewpoint, see George Hildebrand and Gareth Porter's *Cambodia: starvation and revolution* (Monthly Review Press, New York, 1976). For an account of what it was like to live during this period from the standpoint of a Khmer living in Phnom Penh, see the early chapters of Haing S. Ngor's *Surviving the Killing Fields: the Cambodian odyssey of Haing S. Ngor* (with Roger Warner, Pan Books, London, 1989). Henry Kamm's *Cambodia: report from a stricken land* (Arcade, New York, 1998) provides a stark portrait of the corruption of the Lon Nol period and ends with the corruption of the Hun Sen period.

Chapter 8: Pol Pot's savage utopia, 1975–79

Many hundreds of thousands of words have been written about the Khmers Rouges period and what follows does not pretend to be an exhaustive list of books on the subject. Ben Kiernan's *How Pol Pot Came to Power: a history of communism in Kampuchea, 1930–1975* (Verso, London, 1985) was a groundbreaking account of the rise of the Khmers Rouges. It is still indispensable for those seeking to understand the origins of the Pol Pot phenomenon, although other scholars have challenged some of its assumptions. David Chandler's previously cited *Tragedy* provides both detailed background on the rise of the Khmers Rouges and an account of the regime itself, drawing in part on testimonies of survivors to do so. The same author's *Brother Number One: a political biography of Pol Pot* (Allen & Unwin, Sydney, 1993) is a fine study of the life and infamous works of the dictator. More recently, Philip

Short has published his remarkable *Pol Pot: the history of a nightmare* (John Murray, London, 2004). Either of these books would be a good place to start in an attempt to understand the period. An earlier work that draws on interviews is Michael Vickery's *Cambodia: 1975–1982* (Allen & Unwin, Sydney, 1984). Elizabeth Becker's *When the War was Over: Cambodia's revolution and the voices of its people* (Simon and Schuster, New York, 1986) is interesting, particularly because its author was in Cambodia during the last days of the secretive Pol Pot regime. *Kampuchea: decade of the genocide. Report of a Finnish Inquiry Commission*, edited by Kimmo Kiljunen (Zed Books, London, 1984), is still a good source of information on the extent of the killings under Pol Pot. See also the Yale University Cambodia Genocide program website at <http://www.yale.edu/cgp/resources.html>. Valuable documentary evidence on the inside workings of this secretive and paranoid regime is found in David P. Chandler, Ben Kiernan and Chanthou Boua's *Pol Pot Plans the Future: confidential leadership documents from Democratic Kampuchea, 1976–1977* (Yale University Southeast Asian Studies, New Haven, Connecticut, 1988). A translation of Hu Nim's forced confession is contained in this volume.

Although François Ponchaud's *Cambodia Year Zero* (Penguin, Harmondsworth, 1978) has been criticised for romanticising pre-DK Cambodia, it still remains a valuable source. A number of eyewitness accounts by Khmer survivors have been published. These include Haing S. Ngor's previously cited *Surviving the Killing Fields* and Pin Yathay's *Stay Alive My Son* (Arrow Books, London, 1987). To these we should add the Frenchman François Bizot's *The Gate* (trans. Euan Cameron, Vintage, London, 2004). Bizot was captured by the Khmers Rouges during the civil war and is in the strange situation of owing his life to his gaoler, Duch, the mass murderer who later became notorious for his role at the Tuol Sleng torture centre. Bizot's book also contains a hellishly unforgettable record of the evacuation of Phnom Penh in April 1975.

Chapters 9 and 10: Painful transition and Towards an uncertain future

A number of books deal with Democratic Kampuchea's relations with Vietnam and China in the lead-up to the Vietnamese invasion of Christmas Day 1979. These include Nayan Chanda's *Brother Enemy: the war after the war* (Collier Books, New York, 1986); Gary Klintworth's *Vietnam's Intervention in Cambodia in International Law* (Australian Government Publishing Service, Canberra, 1989); P.C. Pradhan's *Foreign Policy of Kampuchea* (Radiant Publishers, New Delhi, 1985); and Grant Evans and Kelvin Rowley's *Red Brotherhood at War: Indochina since the fall of Saigon* (Verso, London, 1984). For a different perspective, see William Shawcross' *The Quality of Mercy: Cambodia, holocaust and modern conscience* (André Deutsch, London, 1984).

Evan Gottesman's eloquent *Cambodia After the Khmer Rouge: inside the politics of nation building* (Yale University Press, New Haven and London, 2003) provides an indispensable overview of events in Cambodia since the fall of Pol Pot. Margaret Slocomb's *The People's Republic of Kampuchea, 1979–1989: the revolution after Pol Pot* (Silkworm Books, Chiang Mai, 2003) is a useful account from the point of view of a writer generally sympathetic, although not uncritically so, to the PRK. On social conditions after Pol Pot, see for instance Eva Myslwiec's *Punishing the Poor: the international isolation of Kampuchea* (Oxfam, Oxford, 1988). Less accessible sources include Darryl Bullen et. al, *Ten Years After Liberation* (Australian Left Review, Sydney, c.1985) and Helen Ester's *Vietnam, Thailand, Kampuchea: a first hand account* (Australian Council for Overseas Aid, Canberra, 1980). Viviane Frings published two useful short studies on aspects of the PRK: *The Failure of Agricultural Collectivization in the People's Republic of Kampuchea, 1979–1989* (Working Paper 80, Centre of South East Asian Studies, Monash University, Melbourne, 1991) and *Allied and Equal: the Kampuchean People's Revolutionary Party's historiography and its relations with Vietnam (1979–1991)*

(CSEAS, Monash, Melbourne, 1994). Books dealing with Cambodia since the end of the PRK include Sorpong Peou's *Intervention and Change in Cambodia: towards democracy?* (Silkworm Books, Chiang Mai, 2000); MacAlister Brown and Joseph J. Zasloff's *Cambodia Confounds the Peacemakers, 1979–1998* (Cornell University Press, Ithaca and London, 1998); and David W. Roberts' *Political Transition in Cambodia, 1991–99* (Curzon Press, Richmond, Surrey, 2001).

Index

CAMBODIA

CAMBODGE

SIEM REAP
BANTEAY SREI
PHOTO: SOK SOTHY

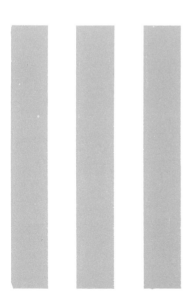